T0302008

Advanced Mathematical Methods in Environmental and Resource Economics

World Scientific Lecture Notes in Economics and Policy

ISSN: 2630-4872

Series Editor: Ariel Dinar *(University of California, Riverside, USA)*

The World Scientific Lecture Notes in Economics and Policy series is aimed to produce lecture note texts for a wide range of economics disciplines, both theoretical and applied at the undergraduate and graduate levels. Contributors to the series are highly ranked and experienced professors of economics who see in publication of their lectures a mission to disseminate the teaching of economics in an affordable manner to students and other readers interested in enriching their knowledge of economic topics. The series was formerly titled World Scientific Lecture Notes in Economics.

Published:

Vol. 13: *Advanced Mathematical Methods in Environmental and Resource Economics*
by Anastasios Xepapadeas

Vol. 12: *Lecture Notes in Global-Local Policy Interactions*
by Ariel Dinar

Vol. 11: *Lecture Notes in Water Policy*
by David Feldman

Vol. 10: *Lecture Notes in International Trade Theory: Classical Trade and Applications*
by Larry S. Karp

Vol. 9: *Lecture Notes in International Trade: An Undergraduate Course*
by Priyaranjan Jha

Vol. 8: *Lecture Notes in State and Local Public Finance: (Parts I and II)*
by John Yinger

Vol. 7: *Economics, Game Theory and International Environmental Agreements: The Ca' Foscari Lectures*
by Henry Tulkens

For the complete list of volumes in this series, please visit
www.worldscientific.com/series/wslnep

World Scientific Lecture Notes in Economics and Policy – Vol. 13

Advanced Mathematical Methods in Environmental and Resource Economics

Anastasios Xepapadeas

University of Bologna, Italy & Athens University
of Economics and Business, Greece

W⬧ World Scientific

NEW JERSEY · LONDON · SINGAPORE · BEIJING · SHANGHAI · HONG KONG · TAIPEI · CHENNAI · TOKYO

Published by

World Scientific Publishing Co. Pte. Ltd.

5 Toh Tuck Link, Singapore 596224

USA office: 27 Warren Street, Suite 401-402, Hackensack, NJ 07601

UK office: 57 Shelton Street, Covent Garden, London WC2H 9HE

Library of Congress Cataloging-in-Publication Data
Names: Xepapadeas, Anastasios, author.
Title: Advanced mathematical methods in environmental and resource economics /
    Anastasios Xepapadeas, University of Bologna, Italy &
    Athens University of Economics and Business, Greece.
Description: New Jersey : World Scientific, [2023] | Series: World Scientific lecture notes in
    economics and policy, 2630-4872 ; vol. 13 | Includes bibliographical references and index.
Identifiers: LCCN 2022035695 | ISBN 9789811262203 (hardcover) |
    ISBN 9789811262210 (ebook) | ISBN 9789811262227 (ebook other)
Subjects: LCSH: Environmental economics--Mathematical models. | Environmental policy--
    Economic aspects--Mathematical models. | Natural resources--Mathetmical models.
Classification: LCC HC79.E5 X47 2023 | DDC 338.9/27015118--dc23/eng/20220811
LC record available at https://lccn.loc.gov/2022035695

British Library Cataloguing-in-Publication Data
A catalogue record for this book is available from the British Library.

For any available supplementary material, please visit
https://www.worldscientific.com/worldscibooks/10.1142/13020#t=suppl

Desk Editors: Aanand Jayaraman/Lai Ann

Typeset by Stallion Press
Email: enquiries@stallionpress.com

Printed in Singapore

Preface

These lectures have been developed during my teaching of advanced mathematical methods for environmental and resource economics in PhD programs and seminars in a number of universities over the last 25 years.

The most interesting issues in environmental and resource economics have an explicit temporal dimension, since variables of interest such as pollutants, greenhouse gases, biomass of biological resources or the stocks of fossil fuels accumulate in the ambient environment or are depleted through human actions and natural processes.

To study the mechanisms driving the interactions between humans and the natural world through unified models of ecological and economic systems, and to design policies to steer these systems toward socially-desirable targets, the temporal dimension should be modeled.

The purpose of these lectures is to provide the mathematical tools for analyzing environmental and resource management issues in a dynamic set-up. In this respect, these lectures start with a brief description of differential equations and then move to describe methods of optimal control and dynamic programming. These methods are extended to stochastic control and differential games with an application to the so-called "lake problem," which has received considerable attention in environmental and resource economics and is regarded as a vehicle for analyzing a wider variety of problems. The final two chapters cover two more recent advances in the area. The first is analysis of the impact of deep uncertainty and aversion to ambiguity using robust control methods which can be useful in studying precautionary policies for resource management and climate change. The second is the study of pollution/resource management and optimal growth in a spatiotemporal domain in which the transport of variables is governed by local linear or nonlinear diffusion and long-range effects through spatial kernels. This allows the analysis of endogenous formation of spatial patterns and clustering, and spatially-dependent optimal policies.

The lectures focus on presenting the tools and the way in which they are applied mainly through the use of optimality conditions, along with examples of their use in optimal control problems using Mathematica code. No proofs are provided.

The lectures would be valuable for advanced graduate students in environmental and resource economics who are studying dynamic problems.

About the Author

Anastasios Xepapadeas is currently Professor of Economics at the Department of Economics of the University of Bologna and Professor Emeritus at the Department of International and European Economic Studies of Athens University of Economics and Business. He is an elected international member of the US National Academy of Sciences, past president of the European Association of Environmental and Resource Economics and past Chair of the Board of Directors of the Beijer Institute of the Royal Swedish Academy of Sciences. He is co-editor of *Environmental and Resource Economics* and member of the editorial committee of *Annual Review of Resource Economics*. He has published more than 150 papers in leading journals and collective volumes. His current research interests include Spatiotemporal Analysis in Economics; Economics of Climate Change; Uncertainty, and Robust Control.

Contents

Chapter 1

Differential Equations

An ordinary differential equation (ODE) of order $n \geq 1$ can be informally defined as an equation involving an unknown function of one independent variable, which in most cases is taken to represent time, $x(t)$, and its derivatives up to order n. The nth order differential equation can be written as

$$\frac{dx^n(t)}{dt} = f\left(x(t), \frac{dx(t)}{dt}, \frac{dx^2(t)}{dt}, \ldots, \frac{dx^{n-1}(t)}{dt}, t \right) \qquad (1)$$

If $x \in \mathbb{R}^n$, then (1) represents a system of n differential equations.

A partial differential equation (PDE) of order $n \geq 1$ can be informally defined as an equation involving an unknown function of more than one independent variables, $x(t, z)$, and its derivatives up to order n.

Let t in an open subset $T \subset \mathbb{R}$, with t interpreted as time and $D = T \otimes \mathbb{R}^n \subset \mathbb{R}^{n+1}$ be a connected set. Let $f : D \to \mathbb{R}^n$ be a continuous vector valued function. The system of n first-order differential equations can be written as

$$\dot{x}_i(t) = f_i(x_1(t), \ldots, x_n(t), t), \quad i = 1, \ldots, n, \ \dot{x} \equiv \frac{dx}{dt}$$

$$= \lim_{\varepsilon \to 0} \frac{x(t + \varepsilon) - x(t)}{\varepsilon} \qquad (2)$$

1

In vector notation, $\dot{\mathbf{x}}(t) = f(\mathbf{x}(t), t)$. The vector $\mathbf{x}(t) = (x_1(t), \ldots, x_n(t))$ is the **state of the dynamical system.**

If we set $x = x_1$, the system

$$\dot{x}_1 = x_2$$
$$\dot{x}_2 = x_3$$
$$\ldots \qquad\qquad (3)$$
$$\dot{x}_n = f(x_1, x_2, \ldots, x_n)$$

is equivalent to the nth order ODE

$$x^{(n)}(t) = f\left(x^{(n-1)}(t), x^{(n-2)}(t), \ldots, \dot{x}(t), x(t), t\right), x^{(n)}(t) = \frac{d^n x(t)}{dt^n} \qquad (4)$$

The second-order ODE $\ddot{x} + a_1 \dot{x} + a_2 x = b$, by setting $x = x_1$, is equivalent to the system,

$$\dot{x}_1 = x_2$$
$$\dot{x}_2 = b - a_1 x_1 - a_2 x_2 \qquad (5)$$

First-Order Linear ODEs

$$\dot{x}(t) + P(t)x(t) = Q(t) \qquad (6)$$
$$x(t) = e^{-\int P(t)dt}\left(Q(t)e^{-\int P(t)dt} + A\right) \qquad (7)$$
$$\dot{x}(t) + \alpha x(t) = b, \quad x(0) = x_0 \qquad (8)$$
$$x(t) = Ae^{-at} + \frac{b}{a}, \quad x_0 = A + \frac{b}{a} \qquad (9)$$

Second-Order Linear ODEs

$$\ddot{x}(t) + a_1\dot{x}(t) + a_2 x(t) = b, \quad x(0) = x_0, \quad \dot{x}(0) = x_1$$

λ_1, λ_2 roots of the characteristic equation

$$\lambda^2 + a_1\lambda + a_2 = 0$$

Solution:

(λ_1, λ_2) real $\quad \lambda_1 \neq \lambda_2 \quad\quad A_1 e^{\lambda_1 t} + A_2 e^{\lambda_2 t} + \frac{b}{a}$

(λ_1, λ_2) real $\quad \lambda_1 = \lambda_2 = \mu \quad\quad A_1 e^{\mu t} + A_2 t e^{\mu t} + \frac{b}{a}$

(λ_1, λ_2) complex $\lambda_{1,2} = u \pm v_i \ e^{ut}[A_1\cos(vt) + A_2\sin(vt)] + \frac{b}{a}$

When f does not explicitly depend on time, $\dot{x}(t) = f(x(t))$, then the system is called **autonomous**.

Linear system

$$\dot{x}(t) = Ax(t) + b(t) \tag{10}$$

$$\dot{x}(t) = \begin{pmatrix} \dot{x}_1(t) \\ \vdots \\ \dot{x}_n(t) \end{pmatrix}, \quad x(t) = \begin{pmatrix} x_1(t) \\ \vdots \\ x_n(t) \end{pmatrix}, \quad A = \begin{pmatrix} a_{11} & \cdots & a_{1n} \\ \vdots & \ddots & \vdots \\ a_{n1} & \cdots & a_{nn} \end{pmatrix}$$

$$b(t) = \begin{pmatrix} b_1(t) \\ \vdots \\ b_n(t) \end{pmatrix}$$

$b(t) = 0$: **homogeneous system**

Solution

A continuously differentiable vector valued function $\varphi(t)$ defined in an open interval (t_1, t_2) with range in $\mathbb{R}^n$ is **a solution** of the system (2) if

$$\dot{\varphi}(t) = f(\varphi(t), t) \tag{11}$$

Let $(t_0, x_0) \in D : x(t_0) = x_0$, the point (t_0, x_0) is an **initial condition or initial state** and the **initial value problem** consists of finding a solution

$$\varphi(t) : \varphi(t_0) = x_0 \tag{12}$$

The solution of the initial value problem is denoted as $\varphi(x_0, t_0 : t)$.

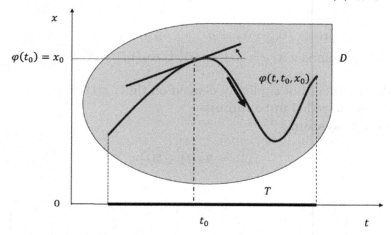

Solution of the ODE $\dot{x} = f(x(t), t)$ for $n = 1$ with initial condition

$$x(t_0) = x_0$$

An Autonomous System on the Plane

$$\dot{x}_1 = f_1(x_1, x_2), \quad x_1(0) = x_{10} \tag{13}$$

$$\dot{x}_2 = f_2(x_1, x_2), \quad x_2(0) = x_{20} \tag{14}$$

Let $(\varphi_1(t), \varphi_2(t)) = (x_1(t), x_2(t))$, a solution that starts at the initial state $x_0 = (x_{10}, x_{20})$.

The curve $(x_1(t), x_2(t))$ in $\mathbb{R}^2$ with t acting as a **parameter** is called **a solution curve, or trajectory, or orbit** from $x_0 =$

(x_{10}, x_{20}). The (x_1, x_2) plane is called the **state space or the phase space**. The family of all trajectories is called the **phase portrait**.

The definitions are extended to $\mathbb{R}^n$.

Parametric Curves

$(\varphi_1(t), \varphi_2(t)) = (\sin(t), \cos(2t))$,
$(\varphi_1(t), \varphi_2(t), \varphi_3(t)) = (5\cos(t), 5\sin(t), t + \sin(t))$

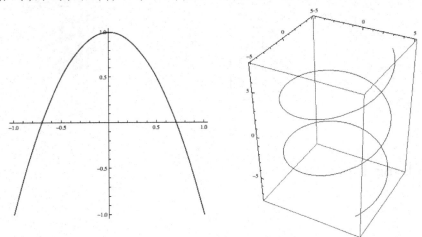

Vector Fields

A vector field is an assignment of a vector to each point in a subset of Euclidean space.

The function f in (2) is called a **vector field** on D because it takes the vector $(t, x) \in \mathbb{R}^{n+1}$ to the vector $\dot{x} \in \mathbb{R}^n$. In $\mathbb{R}^2$ (2) or (13)–(14) determines the slope of $f(x(t), t)$ at each point $(t, x) \in D$. A solution $(\varphi_1(t), \varphi_2(t)) = (x_1(t), x_2(t))$ determines a curve that has the slope of $f(\varphi_1(t), \varphi_2(t), t)$.

By (13)–(14)

$$\frac{dx_2}{dx_1} = \frac{f_2(\varphi_1(t), \varphi_2(t))}{f_1(\varphi_1(t), \varphi_2(t))} \tag{15}$$

The direction of the solution curve $(\varphi_1(t), \varphi_2(t))$ coincides at any point $t \in T$ with the direction of the vector field.

$$\dot{x}_1 = x_1, \quad \dot{x}_2 = -x_2$$
$$\dot{x}_1 = x_1, \quad \dot{x}_2 = x_2, \quad \dot{x}_3 = x_3$$

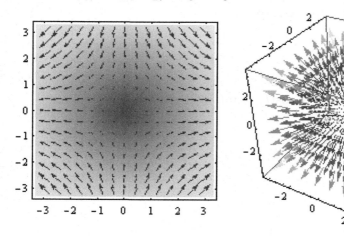

Solving Linear Systems

$$\dot{x} = Ax + b \tag{16}$$

Solution of the homogeneous system $\dot{x} = Ax$.

Assume that A has n real distinct eigenvalues $(\lambda_1, \ldots, \lambda_n)$. Let $P = \{v_1, \ldots, v_n\}$, a set of corresponding eigenvectors, $Ax = \lambda x$. Matrix P is invertible and

$$P^{-1}AP = \mathrm{diag}[\lambda_1, \ldots, \lambda_n] = \begin{pmatrix} \lambda_1 & 0 & \cdots & 0 \\ 0 & \lambda_2 & \cdots & 0 \\ 0 & 0 & \ddots & 0 \\ 0 & 0 & \cdots & \lambda_n \end{pmatrix} \tag{17}$$

Define

$$y = P^{-1}x \Rightarrow x = Py \tag{18}$$
$$\dot{y} = P^{-1}\dot{x} = P^{-1}Ax = P^{-1}APy \tag{19}$$

$$\dot{y} = \text{diag}[\lambda_1, \ldots, \lambda_n]y = \begin{pmatrix} \lambda_1 & 0 & \cdots & 0 \\ 0 & \lambda_2 & \cdots & 0 \\ 0 & 0 & \ddots & 0 \\ 0 & 0 & \cdots & \lambda_n \end{pmatrix} y \qquad (20)$$

$$y(t) = ce^{\Lambda t}, \ e^{\Lambda t} = \begin{pmatrix} e^{\lambda_1 t} & 0 & \cdots & 0 \\ 0 & e^{\lambda_2 t} & \cdots & 0 \\ 0 & 0 & \ddots & 0 \\ 0 & 0 & \cdots & e^{\lambda_n t} \end{pmatrix}, \ c = \begin{pmatrix} c_1 \\ c_2 \\ \cdots \\ c_n \end{pmatrix} \qquad (21)$$

$\Phi = e^{\Lambda t}$ is a **fundamental matrix solution**

$$y(t) = ce^{\Lambda t} = P^{-1}x \Rightarrow x(t) = Pce^{\Lambda t} \qquad (22)$$

The $n = 2$ case

$$x_1(t) = v_{11}c_1 e^{\lambda_1 t} + v_{12}c_2 e^{\lambda_2 t} \qquad (23)$$

$$x_2(t) = v_{21}c_1 e^{\lambda_1 t} + v_{22}c_2 e^{\lambda_2 t} \qquad (24)$$

$$\begin{pmatrix} v_{11} \\ v_{21} \end{pmatrix} \to \lambda_1, \quad \begin{pmatrix} v_{12} \\ v_{22} \end{pmatrix} \to \lambda_2, \quad \begin{pmatrix} c_1 \\ c_1 \end{pmatrix} : \text{ constants} \qquad (25)$$

$$\lambda_1, \lambda_2 = \frac{1}{2}\left[(a_{11} + a_{22}) \pm \sqrt{(a_{11} + a_{22})^2 - 4(a_{11}a_{22} - a_{12}a_{21})}\right]$$

$$\lambda_1, \lambda_2 = \frac{1}{2}\left[\text{trace } A \pm \sqrt{(\text{trace } A)^2 - 4(\det A)}\right] \qquad (26)$$

constants are determined by initial conditions $x_0 = (x_{10}, x_{20})$.

Solution of the non-homogeneous system $\dot{x} = Ax + b$.

The solution is the sum of the solution of the homogeneous part and the **particular solution.**

Set $x = \bar{x}$ fixed for any particular solution, then

$$0 = A\bar{x} + b \Rightarrow \bar{x} = -A^{-1}b \qquad (27)$$

The solution of the non-homogeneous system is

$$x(t) = Pce^{\Lambda t} + \bar{x} \qquad (28)$$

Constants c are determined by initial conditions $x_0 = (x_{10}, x_{20}, \ldots, x_{n0})$.

Real and Distinct Eigenvalues for Matrix A

The $n = 2$ case

$$x_1(t) = v_{11}c_1 e^{\lambda_1 t} + v_{12}c_2 e^{\lambda_2 t} + \bar{x}_1 \tag{29}$$

$$x_2(t) = v_{21}c_1 e^{\lambda_1 t} + v_{22}c_2 e^{\lambda_2 t} + \bar{x}_2 \tag{30}$$

$$\bar{x} = -A^{-1}b \tag{31}$$

$$\begin{pmatrix} c_1 \\ c_1 \end{pmatrix} \quad : \quad \begin{matrix} x_{10} = v_{11}c_1 + v_{12}c_2 + \bar{x}_1 \\ x_{20} = v_{21}c_1 + v_{22}c_2 + \bar{x}_2 \end{matrix} \tag{32}$$

$$\begin{pmatrix} v_{11} \\ v_{21} \end{pmatrix} \to \lambda_1, \quad \begin{pmatrix} v_{12} \\ v_{22} \end{pmatrix} \to \lambda_2 \tag{33}$$

Complex and Repeating Eigenvalues for Matrix A

The $n = 2$ case

Repeating eigenvalues: $\lambda_1 = \lambda_2 = \lambda$

$$x_1(t) = c_1 v_1 e^{\lambda t} + c_2(\eta_1 + v_1)t e^{\lambda t} \tag{34}$$

$$x_2(t) = c_2 v_2 e^{\lambda t} + c_2(\eta_2 + v_2)t e^{\lambda t} \tag{35}$$

$$v = \begin{pmatrix} v_1 \\ v_1 \end{pmatrix} \to \lambda \tag{36}$$

$$(\eta_1, \eta_2) \quad \text{solves} \quad (A - \lambda I)\eta = v \tag{37}$$

Complex eigenvalues: $\lambda_1, \lambda_2 = u \pm vi$

$$x_1(t) = e^{ut}[c_1(\gamma_1 \cos(vt) - \gamma_2 \sin(vt)) \tag{38}$$

$$+ c_2(\gamma_1 \sin(vt) + \gamma_2 \cos(vt))] \tag{39}$$

$$x_2(t) = e^{ut}[c_1(\delta_1 \cos(vt) - \delta_2 \sin(vt)) \tag{40}$$

$$+ c_2(\delta_1 \sin(vt) + \delta_2 \cos(vt))] \tag{41}$$

$$\begin{pmatrix} v_1 \\ v_1 \end{pmatrix} = \begin{pmatrix} \gamma_1 + i\gamma_2 \\ \delta_1 + i\delta_2 \end{pmatrix} \tag{42}$$

For more details for the cases of complex and repeated eigenvalues for matrix A, see any good book in differential equations e.g., M. W. Hirsch and S. Smale, *Differential Equations, Dynamical Systems, and Linear Algebra*, Academic Press, 1974; M. W. Hirsch, S. Smale and R. L. Devaney, *Differential Equations, Dynamical Systems, and an Introduction to Chaos*, Elsevier, 2004.

```
In[9]:= m2 = {{1, 2}, {3, 2}}
        Eigensystem[m2]

Out[9]= {{1, 2}, {3, 2}}

Out[10]= {{4, -1}, {{2, 3}, {-1, 1}}}
```

```
In[11]:= StreamPlot[{x + 2 y, 3 x + 2 y}, {x, -3, 3},
         {y, -3, 3}, VectorPoints → Automatic, StreamStyle → Orange]
```

Out[11]=

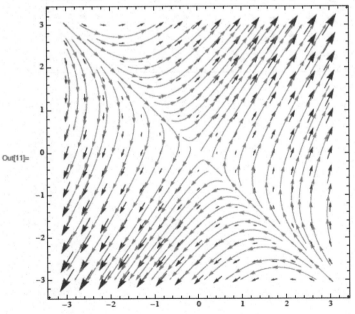

```
In[4]:= m1 = {{7, 1}, {-4, 3}}
        Eigensystem[m1]

Out[4]= {{7, 1}, {-4, 3}}

Out[5]= {{5, 5}, {{-1, 2}, {0, 0}}}

In[6]:= StreamPlot[{7 x + y, 4 x + 3 y}, {x, -3, 3},
        {y, -3, 3}, VectorPoints → Automatic, StreamStyle → Orange]
```

In[1]:= **m = {{3, -9}, {4, -3}}**
Eigensystem[m]

Out[1]= **{{3, -9}, {4, -3}}**

Out[2]= $\left\{\left\{3\,i\,\sqrt{3}\,,\,-3\,i\,\sqrt{3}\,\right\},\,\left\{\left\{\dfrac{3}{4}+\dfrac{3\,i\,\sqrt{3}}{4}\,,\,1\right\},\,\left\{\dfrac{3}{4}-\dfrac{3\,i\,\sqrt{3}}{4}\,,\,1\right\}\right\}\right\}$

In[3]:= **StreamPlot[{3 x - 9 y, 4 x - 3 y}, {x, -3, 3},**
{y, -3, 3}, VectorPoints → Automatic, StreamStyle → Orange]

Out[3]=

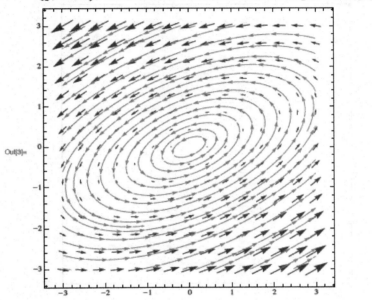

```
m4 = {{3, -13}, {5, -5}}
Eigensystem[m4]

{{3, -13}, {5, -5}}
```

$$\left\{\{-1+7\,i,\ -1-7\,i\},\ \left\{\left\{\frac{4}{5}+\frac{7\,i}{5},\ 1\right\},\ \left\{\frac{4}{5}-\frac{7\,i}{5},\ 1\right\}\right\}\right\}$$

```
StreamPlot[{3 x - 13 y, 5 x - 5 y}, {x, -3, 3},
  {y, -3, 3}, VectorPoints → Automatic, StreamStyle → Orange]
```

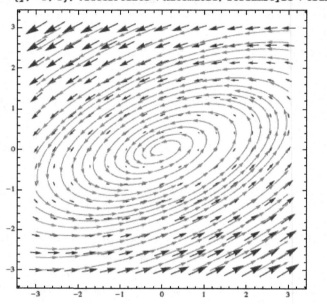

Solution Properties

Existence — Uniqueness: If the coordinate functions f_i, $i = 1, \ldots, n$ are continuous in D and satisfy a Lipschitz condition

$$\|f_i(x^1, t) - f_i(x^2, t)\| \le L\|x^1 - x^2\|, \quad L > 0, \quad \forall i \qquad (43)$$

then a solution to the system

$$\dot{x}_i(t) = f_i(x_1(t), \ldots, x_n(t), t), \quad i = 1, \ldots, n \qquad (44)$$

with initial conditions (x_0, t_0) exists and it is unique. If the fs are differentiable, and have bounded derivatives, then the Lipschitz condition is satisfied.

Dependence on initial values and parameters: Consider the initial value problem $\dot{x} = f(x, t, \alpha)$, where $\alpha \in \mathbb{R}^k$ is a vector of exogenous variables or parameters. Assume that the coordinate functions f_i are continuous in a closed and compact domain $D \in \mathbb{R}^{n+k+1}$ and all partial derivatives of fs with respect to x and α exist and are continuous in D. Then the solution to the initial value problem $\varphi(x_0, t_0, t, \alpha)$ is a continuous function of (x_0, t_0, t, α) and its derivatives with respect to x_0 and α exist.

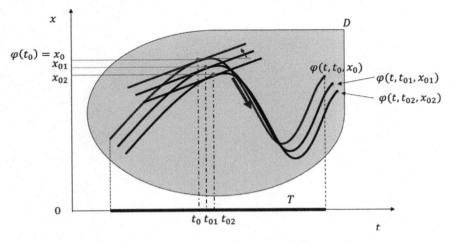

Continuous dependence on initial conditions.

Chapter 2

Stability

Equilibrium

Consider the autonomous system $\dot{x} = f(x)$, and the corresponding initial value problem with initial condition (t_0, x_0), and assume that the conditions for existence, uniqueness and continuous dependence of the solution are satisfied.

Definition: An **equilibrium point** or **fixed point**, or **critical point** or **rest point**, or **steady state** of the system is a point x^* such that $f(x^*) = 0$, or equivalently, a point $x^* : \dot{x} = 0$

An equilibrium point is isolated if there is no other equilibrium point in its neighborhood.

Let $\varphi(x_0, t_0, t)$ be the solution of the initial value problem that at $t = t_0$ passes through the initial point x_0, and let x^* be an equilibrium point. The stability of the equilibrium point is defined with respect to the initial conditions, and the following stability concepts are commonly used:

Stability Concepts: Definitions

- The equilibrium point x^* is stable in the Lyapunov sense if the solution $\varphi(x_0, t_0, t)$ with x_0 'close' to the equilibrium point remains in the neighborhood of x^* for all $t \geq 0$. Or more precisely if for an $\varepsilon > 0$, a $\delta > 0$ exists, such that if $\|x_0 - x^*\| < \delta$, then $\|\varphi(x_0, t_0, t) - x^*\| < \varepsilon, \forall t \geq t_0$.

15

- The equilibrium point is asymptotically stable if it is Lyapunov stable and furthermore $\varphi\left(x_0, t_0, t\right) \to x^*$ as $t \to \infty$.
- The equilibrium point is globally asymptotically stable if it is asymptotically stable and x_0 need not be 'close' to x^*. The solution converges to the equilibrium point for any initial value in the domain of f and not just for initial values in the neighborhood of x^*.

The concept of asymptotic stability is very important in economics since it relates directly to the **steady state long-run equilibrium**.

An equilibrium point is **unstable** if it is not stable.

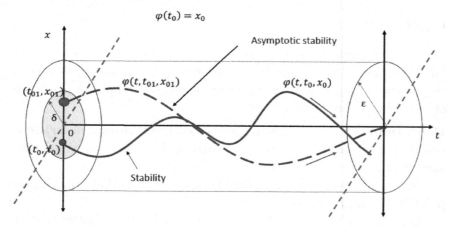

Stability and asymptotic stability (Adapted from W. Brock and A. Malliaris, Differential Equations, Stability and Chaos.)

Stability of Linear Systems

Consider the linear system with constant coefficients $\dot{x} = Ax + b$.
  The equilibrium point is defined as

$$x^* : \dot{x} = 0 \quad \text{or} \quad x^* = -A^{-1}b \tag{1}$$

Definition: The equilibrium point is **globally asymptotically stable** if and only if the real parts of the eigenvalues (characteristic roots) of A are negative. Matrix A is then called a stable matrix.

A real matrix ($n x n$) is stable

(i) if and only if a symmetric positive definite matrix B exists such that $BA + A'B$ is negative definite.
(ii) if A is symmetric and negative definite (see also Ruth–Hurwitz conditions).

Classification of Equilibrium Points ($n = 2$)

$\lambda_1, \lambda_2 = \frac{1}{2}[\text{tr}A \pm \sqrt{\Delta}], \Delta = (\text{tr}A)^2 - 4|A|$

Characteristic Roots	$\text{tr}(A), |A|, \Delta$	Type of Equilibrium
$\lambda_1 < = \lambda_2 = \lambda > 0$	$\text{tr}(A) > 0, |A| > 0, \Delta = 0$	Unstable proper node
$\lambda_1 = \lambda_2 = \lambda < 0$	$\text{tr}(A) < 0, |A| > 0, \Delta = 0$	Stable proper node
$\lambda_1 \neq \lambda_2, \lambda_1, \lambda_2 > 0$	$\text{tr}(A) > 0, |A| > 0, \Delta > 0$	Unstable improper node
$\lambda_1 \neq \lambda_2, \lambda_1, \lambda_2 < 0$	$\text{tr}(A) < 0, |A| > 0, \Delta > 0$	Stable improper node
$\lambda_1 > 0, \lambda_2 < 0,$	$|A| < 0$	Saddle point
λ_1, λ_2 complex positive real parts	$\text{tr}(A) > 0, \Delta < 0$	Unstable focus
λ_1, λ_2 complex negative real parts	$\text{tr}(A) < 0, \Delta < 0$	Stable focus
λ_1, λ_2 complex zero real parts	$\text{tr}(A) = 0, \Delta = 0$	Center

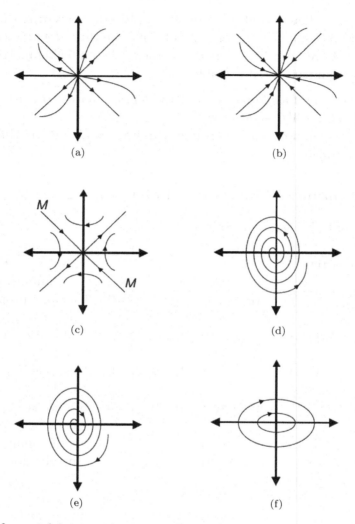

(a)

(b)

(c)

(d)

(e)

(f)

Of special interest in economics is the saddle point equilibrium occurring when one of the characteristic roots is positive while the other is negative. In this case, the general solution of the homogeneous system is

$$\varphi_1\left(t\right) = x_1\left(t\right) = v_{11}c_1 e^{\lambda_1 t} + v_{12}c_2 e^{\lambda_2 t} \tag{2}$$

$$\varphi_2\left(t\right) = x_2\left(t\right) = v_{21}c_1 e^{\lambda_1 t} + v_{22}c_2 e^{\lambda_2 t} \tag{3}$$

$$\begin{pmatrix} v_{11} \\ v_{21} \end{pmatrix} \to \lambda_1 \begin{pmatrix} v_{12} \\ v_{22} \end{pmatrix} \to \lambda_2 \begin{pmatrix} c_1 \\ c_1 \end{pmatrix}: \quad \text{constants} \tag{4}$$

In a saddle point equilibrium, the system converges towards equilibrium only along the trajectory MM, which is called the stable arm of equilibrium. The other arm is the unstable arm. The slope of the arms is given by the ratio v_{1i}/v_{2i}, $i = 1, 2$ for the corresponding eigenvalue λ_i. The stable arm is a special case of a one-dimensional linear subspace (manifold) that appears in saddle point equilibrium.

In the general case of a system of n differential equations, if the matrix A has m eigenvalues with negative real parts and $n - m$ eigenvalues with positive real parts, then an m-dimensional linear subspace exists such that any solution starting on this subspace at $t = 0$ converges to the equilibrium point as $t \to \infty$. Furthermore, any solution starting near the equilibrium point but not on the stable subspace does not converge to equilibrium.

Stability of Nonlinear Systems: Qualitative Analysis

Linearization

Consider the system of nonlinear differential equations $\dot{x} = f(x)$, $f : \mathbb{R}^n \to \mathbb{R}^n$. Assume that x^* is an isolated equilibrium point $f(x^*) = 0$.

Take the first-order Taylor expansion around the equilibrium point. The linearized system can be obtained as

$$\dot{x}(t) = f(x^*) + A(x(t) - x^*) \tag{5}$$

$$\dot{x} = A(x - x^*), \quad A = \left[\frac{\partial f_i(x^*)}{\partial x_j}\right]_{ij} = Df(x^*), \quad i, j = 1, \ldots, n \tag{6}$$

where A is the Jacobian matrix of the system evaluated at the equilibrium point.

Definition: An equilibrium point x^* is called **hyperbolic** if $A = Df(x^*)$ has no eigenvalues with zero real parts. An equilibrium point x^* is called **non-hyperbolic** if at least one eigenvalue of $A = Df(x^*)$ has zero real part.

If a hyperbolic equilibrium point is globally stable in the linear approximation, then it is locally stable at the original nonlinear system.

The converse, however, is not necessarily true (for more details, see Hartman–Grobman theorem in e.g., Arrowsmith and Place: *An Introduction to Dynamical Systems*).

Asymptotic Linear Stability and Perturbations

$\dot{x} = f(x)$, and x^* is an isolated hyperbolic fixed point $f(x^*) = 0$. Introduce a small perturbation $\eta(t)$ at x^*. So, $x(t) = x^* + \eta(t)$, $0 < |\eta(t)| \ll 1$. Then

$$\frac{d(x^* + \eta(t))}{dt} = f(x^* + \eta(t)) \Rightarrow \dot{\eta}(t) = f(x^* + \eta(t)) \tag{7}$$

Take a Taylor expansion around x^*

$$\dot{\eta} = f(x^*) + Df(x^*)(x^* + \eta(t) - x^*) + O\left(|\eta(t)|^2\right) \tag{8}$$

$$\dot{\eta} = Df(x^*)\eta(t) + O\left(|\eta(t)|^2\right) = A\eta + O\left(|\eta|^2\right) \tag{9}$$

The leading order is determined by $\eta(t) = \eta_0 e^{\Lambda t}$. If Λ is a stable matrix (all eigenvalues have negative real parts), then

$$\lim_{t\to\infty} \eta(t) = \lim_{t\to\infty} \eta_0 e^{\Lambda t} = 0 \tag{10}$$

So, the perturbation dies out and the system returns to x^*.

Manifold Theorems

Theorem (Stable manifold): *Let* $\dot{x} = f(x)$, $f(x^*) = 0$ *and* $Df(x^*)$ *has* m *eigenvalues with negative real parts and* $n - m$ *eigenvalues with positive real parts. Then an* m *dimensional differentiable manifold* S *exists which is tangent to the stable linear subspace* E^S *of the linear system* $\dot{x} = Df(x^*)(x - x^*)$ *at* x^*, *and an* $n - m$ *dimensional differentiable manifold* U *exists which is tangent to the unstable linear subspace* E^U *of the linear system* $\dot{x} = Df(x^*)(x - x^*)$ *at* x^*. *For all* $x_0 \in S$ $\lim_{t\to\infty} \varphi(x_0, t_0, t) = x^*$.

Theorem (Center manifold): $Df(x^*)$ *has* m *eigenvalues with negative real parts and* k *eigenvalues with positive real parts and* $n - m - k$ *eigenvalues with zero real parts. Then an* $n - m - k$ *dimensional differentiable manifold center manifold* C *exists which is tangent to the center linear subspace* E^C *of the linear system* $\dot{x} = Df(x^*)(x - x^*)$ *at* x^*.

Stable Manifold and Topological Equivalence

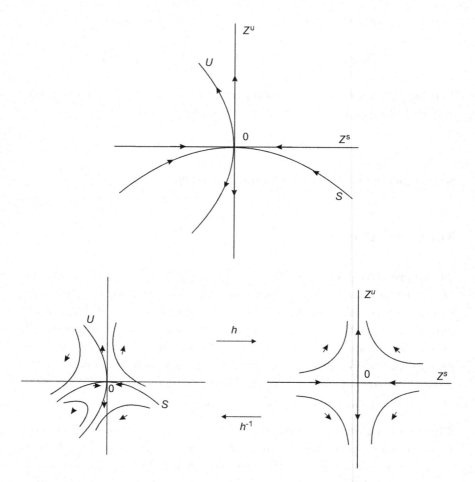

Global Stability (Lyapunov)

Let $\dot{x} = f(x), f(x^*) = 0$. Assume that a Lyapunov function $V(x_1 - x_1^*, \ldots, x_n - x_n^*)$ exists with the following properties:

$V > 0$ if $x_i \neq x_i^*$ for at least one i and $V = 0$ iff $x_i = x_i^*, \forall i$

$V \to +\infty$ as $\| x_i - x_i^* \| \to +\infty$

For the trajectory derivative

$$\frac{dV}{dt} = \dot{V}(t) = \sum_{i=1}^{n} \frac{\partial V}{\partial (x_i - x_i^*)} \frac{d(x_i - x_i^*)}{dt} \text{ it holds that}$$

$\dot{V}(t) < 0$ if $x_i \neq x_i^*$ for at least one i

$\dot{V}(t) = 0$ if $x_i = x_i^*, \forall i$

Then x^* is globally stable. The Euclidean distance $\|x - x^*\|$ or the modified Euclidean distance $\|a(x - x^*)\|$ has been used as a Lyapunov function in applications.

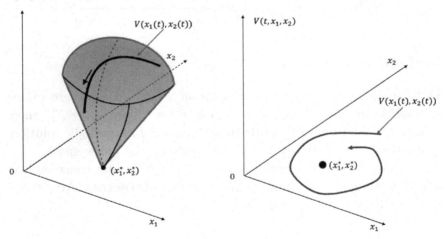

The Lyapunov function (left panel) and its contours (right panel).

Phase Diagram Analysis: Use of Isoclines

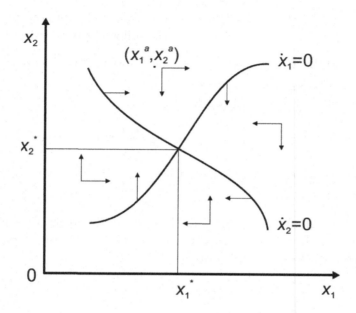

Periodic Solutions

Definition: Let $\dot{y} = f(y)$ with solution $\varphi(y_0, t_0, t)$, if there exists a positive number $T > 0 : \varphi(y_0, t_0, t) = \varphi(y_0, t_0, t + T)$, then $\varphi(y_0, t_0, t)$ is a **periodic solution** with period T. A periodic solution generates a **closed orbit** or a **limit cycle** on the phase space.

A limit cycle is a generalization of the equilibrium concept. Isolated fixed points and limit cycles are called **attractors**. Attractors could be **attracting** or **repelling**.

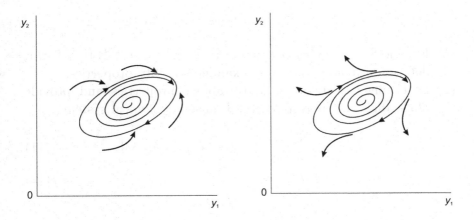

Existence of Limit Cycles on the Plane (Poincare Bendixson)

Let $\dot{y} = f(y), f : E \rightarrow \mathbb{R}^2$, where E is a closed and bounded connected set.

- If E does not contain isolated fixed points, or contains an unstable isolated fixed point and the vector field defined by $f(y)$ points inwards on the boundary of E, then E contains a limit cycle.
- If the divergence $\operatorname{div}(f) = \frac{\partial f}{\partial y_1} + \frac{\partial f}{\partial y_2}$ does not change sign in E, then E does not contain a limit cycle.

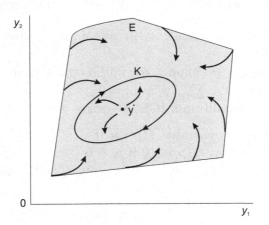

Let $f(k) = k^a$ $0 < a < 1$ be a production function.

(1) For the Solow equation $\dot{k} = sf(k) - \delta k$, $0 < s < 1$, $0 < \delta < 1$, determine steady states and examine stability properties.
(2) Determine steady state and stability properties and provide phase diagram analysis for the Ramsey dynamical system.

$$\dot{c} = \frac{1}{\sigma}\left[f'(k) - (\rho + \delta)\right]c, \rho, \sigma > 0 \tag{11}$$

$$\dot{k} = f(k) - c - \delta k \tag{12}$$

(3) Consider the system

$$\dot{x}_1 = x_1(1 - x_1 - \beta_{12}x_2), \quad x_1(0) = x_{10} \tag{13}$$

$$\dot{x}_2 = \alpha x_2(1 - x_2 - \beta_{21}x_1), \quad x_2(0) = x_{20} \tag{14}$$

$$(\alpha, \beta_{12}, \beta_{21}, x_{10}, x_{20}) > 0 \tag{15}$$

Determine steady states and stability properties. Under what conditions regarding the parameters a positive steady state exists?

Stability of Competitive Equilibrium: Description

- Excess demand functions: $z_i(p) = x_i(p) - y_i(p) - w_i$, $p = (p_1, \ldots, p_n)$
- $x_i(p)$: demand, $y_i(p)$: supply, w_i: initial endowment
- Walras law: $pz(p) = \sum_{i=1}^{n} p_i z_i(p) = 0$
- A competitive equilibrium (CE) p^* exists

  (a) If all goods are desirable $z(p^*) = 0$
  (b) Desirable good i, $z_i(p_i) > 0$ if $p_i = 0$
  (c) If p^* is a CE and $z_i(p_i) < 0$ for some good i then i is a free good

- Tâtonnement $\dot{p} = \beta z(p)$, $\beta > 0$, normalize to $\beta = 1$

- Walras law implies:

$$\frac{d}{dt}\sum_{i=1}^{n}(p_i)^2 = \sum_{i=1}^{n}2p_i\dot{p}_i = \sum_{i=1}^{n}2p_iz_i(p) = 2\sum_{i=1}^{n}p_iz_i(p) = 0 \quad (16)$$

During price adjustment, the sum of square of prices is constant. During price adjustment, prices are on the surface of an n-sphere.

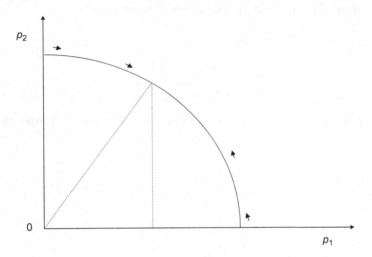

Weak axiom of revealed preference (WARP): If $z_i(p)$ satisfies WARP then $p^*z(p) > 0 \ \forall p \neq p^*$.

Derive conditions for local stability of the CE using linearization.

Derive conditions for global stability using the WARP (use as a Lyapunov function, the function $V(p) = \sum_{i=1}^{n}(p_i - p_i^*)^2$).

Cournot Stability

Profit for firm i: $\pi_i(x) = x_iP(X) - c_i(x_i)$, $x = (x_1,\ldots,x_n)$, $X = \sum_{i=1}^{n}x_i$.

Cournot equilibrium: $x^* = (x_1^*,\ldots,x_n^*)$ is a Cournot equilibrium (CE) if

$$\pi_i(x_1^*,\ldots,x_n^*) \geq \pi_i(x_1^*,\ldots,x_i,\ldots,x_n^*) \quad \forall x_i \neq x_i^* \quad (17)$$

Derive and interpret first- and second-order conditions for CE.

Write first-order conditions in the form of the dynamical system

$$\dot{x}_i = \phi_i (x_1, \ldots, x_n) \tag{18}$$

Link CE with the steady state of $\phi_i (x_1, \ldots, x_n)$ and derive conditions for stability (use linearization).

Predator–Prey, Lotka–Volterra Systems

Consider the predator–prey system

$$\dot{x} = x (1 - y) \tag{19}$$
$$\dot{y} = ay (x - 1) \tag{20}$$

Determine the steady states and characterize stability properties.

Chapter 3

Optimal Control and the Principle of Optimality

Control in Optimization Problems

A fishery problem x: fish biomass, u: fishing (harvesting)

$$\dot{x}(t) = F(x(t)), \quad x(0) = x_0 \tag{1}$$

$$\dot{x}(t) = F(x(t)) - u(t) \tag{2}$$

A capital accumulation problem k: capital stock, $f(k)$: production function, c: consumption

$$\dot{k}(t) = sf(k(t)) - \delta k(t), \quad k(0) = k_0 \tag{3}$$

$$\dot{k}(t) = f(k(t)) - c(t) - \delta k(t), \quad k(0) = k_0 \tag{4}$$

Extracting an exhaustible resource (oil) S: stock of the resource, u: extraction rate.

$$\dot{S}(t) = -u(t), \quad S(0) = S_0 \tag{5}$$

$x(t)$: state variable, $u(t)$: control variable

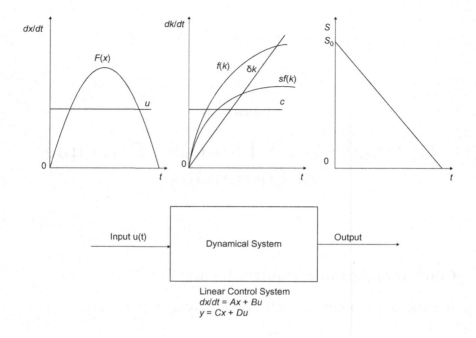

Possible Objectives

Fishery: Maximize profit over a finite time horizon by choosing harvesting $u(t)$

$$J = \int_0^T e^{-\rho t} \left[R(u(t)) - c(x(t), u(t)) \right] dt, \, x(T) = x_T \quad \text{given} \quad (6)$$

Capital accumulation: Maximize utility over an infinite time by choosing consumption $c(t)$

$$J = \int_0^\infty e^{-\rho t} U(c(t)) dt \quad (7)$$

Extraction: Maximize profits from extraction by choosing the extraction rate $u(t)$. Resource is exhausted in finite time

$$J = \int_0^T e^{-\rho t} \left[R(u(t)) - c(x(t), u(t)) \right] dt, \quad S(T) = 0 \quad (8)$$

J or $J[x]$ is a functional.

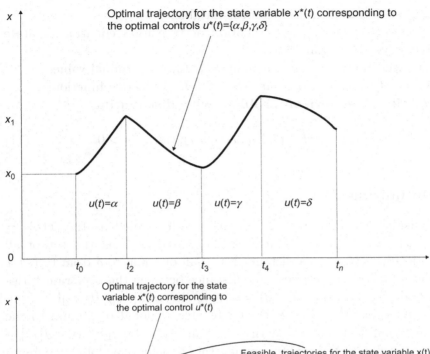

Optimal trajectory for the state variable $x^*(t)$ corresponding to the optimal controls $u^*(t) = \{\alpha, \beta, \gamma, \delta\}$

$u(t) = \alpha$ $u(t) = \beta$ $u(t) = \gamma$ $u(t) = \delta$

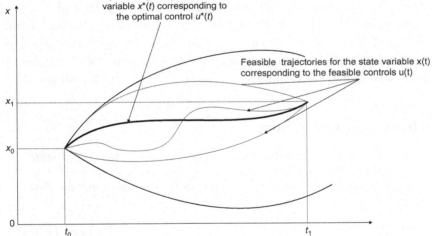

Optimal trajectory for the state variable $x^*(t)$ corresponding to the optimal control $u^*(t)$

Feasible trajectories for the state variable x(t) corresponding to the feasible controls u(t)

The General Control Problem

$$\max_{u(t)} \int_{t_0}^{T} f_0(x(t), u(t), t)dt + S\left(x(T), T\right) \qquad (9)$$

subject to $\dot{x}(t) = f(x(t), u(t), t), \quad x(t_0) = x_0, \quad u \in \mathcal{U}, \quad t \in [t_0, T]$

$$(10)$$

$x(t)$: state variable, $u(t)$: control variable,
$f(x(t), u(t), t)$: equation of motion or transition equation or state dynamics, x_0: initial state,
t_0: initial time, T: terminal time, $S(x(T), T)$: terminal value,
$J(u) = \int_{t_0}^{T} f_0(x(t), u(t), t)dt + S(x(T), T)$: objective functional.

Infinite time horizon problem with discounting

$$\max_{u(t)} \int_{t_0}^{\infty} e^{-\rho t} f_0(x(t), u(t), t)dt, \quad \rho > 0 \tag{11}$$

Optimizing J

Consider the trajectory x and its graph defined as the set $\Gamma = \{(t, x(t)): t \in [t_1, t_2]\}$. The δ neighborhood of Γ is the set of all trajectories (t, x) at a distance less than or equal to δ from Γ. Let x and y be two trajectories. The distance between the two trajectories x and y is defined as $d(x, y) = sup[|y(t) - x(t)|, \ t \in [t_0, t_1]]$.

A trajectory $x^* \in X$ is said to give a global maximum to the functional $J[x]$, and we say that x^* is an optimal trajectory if $J[x^*] \geq J[y]$ for all $y \in X$. The functional is said to achieve a global maximum at x^*. The global maximum is unique if $J[x^*] > J[y]$ for all $y \in X$.

Principle of Optimality

An optimal policy has the property that whatever the initial state and initial decision are, the remaining decisions must constitute an optimal policy with regard to the state resulting from the first decision.

Richard Bellman

Definition: From any point on an optimal trajectory, the remaining trajectory is optimal for the problem initiated at that point.

Let $x^*(t)$ be the optimal trajectory as defined above. Let y^* denote any subarc of the curve x^*, as shown in the following figure, and let Ω_0 be the class of all admissible trajectories $\hat{y}(t), t \in [a, b]$, with initial conditions and terminal conditions the same as y That is $y(a) = y^*(a)$, $y(b) = y^*(b)$. Then y^* is an optimal trajectory for problem in Ω_0. In other words, a truncated part of an optimal trajectory is itself optimal for the time interval corresponding to the truncated part.

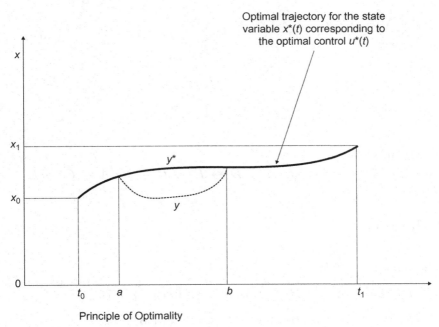

Principle of Optimality

Optimization in Stages

Optimization over time can be thought of as 'optimization in stages'. The best action maximizes (minimizes) the sum of the benefits (costs) obtained at the current stage and the maximum (minimum) total benefits (costs) that can be obtained from all subsequent stages, consequent on this decision. This is known as the Principle of Optimality.

A Shortest Distance Problem

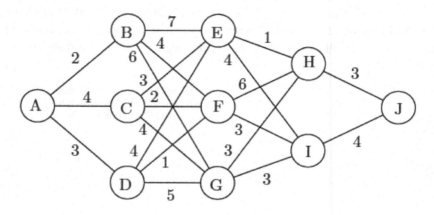

Optimal paths:
$A \to D \to F \to I \to J$, $A \to D \to E \to H \to J$, $A \to C \to E \to H \to J$

Solution

$$V(J) = 0, \quad V(H) = 3, \quad V(I) = 4$$

$$V(F) = \min \{6 + V(H), 3 + V(I)\} = \min \{9, 7\} = 7$$

$$V(E) = \min \{1 + V(H), 4 + V(I)\} = \min \{4, 8\} = 4$$

$$V(G) = \min \{3 + V(H), 3 + V(I)\} = \min \{6, 7\} = 6$$

$$V(D) = \min \{4 + V(E), 1 + V(F), 5 + V(G)\} = \min \{8, 8, 11\} = 8$$

$$V(C) = \min \{3 + V(E), 2 + V(F), 4 + V(G)\} = \min \{7, 9, 10\} = 7$$

$$V(B) = \min \{7 + V(E), 4 + V(F), 6 + V(G)\}$$
$$= \min \{11, 11, 12\} = 11$$

$$V(A) = \min \{2 + V(B), 4 + V(C), 3 + V(D)\}$$
$$= \min \{13, 11, 11\} = 11$$

Optimal paths:
$A \to D \to F \to I \to J$, $A \to D \to E \to H \to J$, $A \to C \to E \to H \to J$

State Structure Optimization and Dynamic Programming

Discrete time approximation

Uncontrolled system or process: $x_t = f(x_{t-1}, t)$, x is the **state variable**, $t = 0, 1, 2, ...$

Controlled system or process:

$$x_t = f(x_{t-1}, u_{t-1}, t) \tag{12}$$

u is the **control variable**.

We optimize from $t = 0$ until $t = T$. Assume we want to minimize costs for $0 \le t \le T$. T is the fixed **horizon**.

The **performance or objective** is

$$\mathbb{C} = \sum_{\tau=0}^{T-1} c(x_\tau, u_\tau, \tau) + \mathbb{C}_T(x_T) \tag{13}$$

$c(x_t, u_t, t)$: **instantaneous cost**, $\mathbb{C}_T(x_T)$: **terminal or closing cost**

Backward Recursion for the Objective

$$\mathbb{C}_t = \sum_{\tau=t}^{T-1} c(x_\tau, u_\tau, t) + \mathbb{C}_T(x_T) \tag{14}$$

$$c(x_t, u_t, t) + \sum_{\tau=t+1}^{T-1} c(x_\tau, u_\tau, t) + \mathbb{C}_T(x_T), \quad \text{or} \tag{15}$$

$$\mathbb{C}_t = c(x_t, u_t, t) + \mathbb{C}_{t+1} \tag{16}$$

Solution Approaches

1. Solve (12) in terms of u and write the cost function as

$$\mathbb{C} = \sum_{\tau=0}^{T-1} g\left(x_\tau, x_{\tau+1}, \tau\right) + \mathbb{C}_T(x_T). \tag{17}$$

This leads to the *calculus of variations*.
2. Minimize $\mathbb{C}$ with respect to both $\{x_t\}$ and $\{u_t\}$ by minimizing (14) subject to (13) by using appropriate Lagrangean multipliers. This provides a route to Pontryagin's maximum principle.

Dynamic Programming

Define the value function $V(x_t, t)$ as the minimal value of $\mathbb{C}_t$ with respect to the remaining control values u_τ $(t \leq \tau \leq T)$ for a given x_t. We regard the value function as a function $V(x, t)$ which is the minimal cost incurred from time t if x_t has value x.

Theorem (Dynamic Programming Equation): *Given (12) and (13), the value function obeys the dynamic programming equation*

$$V(x, t) = \inf_u \left[c(x, u, t) + V\left(x, t+1\right)\right] \tag{18}$$

$$= \inf_u \left[c(x, u, t) + V(f(x, u, t), t+1)\right] \tag{19}$$

$$= \inf_u \left[c(x, u, t) + V(f(x_t, u_t, t+1))\right] \tag{20}$$

with terminal condition

$$V(x, T) = \mathbb{C}_T(x_T) \tag{21}$$

The minimizing value of u in (18) is a function of x and t only, or $u(x, t)$ and the optimal control at time t is $u_t = u(x_t, t)$.

Feedback Control

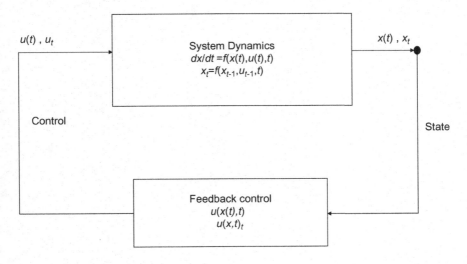

Feedback Control

Discounting and Time Independence

$$\mathbb{C} = \sum_{\tau=0}^{T-1} \beta^\tau c\left(x_\tau, u_\tau, \tau\right) + \beta^T \mathbb{C}_T\left(x_T\right) \qquad (22)$$

$$V(x,t) = \inf_u \left[c(x,u,t) + \beta V\left(f(x,u,t), t+1\right)\right] \qquad (23)$$

If c and f are independent of time, or $f\left(x,u\right), c\left(x,u\right)$ the problem is said to be **time-homogeneous or time-autonomous.** The value function will depend on the difference $s = T - t$ which is **the time to go.** We will write $V(x,t) = V_s\left(x\right)$.

If the problem is time-homogeneous and the time horizon is infinite $T \to \infty$, for well-defined $\mathbb{C}$, the value function is independent of t.

Chapter 4

Calculus of Variations

The Problem

$$\max_{x(t)} \int_{t_0}^{t_1} F\left(t, x(t), \dot{x}(t)\right) dt, \quad \dot{x}(t) = \frac{dx(t)}{dt} \qquad (1)$$

$$\text{subject to } x\left(t_0\right) = x_0, x\left(t_1\right) = x_1 \qquad (2)$$

- F is to be understood as a function of three independent arguments

$$F(u, v, z). \text{ If } F(u, v, z) = u^2 + vz - z^2 \qquad (3)$$

$$F(t, x, \dot{x}) = t^2 + x\dot{x} - (\dot{x})^2 \qquad (4)$$

- F is continuous in $(t, x, \dot{x})$ and has continuous partial derivatives with respect to $(x, \dot{x})$.
- The admissible class of functions $x(t)$, among which the maximum is sought, consists of all continuously differentiable functions defined on the interval $[t_0, t_1]$ satisfying the fixed endpoint conditions $x\left(t_0\right) = x_0, x\left(t_1\right) = x_1$.

The Euler–Lagrange Equation

If $x^*(t)$ is a trajectory that solves problem (1) in the fixed time interval $[t_0, t_1]$, then it satisfies the Euler–Lagrange (or just Euler) equation

$$F_x\left(t, x^*(t), \dot{x}^*(t)\right) = \frac{d}{dt}\left(F_{\dot{x}}\left(t, x^*(t), \dot{x}^*(t)\right)\right) \tag{5}$$

$$F_x = \frac{\partial F\left(t, x^*(t), \dot{x}^*(t)\right)}{\partial x}, \quad F_{\dot{x}} = \frac{\partial F\left(t, x^*(t), \dot{x}^*(t)\right)}{\partial \dot{x}} \tag{6}$$

The Euler equation is a necessary condition for optimization. Since

$$\frac{dF_{\dot{x}}}{dt} = F_{\dot{x}t} + F_{\dot{x}x}\dot{x} + F_{\dot{x}\dot{x}}\ddot{x} \tag{7}$$

the Euler equation becomes the second-order ODE.

$$F_x = F_{\dot{x}t} + F_{\dot{x}x}\dot{x} + F_{\dot{x}\dot{x}}\ddot{x}, \quad t_0 \le t \le t_1 \tag{8}$$

$$x\left(t_0\right) = x_0, \quad x(t_1) = x_1 \tag{9}$$

with all derivatives evaluated at $(t, x^*(t), \dot{x}^*(t))$ and $\dot{x} = \dot{x}(t)$, $\ddot{x} = \ddot{x}(t) = \frac{d^2 x(t)}{dt^2}$. The boundary conditions $x\left(t_0\right) = x_0, x(t_1) = x_1$ are necessary to determine the two arbitrary constants of integration.

Forms of the Euler Equation

- duBois–Reymond equation

$$F_x\left(t, x^*(t), \dot{x}^*(t)\right) = \int_{t_0}^{t_1}\left(F_{\dot{x}}\left(s, x^*(s), \dot{x}^*(s)\right)\right)ds + c \tag{10}$$

- $F = F(x, \dot{x})$. Take the total derivative of $F(x, \dot{x}) - \dot{x}F_{\dot{x}}(x, \dot{x})$ with respect to time

$$\frac{d}{dt}\left(F - \dot{x}F_{\dot{x}}\right) = F_x\dot{x} + F_{\dot{x}}\ddot{x} - \ddot{x}F_{\dot{x}} - \dot{x}\frac{dF_{\dot{x}}}{dt} \tag{11}$$

$$= \dot{x}\left(F_x - \frac{dF_{\dot{x}}}{dt}\right), \quad F_x - \frac{dF_{\dot{x}}}{dt}: \text{Euler equation}$$

$$\frac{d}{dt}\left(F - \dot{x}F_{\dot{x}}\right) = \dot{x}\left(F_x - \frac{dF_{\dot{x}}}{dt}\right)$$

$$= 0 \begin{cases} \text{if } \dot{x} = 0, \text{ or} \\ \text{the Euler equation is satisfied} \end{cases} \tag{12}$$

$$\frac{d}{dt}\left(F - \dot{x}F_{\dot{x}}\right) = 0 \Rightarrow F - \dot{x}F_{\dot{x}} = C \tag{13}$$

If (13) is satisfied then $\forall t \in [t_0, t_1]$

$$(F - \dot{x}F_{\dot{x}}) = C \Leftrightarrow \dot{x} = 0 \quad \text{or} \tag{14}$$

$$F_x - \frac{dF_{\dot{x}}}{dt} = 0 \tag{15}$$

Special Cases of the Euler Equation

(1) $F = F(t, \dot{x})$: then the Euler equation $F_x(t, x^*(t), \dot{x}^*(t)) - \frac{d}{dt}(F_{\dot{x}}(t, x^*(t), \dot{x}^*(t))) = 0$ implies

$$F_{\dot{x}}(t, \dot{x}) = \text{constant} \tag{16}$$

(2) $F = F(x, \dot{x})$ (autonomous problem): From $\frac{d}{dt}(F - \dot{x}F_{\dot{x}}) = \dot{x}\left(F_x - \frac{dF_{\dot{x}}}{dt}\right)$, we obtain

$$F - \dot{x}F_{\dot{x}} = \text{constant} \tag{17}$$

(3) $F = F(\dot{x})$: The Euler equation $F_x = F_{\dot{x}t} + F_{\dot{x}x} + F_{\dot{x}\dot{x}}\ddot{x}$ implies

$$F_{\dot{x}\dot{x}}\ddot{x} = 0 \tag{18}$$

which means that either $F_{\dot{x}\dot{x}}(\dot{x}) = 0$ or $\ddot{x} = 0$.

Canonical Form of the Euler Equation

Define

$$p(t) = F_{\dot{x}}(t, x, \dot{x}) \tag{19}$$

and introduce the **Hamiltonian function**

$$H(t, x, p) = -F(t, x, \dot{x}) + p\dot{x} \tag{20}$$

p in economics is **shadow price**, in physics it refers to generalized momenta.

$$dH = -F_t dt - F_x dx - F_{\dot{x}} d\dot{x} + p d\dot{x} + \dot{x} dp \qquad (21)$$

$$= -F_t dt - F_x dx + \dot{x} dp \qquad (22)$$

$$\text{since } F_{\dot{x}} d\dot{x} = p d\dot{x} \text{ by the definition of } p. \qquad (23)$$

Then

$$\frac{\partial H}{\partial x} = -F_x, \quad \frac{\partial H}{\partial p} = \dot{x} \qquad (24)$$

If $x(t)$ satisfies the Euler equation $-F_x = -\frac{d}{dt} F_{\dot{x}} = -\frac{dp}{dt} = -\dot{p}$. Then the **canonical form** of the Euler equation is

$$\dot{p} = -\frac{\partial H}{\partial x}, \quad \dot{x} = \frac{\partial H}{\partial p} \qquad (25)$$

Second Order Conditions

If $F(t, x, \dot{x})$ is concave in $(x, \dot{x})$ and if $x(t)$ satisfies the Euler equation $F_x = \frac{d}{dt} F_{\dot{x}}$ then $x^*(t)$ maximizes

$$\int_{t_0}^{t_1} F(t, x, \dot{x}) \, dt, \quad \text{subject to } x(t_0) = x_0, \quad x(t_1) = x_1 \qquad (26)$$

Thus, if $F(t, x, \dot{x})$ is concave in $(x, \dot{x})$, the Euler equation is **sufficient** for optimality.

Solve the optimal consumption problem for an individual

$$\max_{C(t)} \int_0^T e^{-rt} U(C(t)) \, dt \quad U' > 0, U'' < 0 \qquad (27)$$

$$iK(t) + w(t) = C(t) + \dot{K}(t) \qquad (28)$$

$$K(0) = K_0, K(T) = K_T \text{ specified} \qquad (29)$$

Solve the same problem with $r = 0$.

Transversality Conditions

Transversality conditions provide along with the initial condition $x(t_0) = x_0$ the required boundary conditions to determine to two arbitrary constants required for the solution of the Euler equation which is a second-order ODE.

When a terminal condition $x(t_1) = x_1$ is given, we have the two boundary conditions required. But we may have more complicated terminal conditions:

(1) t_1 fixed $x(t_1)$ free
(2) t_1 fixed $x(t_1) \geq x_1$, x_1 fixed
(3) t_1 free, $x(t_1) = g(t_1)$, g a given C^1- function
(4) t_1 free, $x(t_1) \geq x_1$, x_1 fixed

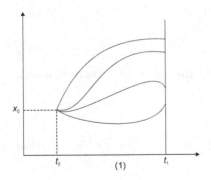

(1)

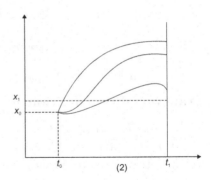

(2)

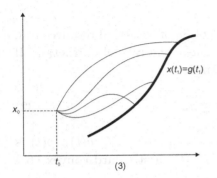

(3)

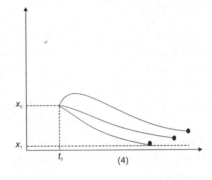

(4)

The corresponding transversality conditions are

(1) $[F_{\dot{x}}]_{t=t_1} = 0.$
(2) $[F_{\dot{x}}]_{t=t_1} \leq 0, \quad (= 0 \text{ if } x^*(t_1) > x_1).$
(3) $[F + (\dot{g} - \dot{x}) F_{\dot{x}}]_{t=t_1} = 0.$
(4) $[F_{\dot{x}}]_{t=t_1} \leq 0, \quad (= 0 \text{ if } x^*(t_1) > x_1)$
    $[F - \dot{x} F_{\dot{x}}]_{t=t_1} = 0.$

The necessary conditions for a function x to solve the optimization problem are that it satisfies the Euler equation, the initial condition $x(t_0) = x_0$, and the transversality condition.

Salvage (Scrap) Value

$$\max_{x(t)} \int_{t_0}^{t_1} F(t, x(t), \dot{x}(t)) \, dt + G(x(t_1)) \tag{30}$$

$$\text{subject to } x(t_0) = x_0 \tag{31}$$

G is a given function $x(t_1)$ is to be determined by the maximization.

Transversality condition:

$[F_{\dot{x}}]_{t=t_1} + G'(x(t_1)) = 0$

If $x^*(t)$ solves problem (), then x^* satisfies the Euler equation and the transversality condition.

Optimal Extraction

At time $t = 0$, there is a fixed amount of S_0 of a natural resource (oil, natural gas) which is extractable. Let $u(t)$ the rate of extraction. If T is the time that extraction stops, then

$$\int_0^T u(t) dt \leq S_0 \tag{32}$$

The rate of profit at time t is $\pi(u(t)) = p(t)u(t) - C(u(t))$, $p(t)$ is the world price of the resource and $C(u(t))$ a standard convex cost function.

Formulate the problem of maximizing discounted profits as a variational problem with $S(T) \geq 0$, T free. Solve it using the transversality conditions 4.

Several Unknown Functions: The Problem

$$\max_{x(t)} \int_{t_0}^{t_1} F(t, x(t), \dot{x}(t))\, dt \tag{33}$$

$$x(t) = (x_1(t), \ldots, x_n(t)), \quad \dot{x}(t) = (\dot{x}_1(t), \ldots, \dot{x}_n(t)) \tag{34}$$

$$x(t_0) = (x_{10}, \ldots, x_{n0}), \tag{35}$$

$$_i(t_1) = x_{i1}, \quad i = 1, \ldots, l \tag{36}$$

$$x_i(t_1) > x_{i1}, \quad i = l+1, \ldots, m \tag{37}$$

$$x_i(t_1) \; free, \quad i = m+1, \ldots, n \tag{38}$$

The Euler Equation (Necessary Conditions)

$$\frac{\partial F}{\partial x_i} - \frac{d}{dt}\left(\frac{\partial F}{\partial \dot{x}_i}\right) = 0, \quad i = 1, \ldots, n$$

Transversality conditions are

$$x_i^*(t_1) = x_{i1}, \quad i = 1, \ldots, l \tag{39}$$

$$\left(\frac{\partial F}{\partial \dot{x}_i}\right)_{t=t_1} \leq 0 \;\; (= 0 \text{ if } x_i^*(t_1) > x_{i1}), \quad i = l+1, \ldots, m \tag{40}$$

$$\left(\frac{\partial F}{\partial \dot{x}_i}\right)_{t=t_1} = 0, \quad i = m+1, \ldots, n \tag{41}$$

The Legendre necessary condition is

$$\sum_{j=1}^{n}\sum_{i=1}^{n} F''_{\dot{x}_i \dot{x}_j}(t, x^*(t), \dot{x}^*(t))\, h_i h_j \leq 0 \tag{42}$$

for all $t \in [t_0, t_1]$ and all numbers $h_i h_j$, $i, j = 1, \ldots, n$.

Chapter 5

Optimal Control

The Problem

$$\max_{u(t)} J(u) = \int_{t_0}^{t_1} F\left(t, x(t), u(t)\right) dt, \quad \dot{x}(t) = \frac{dx(t)}{dt} \tag{1}$$

$$\text{subject to } \dot{x}(t) = g\left(x(t), u(t), t\right) \; x\left(t_0\right) = x_0, \tag{2}$$

$$x\left(t_1\right) = x_1 \text{ fixed, or } \; x\left(t_1\right) \geq x_1, \text{ or } x\left(t_1\right) \text{ free} \tag{3}$$

$$u \in \mathcal{U} \subset \mathbb{R} \tag{4}$$

- $x(t)$ is the state variable, $u(t)$ is the control variable, piecewise continuous function of time, g is the equation of motion or transition equation and $[t_0, t_1]$ is the finite time horizon.

The Pontryagin Maximum Principle

If $u^*(t)$ is piecewise continuous control in the fixed time interval $[t_0, t_1]$ that solves problem (1) and $x^*(t)$ is the associated optimal trajectory or optimal path for the state variable, then there exist a constant p_0 and a continuous and piecewise continuously differentiable function $p(t)$ from $[t_0, t_1]$ to $\mathbb{R}$ such that

$$\left(p_0, p(t)\right) \neq (0, 0) \tag{5}$$

$u^*(t)$ maximizes the Hamiltonian function for $u \in \mathcal{U}$

$$H\left(t, x(t), u(t), p(t)\right) = p_0 F\left(t, x(t), u(t)\right) + p(t)g\left(x(t), u(t), t\right) \quad (6)$$

that is,

$$H\left(t, x^*(t), u^*(t), p(t)\right) \geq H\left(t, x^*(t), u(t), p(t)\right) \quad \forall u \in \mathcal{U} \quad (7)$$

Except at the points of discontinuity of $u^*(t)$, $\{x^*(t), p(t)\}$ solves the Hamiltonian system

$$\dot{p}(t) = -\frac{\partial H^*}{\partial x} \quad (8)$$

$$\dot{x}(t) = \frac{\partial H^*}{\partial p}, \quad x\left(t_0\right) = x_0 \quad (9)$$

$$H^* = H\left(t, x^*(t), u^*(t), p(t)\right) \quad (10)$$

$$u^*(t) = h\left(t, x(t), p(t)\right) \quad (11)$$

$$p_0 = 1 \text{ for economic applications} \quad (12)$$

For interior solutions $u^*(t) = h\left(t, x(t), p(t)\right)$ is determined by:

$$\frac{\partial H^*}{\partial u} = \frac{\partial F}{\partial u} + p\frac{\partial g}{\partial u} = 0 \quad (13)$$

The following transversality conditions are satisfied:

$$\text{If } x\left(t_1\right) = x_1 \text{ fixed} \Rightarrow p\left(t_1\right) \text{ free (no conditions)} \quad (14)$$

$$\text{If } x\left(t_1\right) \geq x_1 \Rightarrow p\left(t_1\right) \geq 0 \left(= 0 \text{ if } x^*\left(t_1\right) \geq x_1\right) \quad (15)$$

$$\text{If } x\left(t_1\right) \text{ free} \Rightarrow p\left(t_1\right) = 0 \quad (16)$$

The variable $p(t)$ is called the **costate** or **auxiliary** variable. Substituting the solutions $u^*(t) = h\left(t, x(t), p(t)\right)$ for the optimal controls into the Hamiltonian system, the following system of first-order differential equations is obtained:

$$\dot{p}(t) = \phi\left(t, x(t), p(t)\right) \quad (17)$$
$$\dot{x}(t) = g\left(t, x(t), h\left(t, x(t), p(t)\right)\right) \quad (18)$$

The solution of this system with boundary conditions is determined by the initial conditions and the transversality conditions determine the optimal path or optimal trajectory for the state variable $x^*(t)$, and the paths for the costate variable $\hat{p}(t)$. The time path for the optimal control is determined as

$$u^*(t) = h\left(t, x^*(t), \hat{p}(t)\right) \tag{19}$$

The optimality conditions of the maximum principle are necessary conditions. Second-order sufficient conditions are stated in the following section.

Sufficient Conditions

Mangasarian sufficient conditions: Let $\{x^*(t), u^*(t)\}$ be an admissible pair of trajectories for problem (1). If auxiliary variable $p(t)$ exists with $p_0 = 1$, such that the conditions of the maximum principle are satisfied and $H(x, u, p, t)$ is concave in (x, u) for all t, then $\{x^*(t), u^*(t)\}$ solves problem (1). If the Hamiltonian is strictly concave, then a unique solution to the problem exists.

Arrow sufficient conditions: Let $\{x^*(t), u^*(t)\}$ be an admissible pair of trajectories for problem (1). Assume that an auxiliary variable $p(t)$ exists with $p_0 = 1$, such that the conditions of the maximum principle are satisfied. Define the maximized Hamiltonian as

$$H^0\left(x, p, t\right) = \max_u H\left(x, u, p, t\right) \tag{20}$$

If $H^0\left(x, p, t\right)$ is concave in x for all t, then $\{x^*(t), u^*(t)\}$ solves problem (1). If $H^0\left(x, p, t\right)$ is strictly concave, then a unique solution to the problem exists.
  Solve

$$\max_{u(t)} \int_0^1 (x + u)\, dt \tag{21}$$

subject to $\dot{x} = 1 - u^2$ $x(0) = 1$, or $x(1)$ free $\tag{22}$

$$\max_{u(t)} \int_0^3 \left(u - \frac{1}{2}u^2 - \frac{1}{2}x^2\right) dt \tag{23}$$

subject to $\dot{x} = -x + u, x(0) = 5$ $\tag{24}$

$$x\left(3\right) = 1, \quad \text{or } x\left(3\right) \text{ free, or } x\left(3\right) \geq 1 \tag{25}$$

Several Unknown Functions: The Problem

$$\max_{x(t)} \int_{t_0}^{t_1} F\left(t, x(t), u(t)\right) dt \qquad (26)$$

subject to $\dot{x}(t) = g\left(x(t), u(t), t\right), \ x\left(t_0\right) = x_0$

$$x(t) = (x_1(t), \dots, x_n(t)), \quad \dot{x}(t) = (\dot{x}_1(t), \dots, \dot{x}_n(t))$$

$$u(t) = (u_1(t), \dots, u_J(t)), \quad u \in \mathcal{U} \subset \mathbb{R}^J$$

$$x\left(t_0\right) = (x_{10}, \dots, x_{n0})$$

$$x_i\left(t_1\right) = x_{i1}, \quad i = 1, \dots, l$$

$$x_i\left(t_1\right) > x_{i1}, \quad i = l+1, \dots, m$$

$$x_i\left(t_1\right) \ \text{free}, \quad i = m+1, \dots, n.$$

The Pontryagin Maximum Principle for Many State Variables

If $u^*(t)$ is piecewise continuous control in the fixed time interval $[t_0, t_1]$ that solves problem (1) and $x^*(t)$ is the associated optimal trajectory or optimal path for the state variable, then there then there exist a constant p_0 and a continuous and piecewise continuously differentiable function $p(t) = (p_1(t), \dots, p_n(t))$ from $[t_0, t_1]$ to $\mathbb{R}^n$ such that:

$$(p_0, p(t)) \neq (0, 0) \qquad (27)$$

$u^*(t)$ maximizes the Hamiltonian function for $u \in \mathcal{U}$

$$H\left(t, x(t), u(t), p(t)\right) = p_0 F\left(t, x(t), u(t)\right)$$

$$+ \sum_{i=1}^{n} p_i(t) g\left(x(t), u(t), t\right) \qquad (28)$$

that is,

$$H\left(t, x^*(t), u^*(t), p(t)\right) \geq H\left(t, x^*(t), u(t), p(t)\right), \quad \forall u \in \mathcal{U} \qquad (29)$$

Except at the points of discontinuity of $u^*(t)$, $\{x^*(t), p(t)\}$ solves the $(2xn)$-dimensional Hamiltonian system as follows:

$$\dot{p}_i(t) = -\frac{\partial H^*}{\partial x}, \quad i = 1, \ldots, n \tag{30}$$

$$\dot{x}_i(t) = \frac{\partial H^*}{\partial p}, \quad i = 1, \ldots, n, \quad x(t_0) = x_0 \tag{31}$$

$$H^* = H(t, x^*(t), u^*(t), p(t)) \tag{32}$$

$$u^*(t) = h(t, x(t), p(t)) \tag{33}$$

$$p_0 = 1 \text{ for economic applications} \tag{34}$$

The following transversality conditions are satisfied:

If $x_i(t_1) = x_{i1}$ fixed $\Rightarrow p_i(t_1)$ free (no conditions)

$$i = 1, \ldots, l$$

If $x_i(t_1) \geq x_{i1} \Rightarrow p(t_{i1}) \geq 0 \, (= 0 \text{ if } x^*(t_1) \geq x_1)$,

$$i = l + 1, \ldots, m$$

If $x_i(t_1)$ free $\Rightarrow p_i(t_1) = 0, \quad i = m + 1, \ldots, n.$

Optimal Control with Discounted Objective: Current Value Hamiltonians

$$\max_{u(t)} J(u) = \int_{t_0}^{t_1} e^{-\rho t} F(t, x(t), u(t)) \, dt, \quad \rho > 0 \tag{35}$$

$$\text{subject to } \dot{x}(t) = g(x(t), u(t), t) \quad x(t_0) = x_0, \tag{36}$$

$$x(t_1) = x_1 \text{ fixed}, \quad \text{or} \quad x(t_1) \geq x_1, \quad \text{or} \quad x(t_1) \text{ free} \tag{37}$$

$$u \in \mathcal{U} \subset \mathbb{R} \tag{38}$$

Current value Hamiltonian with $p_0 = 1$

$$H(t, x(t), u(t), p(t)) = F(t, x(t), u(t)) + \lambda(t) g(x(t), u(t), t)$$

$$\lambda(t) = e^{\rho t} p(t), \quad \lambda(t) e^{-\rho t} = p(t)$$

Pontryagin's maximum principle

- $u^*(t)$ maximizes the **current value** Hamiltonian function for $u \in \mathcal{U}$

$$\dot{\lambda}(t) = \rho\lambda(t) - \frac{\partial H^*}{\partial x} \tag{39}$$

$$\dot{x}(t) = \frac{\partial H^*}{\partial \lambda}, x(t_0) = x_0 \tag{40}$$

$$H^* = H(t, x^*(t), u^*(t), p(t)) \tag{41}$$

$$\text{If } x(t_1) = x_1 \text{ fixed} \Rightarrow p(t_1) \text{ free (no conditions)} \tag{42}$$

$$\text{If } x(t_1) \geq x_1 \Rightarrow p(t_1) \geq 0 \, (= 0 \text{ if } x^*(t_1) \geq x_1) \tag{43}$$

$$\text{If } x(t_1) \text{ free} \Rightarrow p(t_1) = 0 \tag{44}$$

- This is extended in a straightforward way to the many state variables' case.

$$H^P(t, x, u, p) = e^{-\rho t}F(t, x, u) + p(t)g(x, u, t) \tag{45}$$

$$\text{multiply } H^P \text{ by } e^{\rho t} \tag{46}$$

$$H^C(t, x, u, p) = e^{\rho t}H^P(t, x, u, p) \tag{47}$$

$$= F(t, x, u) + \lambda(t)(t)g(x, u, t) \tag{48}$$

$$H^P = e^{-\rho t}H^C \tag{49}$$

If $u^*(t)$ maximizes H^P, it maximizes H^C and reverse

$$\text{If } \frac{\partial H^C}{\partial u} = 0 \Leftrightarrow \frac{\partial(e^{\rho t}H^P)}{\partial u} = e^{\rho t}\frac{\partial H^P}{\partial u} = 0 \tag{50}$$

$$\frac{\partial H^P}{\partial u} = 0 \Leftrightarrow \frac{\partial H^C}{\partial u} \tag{51}$$

$$\dot{p} = -\frac{\partial H^P}{\partial x} \quad \text{or} \quad \frac{d}{dt}\left(\lambda e^{-\rho t}\right) = -\frac{\partial(e^{-\rho t}H^C)}{\partial x} \tag{52}$$

$$\dot{\lambda}e^{-\rho t} - \rho\lambda e^{-\rho t} = -e^{-\rho t}\frac{\partial H^C}{\partial x} \tag{53}$$

$$\dot{\lambda} = \rho\lambda - \frac{\partial H^C}{\partial x} \tag{54}$$

TVC: If $x(t_1)$ is free, then $\lambda(t_1) = e^{-\rho t_1}p(t_1) = 0 \Rightarrow p(t_1) = 0$.

All sufficiency theorems and TVCs apply to the current value of Hamiltonian.

Interpretation of the Costate Variables

Consider the maximum value function for optimal control problem with terminal conditions $x(t_1) = x_1$, defined as

$$V(x_0, x_1, t_0, t_1) = \max_{u(t)} \int_{t_0}^{t_1} F(t, x(t), u(t))\, dt \tag{55}$$

Then it can be shown that

$$\frac{\partial V}{\partial x_0} = p(0), \quad \frac{\partial V}{\partial x_1} = p(t_1) \tag{56}$$

Thus, the costate variable can be interpreted as the dynamic shadow value, or the opportunity cost of the state variable x at the initial and terminal state. The result can be generalized to any time τ. Then $p(\tau)$ is the dynamic shadow value of the state variable at any instant of time in the given time horizon.

$$\frac{\partial V}{\partial x(\tau)} = p(\tau) \tag{57}$$

Open Final Time Problems

$$\max_{u(t)} J(u) = \int_{t_0}^{t_1} F(t, x(t), u(t))\, dt \tag{58}$$

$$\text{subject to } \dot{x}(t) = g(x(t), u(t), t) \quad x(t_0) = x_0, \tag{59}$$

$$x(t_1) = x_1 \text{ fixed}, \quad \text{or} \quad x(t_1) \geq x_1, \quad \text{or} \quad x(t_1) \text{ free} \tag{60}$$

In the problem, both initial and terminal times are fixed. There are however problems where the optimal time is open and should be chosen optimally. In this case, the necessary conditions for the maximum principle are the same as (5)–(16) with one additional condition. If $t_1^* \in (t_0, \infty)$ is the optimal final time, then the following

$$H\left(t_1^*, x\left(t_1^*\right), u\left(t_1^*\right), p\left(t_1^*\right)\right) = F\left(t_1^*, x\left(t_1^*\right), u\left(t_1^*\right)\right) \tag{61}$$

$$+\lambda\left(t_1^*\right) g\left(x\left(t_1^*\right), u\left(t_1^*\right), t_1^*\right) = 0$$

condition should be satisfied (necessary condition). Solving this condition for t_1^* will determine the optimal final time.

Infinite Horizon Optimal Control

The infinite horizon optimal control problem can be stated for $t_0 = 0$ as

$$\max_{u(t)} \int_0^\infty e^{-\rho t} F\left(x(t), u(t)\right) dt \tag{62}$$

$$\text{subject to } \dot{x}(t) = g\left(x(t), u(t)\right) \quad x(0) = x_0 \text{ fixed} \tag{63}$$

$$x \in \mathcal{A} \subset \mathbb{R}^n, \quad u \in \mathcal{U} \subset \mathbb{R}^m \tag{64}$$

Problem (62) is an autonomous optimal control problem, since the F, g functions do not explicitly depend on time t, which is a case very often encountered in economic models.

Pontryagin's Maximum Principle

If the trajectory $\{x^*(t), u^*(t)\}$ with $x(0) = x_0$ solves problem (62), then $u^*(t)$ maximizes the current value Hamiltonian (interior solutions for the optimal controls $u^*(t)$ are assumed).

$$H\left(x, u, \lambda\right) = F\left(x, u\right) + \sum_{i=1}^n \lambda_i(t)(t) g\left(x, u\right) \tag{65}$$

$$\text{or } \frac{\partial H}{\partial u_j} = 0, \quad u_j^* = h_j\left(x, \lambda\right), \quad j = 1, \ldots, m \tag{66}$$

The triplet $\{x^*(t), u^*(t), \lambda(t)\}$ solves the modified Hamiltonian dynamic system (MHDS)

$$\dot{x}_i = \frac{\partial H^*}{\partial \lambda_i}, \quad H^* = H(x, u^*, \lambda), \quad i = 1, \ldots, n \tag{67}$$

$$\dot{\lambda}_i = \rho \lambda_i - \frac{\partial H^*}{\partial x_i}, \quad i = 1, \ldots, n \tag{68}$$

Transversality Conditions

Benveniste and Scheinkman (B–S) type transversality conditions are satisfied at infinity

$$\lim_{t \to \infty} \sum_{i=1}^{n} e^{-\rho t} \lambda_i(t) x_i(t) = 0 \tag{69}$$

or

$$\lim_{t \to \infty} e^{-\rho t} \lambda(t) x(t) = 0 \tag{70}$$

for one state variable.

The transversality condition for an infinite horizon dynamic optimization problem is the boundary condition determining a solution to the problem's first-order conditions together with the initial condition. The transversality condition requires the present value of the state variables to converge to zero as the planning horizon recedes towards infinity. The first-order and transversality conditions are sufficient to identify an optimum in a concave optimization problem. Given an optimal path, the necessity of the transversality condition reflects the impossibility of finding an alternative feasible path for which each state variable deviates from the optimum at each time and increases discounted utility.

- In general, the finite time horizon $\lambda_i(t_1) = 0$ TVC does not carry over to infinite horizon as $\lim_{t \to \infty} \lambda_i(t) e^{-\rho t} = 0$ (see Halkin's counter example).

- Under concavity assumption about F as a function of $x, \dot{x}$ the TVC at infinity $\lim_{t \to \infty} \sum_i e^{-\rho t} \lambda_i(t) x_i(t) = 0$ is a necessary condition (Benveniste and Scheinkman, *JET* 1982).
- Michel (*Econometrica* 1982) Necessary TVC at infinity under concavity assumption $\lim_{t \to \infty} H(t) = 0$.

Solution in the Control-State Space

This is convenient when $F = F(u)$ is independent of the state variable and $g(x, u)$ is separable in (x, u). The problem in this case is as follows:

$$\max_{u(t)} \int_0^\infty e^{-\rho t} F(u(t)) \, dt \tag{71}$$

$$\text{subject to } \dot{x}(t) = g(x(t))) + f(u(t)) \quad x(0) = x_0 \text{ fixed} \tag{72}$$

$$x \in \mathcal{A} \subset \mathbb{R}, \ u \in \mathcal{U} \subset \mathbb{R} \tag{73}$$

$$H = F(u) + \lambda(g(x) + f(u)) \tag{74}$$

$$F'(u) = -\lambda f'(u) \ \Rightarrow \lambda = -\frac{F'(u)}{f'(u)} = B(u) \tag{75}$$

$$\dot{x} = g(x) + f(u) \tag{76}$$

$$\dot{\lambda} = (\rho - g'(x))\lambda \tag{77}$$

Differentiate $F'(u) = -\lambda f'(u)$ with respect to time to obtain

$$F''(u)\dot{u} = -\lambda f''(u)\dot{u} - \dot{\lambda}f'(u) \Rightarrow \dot{\lambda} = \frac{(F''(u) - f''(u)\lambda)\dot{u}}{f'(u)} \tag{78}$$

$$\text{or } \dot{\lambda} = \frac{\left(F''(u) - f''(u)\left(-\frac{F'(u)}{f'(u)}\right)\right)\dot{u}}{f'(u)} = A(u)\dot{u} \tag{79}$$

The MHDS becomes

$$\dot{x} = g(x) + f(u) \tag{80}$$

$$A(u)\dot{u} = \left(\rho - g'\left(x\right)\right) B(u) \text{ or} \tag{81}$$

$$\dot{u} = \left(\rho - g'\left(x\right)\right) \frac{B(u)}{A(u)} \tag{82}$$

The transformed MHDS is defined in the control-state space.

Example: The Ramsey problem

$$\max_{\{c(t)\}} \int_0^\infty e^{-\rho t} U\left(c(t)\right) dt \tag{83}$$

$$\text{subject to} \tag{84}$$

$$\dot{k}(t) = f\left(k(t)\right) - c(t) - \delta k(t), \quad k(0) = k_0 \tag{85}$$

References

Benveniste, L.M. and Scheinkman, J.A. 1982. Duality theory for dynamic optimization models of economics: The continuous time case. *Journal of Economic Theory*, 27(1), pp. 1–19.

Michel, P. 1982. On the transversality condition in infinite horizon optimal problems. *Econometrica: Journal of the Econometric Society*, pp. 975–985.

```
(* max∫₀³ (u-½u²-x²) dt,  subject to ẋ=-x-u ,
x(0)=5,  x(3)=1,  or x(3)free,  or x(3)≥1 *)
(* H(x,u,p)=u-½u²-x²+p(-x+u)
    u=1+p,  ẋ=-x+p+1,  ṗ=x+p*)


Clear[p0, c1, c2]

m = {{-1, 1}, {1, 1}}
Eigensystem[m]
```

$$\{\{-1, 1\}, \{1, 1\}\}$$

$$\left\{\left\{-\sqrt{2}, \sqrt{2}\right\}, \left\{\left\{-1-\sqrt{2}, 1\right\}, \left\{-1+\sqrt{2}, 1\right\}\right\}\right\}$$

```
b = {-1, 0}
LinearSolve[m, b]
```

$$\{-1, 0\}$$

$$\left\{\frac{1}{2}, -\frac{1}{2}\right\}$$

```
v11 = -1 - √2 ;
v12 = -1 + √2 ;
v21 = 1;
v22 = 1;
l1 = -√2 ;
l2 = √2 ;
xbar = 1 / 2;
pbar = 1 / 2;
x[t_, c1_, c2_] = c1 * v11 * Exp[l1 * t] + c2 * v12 * Exp[l2 * t] + xbar
p[t_, c1_, c2_] = c1 * v21 * Exp[l1 * t] + c2 * v22 * Exp[l2 * t] + pbar
```

$$\frac{1}{2} + \left(-1 - \sqrt{2}\right) c1\, e^{-\sqrt{2}\, t} + \left(-1 + \sqrt{2}\right) c2\, e^{\sqrt{2}\, t}$$

$$\frac{1}{2} + c1\, e^{-\sqrt{2}\, t} + c2\, e^{\sqrt{2}\, t}$$

```
(*solve for intial values*)
Solve[{x[0, c1, c2] = 5, p[0, c1, c2] = p0}, {c1, c2}]
```

$$\left\{\left\{c1 \to \frac{-8 - \sqrt{2} - 2\,p0 + 2\sqrt{2}\,p0}{4\sqrt{2}}, \ c2 \to -\frac{1}{4} + \sqrt{2} + \frac{p0}{2} + \frac{p0}{2\sqrt{2}}\right\}\right\}$$

$$c1 = \frac{-8 - \sqrt{2} - 2\,p0 + 2\sqrt{2}\,p0}{4\sqrt{2}};$$

$$c2 = -\frac{1}{4} + \sqrt{2} + \frac{p0}{2} + \frac{p0}{2\sqrt{2}};$$

```
x1[t_, p0_] = x[t, c1, c2]
p1[t_, p0_] = p[t, c1, c2]
```

$$\frac{1}{2} + \left(-1+\sqrt{2}\right) e^{\sqrt{2}\,t} \left(-\frac{1}{4}+\sqrt{2}+\frac{p0}{2}+\frac{p0}{2\sqrt{2}}\right) +$$

$$\frac{1}{4\sqrt{2}}\left(-1-\sqrt{2}\right) e^{-\sqrt{2}\,t}\left(-8-\sqrt{2}-2\,p0+2\sqrt{2}\,p0\right)$$

$$\frac{1}{2} + e^{\sqrt{2}\,t}\left(-\frac{1}{4}+\sqrt{2}+\frac{p0}{2}+\frac{p0}{2\sqrt{2}}\right) + \frac{e^{-\sqrt{2}\,t}\left(-8-\sqrt{2}-2\,p0+2\sqrt{2}\,p0\right)}{4\sqrt{2}}$$

```
(* x(3)=1, p[3] free*)
Solve[x1[3, p0] = 1, p0]
```

$$\left\{\left\{p0 \to \frac{-9-5\sqrt{2}+2\,e^{3\sqrt{2}}-9\,e^{6\sqrt{2}}+5\sqrt{2}\,e^{6\sqrt{2}}}{\sqrt{2}\left(-1+e^{6\sqrt{2}}\right)}\right\}\right\}$$

```
p0 =
```
$$\frac{-9-5\sqrt{2}+2\,e^{3\sqrt{2}}-9\,e^{6\sqrt{2}}+5\sqrt{2}\,e^{6\sqrt{2}}}{\sqrt{2}\left(-1+e^{6\sqrt{2}}\right)};$$

```
c1
c2
```

$$\frac{1}{4\sqrt{2}}\left(-8-\sqrt{2}+1\Big/\left(-1+e^{6\sqrt{2}}\right)2\left(-9-5\sqrt{2}+2\,e^{3\sqrt{2}}-9\,e^{6\sqrt{2}}+5\sqrt{2}\,e^{6\sqrt{2}}\right)-\right.$$

$$\left.1\Big/\left(-1+e^{6\sqrt{2}}\right)\sqrt{2}\left(-9-5\sqrt{2}+2\,e^{3\sqrt{2}}-9\,e^{6\sqrt{2}}+5\sqrt{2}\,e^{6\sqrt{2}}\right)\right)$$

$$-\frac{1}{4}+\sqrt{2}+\frac{-9-5\sqrt{2}+2\,e^{3\sqrt{2}}-9\,e^{6\sqrt{2}}+5\sqrt{2}\,e^{6\sqrt{2}}}{4\left(-1+e^{6\sqrt{2}}\right)}+$$

$$\frac{-9-5\sqrt{2}+2\,e^{3\sqrt{2}}-9\,e^{6\sqrt{2}}+5\sqrt{2}\,e^{6\sqrt{2}}}{2\sqrt{2}\left(-1+e^{6\sqrt{2}}\right)}$$

$$c1 = \frac{1}{4\sqrt{2}}\left(-8-\sqrt{2}+1\Big/\left(-1+e^{6\sqrt{2}}\right)2\left(-9-5\sqrt{2}+2e^{3\sqrt{2}}-9e^{6\sqrt{2}}+5\sqrt{2}\ e^{6\sqrt{2}}\right)-\right.$$
$$\left.1\Big/\left(-1+e^{6\sqrt{2}}\right)\sqrt{2}\left(-9-5\sqrt{2}+2e^{3\sqrt{2}}-9e^{6\sqrt{2}}+5\sqrt{2}\ e^{6\sqrt{2}}\right)\right);$$

$$c2 = -\frac{1}{4}+\sqrt{2}+\frac{-9-5\sqrt{2}+2e^{3\sqrt{2}}-9e^{6\sqrt{2}}+5\sqrt{2}\ e^{6\sqrt{2}}}{4\left(-1+e^{6\sqrt{2}}\right)}+$$

$$\frac{-9-5\sqrt{2}+2e^{3\sqrt{2}}-9e^{6\sqrt{2}}+5\sqrt{2}\ e^{6\sqrt{2}}}{2\sqrt{2}\left(-1+e^{6\sqrt{2}}\right)};$$

`x1[t, p0]`
`p1[t, p0]`

$$\frac{1}{2}+\left(-1+\sqrt{2}\right)e^{\sqrt{2}\,t}$$

$$\left(-\frac{1}{4}+\sqrt{2}+\left(-9-5\sqrt{2}+2e^{3\sqrt{2}}-9e^{6\sqrt{2}}+5\sqrt{2}\ e^{6\sqrt{2}}\right)\Big/\left(4\left(-1+e^{6\sqrt{2}}\right)\right)+\right.$$
$$\left(-9-5\sqrt{2}+2e^{3\sqrt{2}}-9e^{6\sqrt{2}}+5\sqrt{2}\ e^{6\sqrt{2}}\right)\Big/\left(2\sqrt{2}\left(-1+e^{6\sqrt{2}}\right)\right)\Big)+\frac{1}{4\sqrt{2}}\Big(-1-$$
$$\sqrt{2}\Big)e^{-\sqrt{2}\,t}\left(-8-\sqrt{2}+1\Big/\left(-1+e^{6\sqrt{2}}\right)2\left(-9-5\sqrt{2}+2e^{3\sqrt{2}}-9e^{6\sqrt{2}}+5\sqrt{2}\ e^{6\sqrt{2}}\right)-\right.$$
$$\left.1\Big/\left(-1+e^{6\sqrt{2}}\right)\sqrt{2}\left(-9-5\sqrt{2}+2e^{3\sqrt{2}}-9e^{6\sqrt{2}}+5\sqrt{2}\ e^{6\sqrt{2}}\right)\right)$$

$$\frac{1}{2}+e^{\sqrt{2}\,t}\left(-\frac{1}{4}+\sqrt{2}+\left(-9-5\sqrt{2}+2e^{3\sqrt{2}}-9e^{6\sqrt{2}}+5\sqrt{2}\ e^{6\sqrt{2}}\right)\Big/\left(4\left(-1+e^{6\sqrt{2}}\right)\right)+\right.$$
$$\left(-9-5\sqrt{2}+2e^{3\sqrt{2}}-9e^{6\sqrt{2}}+5\sqrt{2}\ e^{6\sqrt{2}}\right)\Big/\left(2\sqrt{2}\left(-1+e^{6\sqrt{2}}\right)\right)\Big)+\frac{1}{4\sqrt{2}}$$
$$e^{-\sqrt{2}\,t}\left(-8-\sqrt{2}+1\Big/\left(-1+e^{6\sqrt{2}}\right)2\left(-9-5\sqrt{2}+2e^{3\sqrt{2}}-9e^{6\sqrt{2}}+5\sqrt{2}\ e^{6\sqrt{2}}\right)-\right.$$
$$\left.1\Big/\left(-1+e^{6\sqrt{2}}\right)\sqrt{2}\left(-9-5\sqrt{2}+2e^{3\sqrt{2}}-9e^{6\sqrt{2}}+5\sqrt{2}\ e^{6\sqrt{2}}\right)\right)$$

`FullSimplify[x1[0, p0]]`

5

`N[x1[3, p0]]`

1.

`Plot[{x1[t, p0], p1[t, p0]}, {t, 0, 3}]`

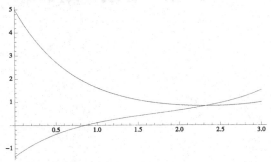

```
(* optimal control*)
u1[t_] = 1 + p1[t, p0]
Plot[u1[t], {t, 0, 3}, PlotRange → {-1, 3}]
```

$$\frac{3}{2} + e^{\sqrt{2}\,t} \left(-\frac{1}{4} + \sqrt{2} + \left(-9 - 5\sqrt{2} + 2\,e^{3\sqrt{2}} - 9\,e^{6\sqrt{2}} + 5\sqrt{2}\,e^{6\sqrt{2}} \right) \middle/ \left(4\left(-1 + e^{6\sqrt{2}}\right) \right) + \right.$$

$$\left. \left(-9 - 5\sqrt{2} + 2\,e^{3\sqrt{2}} - 9\,e^{6\sqrt{2}} + 5\sqrt{2}\,e^{6\sqrt{2}} \right) \middle/ \left(2\sqrt{2}\left(-1 + e^{6\sqrt{2}}\right) \right) \right) + \frac{1}{4\sqrt{2}}$$

$$e^{-\sqrt{2}\,t} \left(-8 - \sqrt{2} + 1 \middle/ \left(-1 + e^{6\sqrt{2}}\right) 2 \left(-9 - 5\sqrt{2} + 2\,e^{3\sqrt{2}} - 9\,e^{6\sqrt{2}} + 5\sqrt{2}\,e^{6\sqrt{2}} \right) - \right.$$

$$\left. 1 \middle/ \left(-1 + e^{6\sqrt{2}}\right) \sqrt{2} \left(-9 - 5\sqrt{2} + 2\,e^{3\sqrt{2}} - 9\,e^{6\sqrt{2}} + 5\sqrt{2}\,e^{6\sqrt{2}} \right) \right)$$

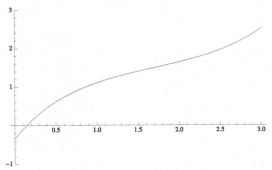

```
(* x(3) free, p[3]=0 *)

p0 =.
Solve[p1[3, p0] == 0, p0]
```

$$\left\{ \left\{ p0 \to -\left(\left(-1 + e^{3\sqrt{2}}\right) \left(1 + 4\sqrt{2} - e^{3\sqrt{2}} + 4\sqrt{2}\,e^{3\sqrt{2}}\right) \right) \middle/ \left(2 - \sqrt{2} + 2\,e^{6\sqrt{2}} + \sqrt{2}\,e^{6\sqrt{2}} \right) \right\} \right\}$$

$$\mathbf{p0} = -\left(\left(-1 + e^{3\sqrt{2}}\right)\left(1 + 4\sqrt{2} - e^{3\sqrt{2}} + 4\sqrt{2}\,e^{3\sqrt{2}}\right)\right) \Big/ \left(2 - \sqrt{2} + 2\,e^{6\sqrt{2}} + \sqrt{2}\,e^{6\sqrt{2}}\right);$$

$\mathbf{c1}$

$\mathbf{c2}$

$$\frac{1}{4\sqrt{2}}\left(-8 - \sqrt{2} + 1\Big/\left(-1 + e^{6\sqrt{2}}\right)2\left(-9 - 5\sqrt{2} + 2\,e^{3\sqrt{2}} - 9\,e^{6\sqrt{2}} + 5\sqrt{2}\,e^{6\sqrt{2}}\right) - \right.$$

$$\left. 1\Big/\left(-1 + e^{6\sqrt{2}}\right)\sqrt{2}\left(-9 - 5\sqrt{2} + 2\,e^{3\sqrt{2}} - 9\,e^{6\sqrt{2}} + 5\sqrt{2}\,e^{6\sqrt{2}}\right)\right)$$

$$-\frac{1}{4} + \sqrt{2} + \frac{-9 - 5\sqrt{2} + 2\,e^{3\sqrt{2}} - 9\,e^{6\sqrt{2}} + 5\sqrt{2}\,e^{6\sqrt{2}}}{4\left(-1 + e^{6\sqrt{2}}\right)} +$$

$$\frac{-9 - 5\sqrt{2} + 2\,e^{3\sqrt{2}} - 9\,e^{6\sqrt{2}} + 5\sqrt{2}\,e^{6\sqrt{2}}}{2\sqrt{2}\left(-1 + e^{6\sqrt{2}}\right)}$$

$$c1 = \frac{1}{4\sqrt{2}}\left(-8-\sqrt{2}+1\Big/\left(-1+e^{6\sqrt{2}}\right)2\left(-9-5\sqrt{2}+2e^{3\sqrt{2}}-9e^{6\sqrt{2}}+5\sqrt{2}\,e^{6\sqrt{2}}\right)-\right.$$
$$\left.1\Big/\left(-1+e^{6\sqrt{2}}\right)\sqrt{2}\left(-9-5\sqrt{2}+2e^{3\sqrt{2}}-9e^{6\sqrt{2}}+5\sqrt{2}\,e^{6\sqrt{2}}\right)\right);$$

$$c2 = -\frac{1}{4}+\sqrt{2}+\frac{-9-5\sqrt{2}+2e^{3\sqrt{2}}-9e^{6\sqrt{2}}+5\sqrt{2}\,e^{6\sqrt{2}}}{4\left(-1+e^{6\sqrt{2}}\right)}+$$

$$\frac{-9-5\sqrt{2}+2e^{3\sqrt{2}}-9e^{6\sqrt{2}}+5\sqrt{2}\,e^{6\sqrt{2}}}{2\sqrt{2}\left(-1+e^{6\sqrt{2}}\right)};$$

```
x1[t, p0]
p1[t, p0]
```

$$\frac{1}{2}+\left(-1+\sqrt{2}\right)e^{\sqrt{2}\,t}\left(-\frac{1}{4}+\sqrt{2}-\left(\left(-1+e^{3\sqrt{2}}\right)\left(1+4\sqrt{2}-e^{3\sqrt{2}}+4\sqrt{2}\,e^{3\sqrt{2}}\right)\right)\right/$$
$$\left(2\left(2-\sqrt{2}+2e^{6\sqrt{2}}+\sqrt{2}\,e^{6\sqrt{2}}\right)\right)-\left(\left(-1+e^{3\sqrt{2}}\right)\left(1+4\sqrt{2}-e^{3\sqrt{2}}+4\sqrt{2}\,e^{3\sqrt{2}}\right)\right)\Big/$$
$$\left(2\sqrt{2}\left(2-\sqrt{2}+2e^{6\sqrt{2}}+\sqrt{2}\,e^{6\sqrt{2}}\right)\right)\right)+\frac{1}{4\sqrt{2}}$$
$$\left(-1-\sqrt{2}\right)e^{-\sqrt{2}\,t}\left(-8-\sqrt{2}+\left(2\left(-1+e^{3\sqrt{2}}\right)\left(1+4\sqrt{2}-e^{3\sqrt{2}}+4\sqrt{2}\,e^{3\sqrt{2}}\right)\right)\right/$$
$$\left(2-\sqrt{2}+2e^{6\sqrt{2}}+\sqrt{2}\,e^{6\sqrt{2}}\right)-$$
$$\left(2\sqrt{2}\left(-1+e^{3\sqrt{2}}\right)\left(1+4\sqrt{2}-e^{3\sqrt{2}}+4\sqrt{2}\,e^{3\sqrt{2}}\right)\right)\Big/\left(2-\sqrt{2}+2e^{6\sqrt{2}}+\sqrt{2}\,e^{6\sqrt{2}}\right)\right)$$

$$\frac{1}{2}+e^{\sqrt{2}\,t}\left(-\frac{1}{4}+\sqrt{2}-\left(\left(-1+e^{3\sqrt{2}}\right)\left(1+4\sqrt{2}-e^{3\sqrt{2}}+4\sqrt{2}\,e^{3\sqrt{2}}\right)\right)\right/$$
$$\left(2\left(2-\sqrt{2}+2e^{6\sqrt{2}}+\sqrt{2}\,e^{6\sqrt{2}}\right)\right)-\left(\left(-1+e^{3\sqrt{2}}\right)\left(1+4\sqrt{2}-e^{3\sqrt{2}}+4\sqrt{2}\,e^{3\sqrt{2}}\right)\right)\Big/$$
$$\left(2\sqrt{2}\left(2-\sqrt{2}+2e^{6\sqrt{2}}+\sqrt{2}\,e^{6\sqrt{2}}\right)\right)\right)+\frac{1}{4\sqrt{2}}$$
$$e^{-\sqrt{2}\,t}\left(-8-\sqrt{2}+\left(2\left(-1+e^{3\sqrt{2}}\right)\left(1+4\sqrt{2}-e^{3\sqrt{2}}+4\sqrt{2}\,e^{3\sqrt{2}}\right)\right)\right/$$
$$\left(2-\sqrt{2}+2e^{6\sqrt{2}}+\sqrt{2}\,e^{6\sqrt{2}}\right)-$$
$$\left(2\sqrt{2}\left(-1+e^{3\sqrt{2}}\right)\left(1+4\sqrt{2}-e^{3\sqrt{2}}+4\sqrt{2}\,e^{3\sqrt{2}}\right)\right)\Big/\left(2-\sqrt{2}+2e^{6\sqrt{2}}+\sqrt{2}\,e^{6\sqrt{2}}\right)\right)$$

```
N[x1[0, p0]]
```
5.

```
N[x1[3, p0]]
```
0.368698

```
N[p1[3, p0]]
```
7.79585×10^{-15}

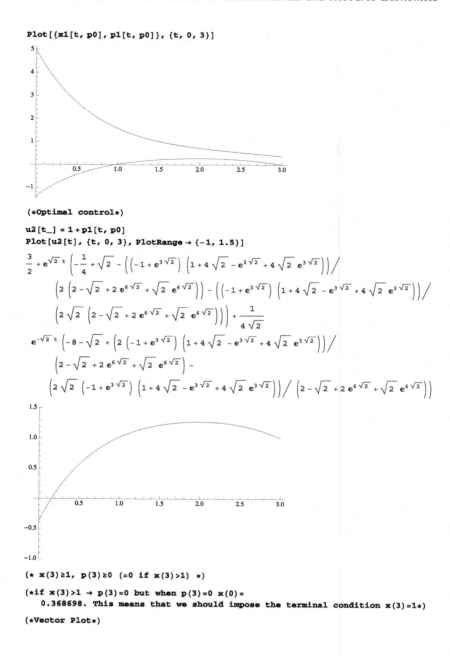

```
Plot[{x1[t, p0], p1[t, p0]}, {t, 0, 3}]
```

```
(*Optimal control*)
```

```
u2[t_] = 1 + p1[t, p0]
Plot[u2[t], {t, 0, 3}, PlotRange → {-1, 1.5}]
```

$$\frac{3}{2} + e^{\sqrt{2}\,t}\left(-\frac{1}{4} + \sqrt{2} - \left(\left(-1 + e^{3\sqrt{2}}\right)\left(1 + 4\sqrt{2} - e^{3\sqrt{2}} + 4\sqrt{2}\,e^{3\sqrt{2}}\right)\right)\Big/\right.$$
$$\left(2\left(2 - \sqrt{2} + 2\,e^{6\sqrt{2}} + \sqrt{2}\,e^{6\sqrt{2}}\right)\right) - \left(\left(-1 + e^{3\sqrt{2}}\right)\left(1 + 4\sqrt{2} - e^{3\sqrt{2}} + 4\sqrt{2}\,e^{3\sqrt{2}}\right)\right)\Big/$$
$$\left.\left(2\sqrt{2}\left(2 - \sqrt{2} + 2\,e^{6\sqrt{2}} + \sqrt{2}\,e^{6\sqrt{2}}\right)\right)\right) + \frac{1}{4\sqrt{2}}$$
$$e^{-\sqrt{2}\,t}\left(-8 - \sqrt{2} + \left(2\left(-1 + e^{3\sqrt{2}}\right)\left(1 + 4\sqrt{2} - e^{3\sqrt{2}} + 4\sqrt{2}\,e^{3\sqrt{2}}\right)\right)\Big/\right.$$
$$\left(2 - \sqrt{2} + 2\,e^{6\sqrt{2}} + \sqrt{2}\,e^{6\sqrt{2}}\right) -$$
$$\left.\left(2\sqrt{2}\left(-1 + e^{3\sqrt{2}}\right)\left(1 + 4\sqrt{2} - e^{3\sqrt{2}} + 4\sqrt{2}\,e^{3\sqrt{2}}\right)\right)\Big/\left(2 - \sqrt{2} + 2\,e^{6\sqrt{2}} + \sqrt{2}\,e^{6\sqrt{2}}\right)\right)$$

```
(* x(3)≥1, p(3)≥0 (=0 if x(3)>1) *)
```

```
(*if x(3)>1 → p(3)=0 but when p(3)=0 x(0)=
    0.368698. This means that we should impose the terminal condition x(3)=1*)
```

```
(*Vector Plot*)
```

```
Clear[p0, c1, c2]
```

```
StreamDensityPlot[{-x+p+1, x+p}, {x, -6, 6}, {p, -3, 3}]
```

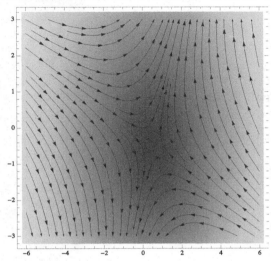

(*parametric plots*)

$x11[t\_] = \frac{1}{2} + \left(-1 + \sqrt{2}\right) e^{\sqrt{2}\,t}$

$$\left(-\frac{1}{4} + \sqrt{2} + \left(-9 - 5\sqrt{2} + 2 e^{3\sqrt{2}} - 9 e^{6\sqrt{2}} + 5\sqrt{2}\,e^{6\sqrt{2}}\right) \big/ \left(4\left(-1 + e^{6\sqrt{2}}\right)\right) +$$

$$\left(-9 - 5\sqrt{2} + 2 e^{3\sqrt{2}} - 9 e^{6\sqrt{2}} + 5\sqrt{2}\,e^{6\sqrt{2}}\right) \big/ \left(2\sqrt{2}\left(-1 + e^{6\sqrt{2}}\right)\right) \right) + \frac{1}{4\sqrt{2}}$$

$$\left(-1 - \sqrt{2}\right) e^{-\sqrt{2}\,t} \left(-8 - \sqrt{2} + \left(2\left(-9 - 5\sqrt{2} + 2 e^{3\sqrt{2}} - 9 e^{6\sqrt{2}} + 5\sqrt{2}\,e^{6\sqrt{2}}\right)\right) \big/\right.$$

$$\left.\left(-1 + e^{6\sqrt{2}}\right) - \left(\sqrt{2}\left(-9 - 5\sqrt{2} + 2 e^{3\sqrt{2}} - 9 e^{6\sqrt{2}} + 5\sqrt{2}\,e^{6\sqrt{2}}\right)\right) \big/ \left(-1 + e^{6\sqrt{2}}\right)\right);$$

$p11[t\_] = \frac{1}{2} + e^{\sqrt{2}\,t} \left(-\frac{1}{4} + \sqrt{2} + \left(-9 - 5\sqrt{2} + 2 e^{3\sqrt{2}} - 9 e^{6\sqrt{2}} + 5\sqrt{2}\,e^{6\sqrt{2}}\right) \big/\right.$

$$\left(4\left(-1 + e^{6\sqrt{2}}\right)\right) +$$

$$\left.\left(-9 - 5\sqrt{2} + 2 e^{3\sqrt{2}} - 9 e^{6\sqrt{2}} + 5\sqrt{2}\,e^{6\sqrt{2}}\right) \big/ \left(2\sqrt{2}\left(-1 + e^{6\sqrt{2}}\right)\right) \right) + \frac{1}{4\sqrt{2}}$$

$$e^{-\sqrt{2}\,t} \left(-8 - \sqrt{2} + \left(2\left(-9 - 5\sqrt{2} + 2 e^{3\sqrt{2}} - 9 e^{6\sqrt{2}} + 5\sqrt{2}\,e^{6\sqrt{2}}\right)\right) \big/ \left(-1 + e^{6\sqrt{2}}\right) -\right.$$

$$\left.\left(\sqrt{2}\left(-9 - 5\sqrt{2} + 2 e^{3\sqrt{2}} - 9 e^{6\sqrt{2}} + 5\sqrt{2}\,e^{6\sqrt{2}}\right)\right) \big/ \left(-1 + e^{6\sqrt{2}}\right)\right);$$

```
N[x11[0]]
N[x11[3]]
N[p11[0]]
N[p11[3]]
```

5.

1.

-1.34626

1.52447

```
ParametricPlot[{x11[t], p11[t]}, {t, 0, 3}, AxesOrigin → {0, 0}]
```

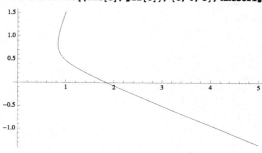

```
x22[t_] =
```

$$\frac{1}{2} + \left(-1 + \sqrt{2}\right) e^{\sqrt{2}\,t} \left(-\frac{1}{4} + \sqrt{2} - \left(\left(-1 + e^{3\sqrt{2}}\right)\left(1 + 4\sqrt{2} - e^{3\sqrt{2}} + 4\sqrt{2}\,e^{3\sqrt{2}}\right)\right) \right/$$
$$\left(2\left(2 - \sqrt{2} + 2\,e^{6\sqrt{2}} + \sqrt{2}\,e^{6\sqrt{2}}\right)\right) -$$
$$\left(\left(-1 + e^{3\sqrt{2}}\right)\left(1 + 4\sqrt{2} - e^{3\sqrt{2}} + 4\sqrt{2}\,e^{3\sqrt{2}}\right)\right)/$$
$$\left(2\sqrt{2}\left(2 - \sqrt{2} + 2\,e^{6\sqrt{2}} + \sqrt{2}\,e^{6\sqrt{2}}\right)\right) + \frac{1}{4\sqrt{2}}\left(-1 - \sqrt{2}\right)e^{-\sqrt{2}\,t}\left(-8 - \sqrt{2} + \right.$$
$$\left.2\left(-1 + e^{3\sqrt{2}}\right)\left(1 + 4\sqrt{2} - e^{3\sqrt{2}} + 4\sqrt{2}\,e^{3\sqrt{2}}\right)\right)/\left(2 - \sqrt{2} + 2\,e^{6\sqrt{2}} + \sqrt{2}\,e^{6\sqrt{2}}\right) - $$
$$\left(2\sqrt{2}\left(-1 + e^{3\sqrt{2}}\right)\left(1 + 4\sqrt{2} - e^{3\sqrt{2}} + 4\sqrt{2}\,e^{3\sqrt{2}}\right)\right)/$$
$$\left(2 - \sqrt{2} + 2\,e^{6\sqrt{2}} + \sqrt{2}\,e^{6\sqrt{2}}\right));$$

```
p22[t_] =
```
$$\frac{1}{2} + e^{\sqrt{2}\,t}\left(-\frac{1}{4} + \sqrt{2} - \left(\left(-1 + e^{3\sqrt{2}}\right)\left(1 + 4\sqrt{2} - e^{3\sqrt{2}} + 4\sqrt{2}\,e^{3\sqrt{2}}\right)\right)\right/$$
$$\left(2\left(2 - \sqrt{2} + 2\,e^{6\sqrt{2}} + \sqrt{2}\,e^{6\sqrt{2}}\right)\right) -$$
$$\left(\left(-1 + e^{3\sqrt{2}}\right)\left(1 + 4\sqrt{2} - e^{3\sqrt{2}} + 4\sqrt{2}\,e^{3\sqrt{2}}\right)\right)/$$
$$\left(2\sqrt{2}\left(2 - \sqrt{2} + 2\,e^{6\sqrt{2}} + \sqrt{2}\,e^{6\sqrt{2}}\right)\right) + \frac{1}{4\sqrt{2}}$$
$$e^{-\sqrt{2}\,t}\left(-8 - \sqrt{2} + 2\left(-1 + e^{3\sqrt{2}}\right)\left(1 + 4\sqrt{2} - e^{3\sqrt{2}} + 4\sqrt{2}\,e^{3\sqrt{2}}\right)\right)/$$
$$\left(2 - \sqrt{2} + 2\,e^{6\sqrt{2}} + \sqrt{2}\,e^{6\sqrt{2}}\right) - \left(2\sqrt{2}\left(-1 + e^{3\sqrt{2}}\right)\right.$$
$$\left.\left(1 + 4\sqrt{2} - e^{3\sqrt{2}} + 4\sqrt{2}\,e^{3\sqrt{2}}\right)\right)/\left(2 - \sqrt{2} + 2\,e^{6\sqrt{2}} + \sqrt{2}\,e^{6\sqrt{2}}\right));$$

```
N[x22[0]]
N[x22[3]]
N[p22[0]]
N[p22[3]]
```

```
5.
```

```
0.368698
```

```
-1.37193
```

$$7.79585 \times 10^{-15}$$

```
ParametricPlot[{x22[t], p22[t]}, {t, 0, 3}, AxesOrigin -> {0, 0}]
```

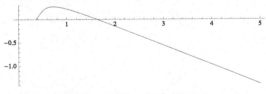

```
(*Which terminal condition is better?*)
```

```
(*x(3)=1*)
```

```
u11[t_] =
```

$$\frac{3}{2} + e^{\sqrt{2}\,t}\left(-\frac{1}{4} + \sqrt{2} + \left(-9 - 5\sqrt{2} + 2\,e^{3\sqrt{2}} - 9\,e^{6\sqrt{2}} + 5\sqrt{2}\,e^{6\sqrt{2}}\right)\big/\left(4\left(-1 + e^{6\sqrt{2}}\right)\right) + \right.$$

$$\left.\left(-9 - 5\sqrt{2} + 2\,e^{3\sqrt{2}} - 9\,e^{6\sqrt{2}} + 5\sqrt{2}\,e^{6\sqrt{2}}\right)\big/\left(2\sqrt{2}\left(-1 + e^{6\sqrt{2}}\right)\right)\right) + \frac{1}{4\sqrt{2}}$$

$$e^{-\sqrt{2}\,t}\left(-8 - \sqrt{2} + \left(2\left(-9 - 5\sqrt{2} + 2\,e^{3\sqrt{2}} - 9\,e^{6\sqrt{2}} + 5\sqrt{2}\,e^{6\sqrt{2}}\right)\right)\big/\left(-1 + e^{6\sqrt{2}}\right) - \right.$$

$$\left.\left(\sqrt{2}\left(-9 - 5\sqrt{2} + 2\,e^{3\sqrt{2}} - 9\,e^{6\sqrt{2}} + 5\sqrt{2}\,e^{6\sqrt{2}}\right)\right)\big/\left(-1 + e^{6\sqrt{2}}\right)\right);$$

```
(*Optimal value*)
```

$$\int_0^3 (u11[t] - 0.5\,(u11[t])^2 - 0.5\,(x11[t])^2)\,dt$$

```
-5.09558

(*x(3) free *)
(*Optimal value*)
u22[t_] =
```

$$\frac{3}{2} + e^{\sqrt{2}\,t}\left(-\frac{1}{4} + \sqrt{2} - \left(\left(-1 + e^{3\sqrt{2}}\right)\left(1 + 4\sqrt{2} - e^{3\sqrt{2}} + 4\sqrt{2}\,e^{3\sqrt{2}}\right)\right)\big/\left(2\left(2 - \sqrt{2} + \right.\right.\right.$$

$$\left.\left.2\,e^{6\sqrt{2}} + \sqrt{2}\,e^{6\sqrt{2}}\right)\right) - \left(\left(-1 + e^{3\sqrt{2}}\right)\left(1 + 4\sqrt{2} - e^{3\sqrt{2}} + 4\sqrt{2}\,e^{3\sqrt{2}}\right)\right)\big/$$

$$\left(2\sqrt{2}\left(2 - \sqrt{2} + 2\,e^{6\sqrt{2}} + \sqrt{2}\,e^{6\sqrt{2}}\right)\right)\right) + \frac{1}{4\sqrt{2}}\,e^{-\sqrt{2}\,t}\left(-8 - \sqrt{2} + \right.$$

$$\left(2\left(-1 + e^{3\sqrt{2}}\right)\left(1 + 4\sqrt{2} - e^{3\sqrt{2}} + 4\sqrt{2}\,e^{3\sqrt{2}}\right)\right)\big/\left(2 - \sqrt{2} + 2\,e^{6\sqrt{2}} + \sqrt{2}\,e^{6\sqrt{2}}\right) -$$

$$\left(2\sqrt{2}\left(-1 + e^{3\sqrt{2}}\right)\left(1 + 4\sqrt{2} - e^{3\sqrt{2}} + 4\sqrt{2}\,e^{3\sqrt{2}}\right)\right)\big/$$

$$\left(2 - \sqrt{2} + 2\,e^{6\sqrt{2}} + \sqrt{2}\,e^{6\sqrt{2}}\right)\right);$$

$$\int_0^3 (u22[t] - 0.5\,(u22[t])^2 - 0.5\,(x22[t])^2)\,dt$$

```
-4.18063
```

Chapter 6

Optimal Control: Steady State Analysis

Infinite Horizon Optimal Control

$$\max_{u(t)} \int_0^\infty e^{-\rho t} F\left(x(t), u(t)\right) dt \tag{1}$$

subject to $\dot{x}(t) = g\left(x(t), u(t)\right) \;\; x(0) = x_0$ fixed $\tag{2}$

$$x \in \mathcal{A} \subset \mathbb{R}^n, \; u \in \mathcal{U} \subset \mathbb{R}^m \tag{3}$$

MHDS

$$\dot{x}_i = \frac{\partial H^*}{\partial \lambda_i}, \quad x_i(0) = x_{i0} \quad i = 1, \ldots, n \tag{4}$$

$$\dot{\lambda}_i = \rho \lambda_i - \frac{\partial H^*}{\partial x_i}, \quad H^* = H\left(x, u^*, \lambda\right), \tag{5}$$

Steady State

The MHDS is a $2n$-dimensional nonlinear dynamical system. With initial values $x_i(0) = x_{i0}, \; i = 1, \ldots, n$ for the state variables. The **steady state (or long-run equilibrium)** for the MHDS is defined as a point $(x^*, \lambda^*) \in \mathbb{R}^{2n}$ such that

$$0 = \frac{\partial H^*}{\partial \lambda_i}, \quad x_i(0) = x_{i0}, \quad i = 1, \ldots, n \tag{6}$$

$$0 = \rho \lambda_i - \frac{\partial H^*}{\partial x_i} \tag{7}$$

Existence, uniqueness and stability can be analyzed by using standard methods applied to dynamical systems. If a steady state (x^*, λ^*) exists then the MHDS is a dynamical system with initial values $x_i(0) = x_{i0}$ and terminal values $(x_1^*, \ldots, x_n^*, \lambda_1^*, \ldots, \lambda_n^*)$ for the state and the costate variables, (two-point boundary problem).

- If a (x^*, λ^*) exists then the B–S TVCs are satisfied for the trajectories $(x(t), \lambda(t))$ converging to (x^*, λ^*) as $t \to \infty$.

Properties of the Steady State

$$\dot{x} = g(x, u^*(x, \lambda)) = H_\lambda(x, \lambda), \quad x(0) = x_0 \tag{8}$$

$$\dot{\lambda} = \rho \lambda - H_x(x, \lambda) \tag{9}$$

Assume that a steady state exists

$$(x^*, \lambda^*): \tag{10}$$

$$0 = H_\lambda(x^*, \lambda^*) \tag{11}$$

$$0 = \rho \lambda - H_x(x^*, \lambda^*) \tag{12}$$

We can check for local stability.

Local Stability

Linearize the MHDS around (x^*, λ^*)

$$\dot{x} = H_{\lambda x}(x - x^*) + H_{\lambda \lambda}(\lambda - \lambda^*) \tag{13}$$

$$\dot{\lambda} = -H_{xx}(x - x^*) + (\rho - H_{\lambda \lambda})(\lambda - \lambda^*) \tag{14}$$

The Jacobian matrix is

$$J = \begin{pmatrix} H_{\lambda x} & H_{\lambda \lambda} \\ -H_{xx} & \rho - H_{x\lambda} \end{pmatrix} \tag{15}$$

we have trace$(J) = \rho > 0$, Assume $n = 1$, the characteristic equation for J is

$$s^2 - \text{trace}\,(J)\,s + \det\,(J) = 0 \tag{16}$$

$$s_{1,2} = \frac{\rho}{2} \pm \frac{1}{2}\sqrt{\rho^2 - 4\left[(H_{\lambda x}\,(\rho - H_{x\lambda}) + H_{xx}H_{\lambda\lambda})\right]} \tag{17}$$

$$s_{1,2} = \frac{\rho}{2} \pm \frac{1}{2}\sqrt{(\rho - 2H_{\lambda x})^2 - 4\left[(H_{xx}H_{\lambda\lambda})\right]} \tag{18}$$

- Real and distinct eigenvalues: either $\begin{cases} s_1, s_2 > 0 & \text{unstable} \\ s_1 > 0, s_2 < 0 & \text{saddle point} \end{cases}$
  since trace$(J) = \rho > 0$ if $\det\,(J) < 0$ saddle point, otherwise instability (unstable node).
- Repeating eigenvalues $s_1 = s_2 = \frac{\rho}{2} > 0$ instability (unstable node).
- If $(\rho - 2H_{\lambda x})^2 - 4\left[(H_{xx}H_{\lambda\lambda})\right] < 0$ we have complex roots. Since the real part is $\frac{\rho}{2} > 0$, we have instability (unstable spiral).
- Since $\rho > 0$, we cannot have a center.
- Thus, the steady state of the MHDS is either a saddle point or completely unstable. (Kurz theorem).
- Since $\lim_{t\to\infty} e^{-\rho t}\lambda(t) = 0$ and $\lim_{t\to\infty} e^{-\rho t}\lambda(t)x(t) = 0$, TVCs at infinity are satisfied.

Stable Manifold

If (x^*, λ^*) is a saddle point then there exists a one-dimensional stable manifold W^S such that or any $x(0)$ on the neighborhood of (x^*, λ^*) there exist a $\lambda(0)$ such that $(x(0), \lambda(0))$ are on the stable manifold and the initial state $(x(0), \lambda(0)) \to (x^*, \lambda^*)$ as $t \to \infty$. E^S is the tangent linear subspace.

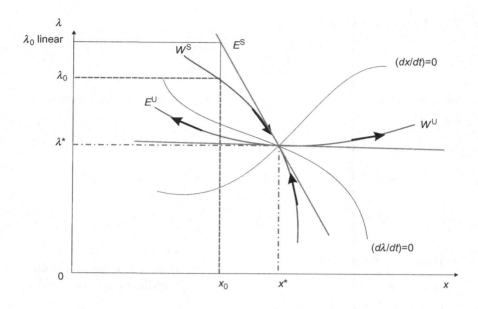

Solving for the Linearization Around the Steady State: Linear Quadratic Optimal Control Problem

Assume $s_1 > 0, s_2 < 0$. The solution of the linearized system in the neighborhood of (x^*, λ^*) will be

$$x(t) = c_1 v_{11} e^{s_1 t} + c_2 v_{12} e^{s_2 t} + x^* \tag{19}$$

$$\lambda(t) = c_1 v_{21} e^{s_1 t} + c_2 v_{22} e^{s_2 t} + \lambda^* \tag{20}$$

For convergence, we need to set $c_1 = 0$. Then

$$x(t) = c_2 v_{12} e^{s_2 t} + x^*, \quad \lim_{t \to \infty} x(t) = x^* \tag{21}$$

Since $x(0) = x_0$, $x_0 = c_2 v_{12} + x^* \Rightarrow c_2 = \frac{x_0 - x^*}{v_{12}} \tag{22}$

$$\lambda(t) = \left(\frac{x_0 - x^*}{v_{12}}\right) v_{22} e^{s_2 t} + \lambda^*, \quad \lim_{t \to \infty} \lambda(t) = \lambda^* \tag{23}$$

$$\lambda(0) = \left(\frac{x_0 - x^*}{v_{12}}\right) v_{22} + \lambda^* = \lambda_0 \tag{24}$$

Linear Stable Manifold — Linear Policy Function

From the solution of the linearized system

$$x(t) = c_2 v_{12} e^{s_2 t} + x^* \tag{25}$$

$$\lambda(t) = c_2 v_{22} e^{s_2 t} + \lambda^* \tag{26}$$

we obtain the linear manifold tangent to the nonlinear manifold of the problem

$$\frac{\lambda(t) - \lambda^*}{x(t) - x^*} = \frac{v_{22}}{v_{12}} \Rightarrow \lambda(t) = \frac{v_{22}}{v_{12}} \left(x(t) - x^* \right) + \lambda^* = \phi\left(x(t) \right) \tag{27}$$

This is a policy function relating costate-state. It is straightforward to define the policy function in terms of control-state. Since from the maximum principle $u = h\left(x, \lambda \right)$, solve for λ to obtain $\lambda = \psi\left(x, u \right)$. Substituting the above and solving in terms of u, we obtain the policy function (linearized) as

$$u(t) = \Phi\left(x(t); x^*, \lambda^* \right) \tag{28}$$

Nonlinear Stable Manifold

This a difficult problem. We need to solve the nonlinear MHDS

$$\dot{x} = \gamma_1(x, \lambda), \quad x(0) = x_0 \tag{29}$$

$$\dot{\lambda} = \gamma_2\left(x, \lambda \right), \quad \left(x(t), \lambda(t) \right) \to \left(x^*, \lambda^* \right) \text{ as } t \to \infty. \tag{30}$$

1. **Multiple shooting:** Start with $x(0)$, guess a $\lambda(0)$, solve numerically the MHDS and check whether $(x(t), \lambda(t)) \to (x^*, \lambda^*)$ *as* $t \to \infty$. Iterate until convergence is achieved for some $\lambda(0)$. The policy function is the pairs

$$\{(x(t), \lambda(t))\} \quad t = 0, 1, 2, \ldots \tag{31}$$

2. Time elimination

$$\frac{d\lambda/dt}{dx/dt} = \frac{d\lambda}{dx} = \frac{\gamma_2(x,\lambda)}{\gamma_1(x,\lambda)} \tag{32}$$

If we solve this ODE, we can obtain the policy function $\lambda(t) = \phi(x(t))$. We do not have initial conditions, but we know that $(x(t), \lambda(t)) \to (x^*, \lambda^*)$ *as* $t \to \infty$. This is problematic however since

$$\frac{d\lambda}{dx} = \frac{\gamma_2(x^*, \lambda^*)}{\gamma_1(x^*, \lambda^*)} = \frac{0}{0} \tag{33}$$

Approximation:

(1) For $x = x^* + \varepsilon$, evaluate from the approximating linear manifold $\lambda_{\varepsilon+} = \frac{v_{22}}{v_{12}}(x + \varepsilon - x^*) + \lambda^*$. Use $\lambda_{\varepsilon+}$ as initial value to solve (32) for $x > x^*$.
(2) For $x = x^* - \varepsilon$ evaluate from the approximating linear manifold $\lambda_{\varepsilon-} = \frac{v_{22}}{v_{12}}(x - \varepsilon - x^*) + \lambda^*$. Use $\lambda_{\varepsilon-}$ as initial value to solve (32) for $x > x^*$.
(3) Connect the two solutions to obtain the nonlinear stable manifold. This is the nonlinear policy function.

Global Asymptotic Stability

Let $\varphi(x_0, \lambda_0; t)$ be a solution of the MHDS. The solution will be called **bounded** if it belongs to a compact set. The steady state (x^*, λ^*) is said to be **globally asymptotically stable** (GAS) for all bounded solutions if for all initial conditions (x_0, λ_0) such that $\varphi(x_0, \lambda_0; t)$ is bounded, it holds that

$$\varphi(x_0, \lambda_0; t) \to (x^*, \lambda^*) \text{ as } t \to \infty \tag{34}$$

Assume that the steady state (x^*, λ^*) is isolated and define the **curvature matrix**

$$Q = \begin{pmatrix} H_{xx} & -\frac{\rho}{2}I_n \\ -\frac{\rho}{2}I_n & -H_{\lambda\lambda} \end{pmatrix} \tag{35}$$

where I is an $(n \times n)$ identity matrix. If Q, evaluated at the steady state, is negative definite, then all bounded solutions of the MHDS converge to the steady state as $t \to \infty$. Thus, the steady state has the global saddle point property and the stable manifold is globally asymptotically stable irrespective of "how far" from the steady state the initial conditions are. If they are on the stable manifold, the initial state will converge to the steady state.

The Globally Stable Manifold

If Q, evaluated at the steady state, is negative definite then all bounded solutions of the MHDS converge to the steady state as $t \to \infty$. Thus, the steady state has the global saddle point property and the stable manifold is globally asymptotically stable. That is irrespective of "how far" from the steady state the initial conditions are. If they are on the stable manifold, the initial state will converge to the steady state.

The Ramsey Problem

Output Y, K capital, C consumption. Population is constant, capital depreciates at a rate δ, output is produced using capital and labor with a standard neoclassical production function $F(K, N)$ with CRS, no productivity growth. Accumulation of capital stock in per capita terms

$$\dot{k} = f(k) - c - \delta k, \quad k_0 > 0 \tag{36}$$

$$f(0) = 0, \quad f'(0) = \infty, \quad f'(\infty) = 0, \quad f''(k) < 0 \tag{37}$$

Preferences

$$U_0 = \int_0^\infty e^{-\rho t} u\left(c(t)\right) dt \tag{38}$$

$u(c(t))$ is the instantaneous utility function and ρ is the rate of time preference or subjective discount rate.

Social Planner

$$\max_{c(t)} U_0 = \int_0^\infty e^{-(\rho+n)t} u\left(c(t)\right) dt \tag{39}$$

$$\text{subject to } \dot{k} = f(k) - c - \delta k, \quad k_0 > 0 \tag{40}$$

$$k(t), c(t) \geq 0 \quad \text{for all } t \tag{41}$$

Current value Hamiltonian

$$H = u(c) + p\left(f(k) - c - \delta k\right) \tag{42}$$

Pontryagin's maximum principle

$$u'(c) = p \tag{43}$$

$$\dot{k} = f(k) - c - \delta k \tag{44}$$

$$\dot{p} = \left[\rho + \delta - f'(k)\right] p \tag{45}$$

From $u'(c) = p \Rightarrow u''(c)\dot{c} = \dot{p}$, the MHDS becomes

$$\dot{k} = f(k) - c - \delta k \tag{46}$$

$$\frac{\dot{c}}{c} = \left[f'(k) - \rho - \delta\right]\sigma(c) \tag{47}$$

$$\sigma(c) = -\frac{u'(c)}{u''(c)}\frac{1}{c} \quad \text{The inverse of the negative} \tag{48}$$

$$\text{of the elasticity of marginal utility} \tag{49}$$

$$\lim_{t \to \infty} k(t)u'(c)e^{-\rho t} = 0 \quad \text{TVC at infinity} \tag{50}$$

(45) or (47) is the Euler equation.

- Constant relative risk aversion (CRRA) utility function

$$u(c) = \begin{cases} \frac{c^{1-\theta}}{1-\theta} & \theta > 0, \quad \theta \neq 1 \\ \ln c & \theta = 1 \end{cases} \quad , \quad \sigma(c) = \frac{1}{\theta} \tag{51}$$

$$\frac{\dot{c}}{c} = \frac{1}{\theta}\left[f'(k) - \rho - \delta\right] \tag{52}$$

- Constant absolute risk aversion (CARA) utility function

$$u(c) = -\left(\frac{1}{\alpha}\right)e^{-\alpha c}, \quad \alpha > 0, \quad \sigma(c) = \frac{1}{\alpha} \tag{53}$$

$$\dot{c} = \frac{1}{\alpha}\left[f'(k) - \rho - \delta\right] \tag{54}$$

Steady State Analysis

$$(k^*, c^*) \ : \ f'(k^*) = \rho + \delta, \tag{55}$$

$$c^* = f(k^*) - \delta k^* \tag{56}$$

Jacobian matrix at the steady state (assume CRRA)

$$J|_{(k^*,c^*)} = \begin{pmatrix} f'(k^*) - \delta & -1 \\ \frac{1}{\theta} f''(k^*) & f'(k^*) - \rho - \delta \end{pmatrix} \tag{57}$$

$$J|_{(k^*,c^*)} = \begin{pmatrix} f(k^*) - \delta k^* & -1 \\ \frac{1}{\theta} f''(k^*) & 0 \end{pmatrix} \tag{58}$$

$$\det\left(J|_{(k^*,c^*)} \right) = \frac{1}{\theta} f''(k^*) < 0 \quad (k^*, c^*) \text{ is a saddle point} \tag{59}$$

Exercise: Derive phase diagram; the approximating linear stable manifold. How are you going to apply time elimination for the nonlinear stable manifold?

(*The system of differential equations for the Cass–Shell optimal growth model is:

$$\frac{c}{c} = \frac{1}{\theta}[f'(k) - \delta - \rho - \theta g],$$

$$k = [f(k) - c - (n + \delta + g)k],$$

$$f(k) = k^a, \quad u(c) = \frac{c - \theta}{1 - \theta},$$

$\bar{c}$ is measured in per effective worker terms, $\quad h = n + \delta + g$

$a = 0.33, \quad n = 0.01, \quad \delta = 0.02, \quad g = 0.03, \quad \theta = 2, \quad \rho = 0.01,$

$w = [\rho - n - (1 - \theta)g] = 0.03^*).$

ln[849] :=

$a = .; \quad h = .; \quad s = .; \quad theta = .;$

$$a = 0.33; \quad h = 0.06; \quad s = 0.2; \quad theta = 2; \quad w = 0.03; \quad g = 0.03;$$

$$rho = 0.01; \quad delta = 0.02;$$

$$k \longrightarrow 6.95338, \quad c \longrightarrow 1.47917$$

The Decentralized Economy

We denote wage by $w(t)$ and the rental price of capital by $r(t)$. Firms rent the services of capital and labor to produce output. Families and firms know current and future prices of w, r and take them as given (Perfect foresight).

Each household solves

$$\max_{c(t)} U_0 = \int_0^\infty e^{-\rho t} u(c(t)) dt \tag{60}$$

subject to the flow budget constraint

$$\dot{a}(t) = w(t) - c(t) + r(t) a(t) \tag{61}$$

$$a(t) \equiv k(t) - b(t) \tag{62}$$

$$\text{wealth equals capital holdings minus dept.} \tag{63}$$

capital and labor are supplied inelastically. Only consumption is a decision variable.

Firms Maximize Profits

Profit maximization and CRS imply

$$f'(k) = r + \delta \tag{64}$$

$$f(k) - k f'(k) = w \tag{65}$$

No-Ponzi-Game Condition is as follows:

$$\lim_{t \to \infty} a(t) \exp\left[-\int_0^t (r(v)) dv \right] = 0 \tag{66}$$

The rate of growth of assets is less than the interest rate.

TVC and No-Ponzi-Game Condition

$$\dot{p} = (\rho - r)\, p \Rightarrow p(t) = p(0) \exp\left[-\int_0^t (r\,(v) - \rho)\, dv\right] \qquad (67)$$

Then TVC becomes

$$\lim_{t\to\infty} a(t)p(0) \exp\left[-\int_0^t (r\,(v) - \rho)\, dv\right] e^{-\rho t} =$$

$$\lim_{t\to\infty} a(t)p(0) \exp\left[-\int_0^t (r\,(v))\, dv\right] = 0 \qquad (68)$$

$$\text{since } p(0) = u'\,(c(0)) > 0 \qquad (69)$$

which is the No-Ponzi-Game Condition.

In[87]:= (*Optimal Control, Finite Time,
Alternative terminal conditions Linear Quadratic Problem *)
(* max$\int_{0}^{3}\left(u-\frac{1}{2}u^2-x^2\right)$ dt, subject to $\dot{x}=-x-u$,
x(0)=5, x(3)=1, or x(3) free, or x$(3)\geq 1$ *)
(* H$(x,u,p)=u-\frac{1}{2}u^2-x^2+p(-x+u)$
$u=1+p$, $\dot{x}=-x+p+1$, $\dot{p}=x+p$*)

In[67]:= (*Solution of the Hamiltonian system*)

In[68]:= Clear[p0, c1, c2]

In[89]:= m = {{-1, 1}, {1, 1}}
Eigensystem[m]

Out[69]= {{-1, 1}, {1, 1}}

Out[70]= $\left\{\left\{-\sqrt{2}, \sqrt{2}\right\}, \left\{\left\{-1-\sqrt{2}, 1\right\}, \left\{-1+\sqrt{2}, 1\right\}\right\}\right\}$

In[71]:= (*Solving for xbar,pbar*)

In[72]:= b = {-1, 0}
LinearSolve[m, b]

Out[72]= {-1, 0}

Out[73]= $\left\{\frac{1}{2}, -\frac{1}{2}\right\}$

In[74]:= v11 = $-1-\sqrt{2}$;
v12 = $-1+\sqrt{2}$;
v21 = 1;
v22 = 1;
l1 = $-\sqrt{2}$;
l2 = $\sqrt{2}$;
xbar = 1/2;
pbar = 1/2;
x[t_, c1_, c2_] = c1 * v11 * Exp[l1 * t] + c2 * v12 * Exp[l2 * t] + xbar
p[t_, c1_, c2_] = c1 * v21 * Exp[l1 * t] + c2 * v22 * Exp[l2 * t] + pbar

Out[82]= $\frac{1}{2} + \left(-1-\sqrt{2}\right)$ c1 $e^{-\sqrt{2}\,t} + \left(-1+\sqrt{2}\right)$ c2 $e^{\sqrt{2}\,t}$

Out[83]= $\frac{1}{2} +$ c1 $e^{-\sqrt{2}\,t} +$ c2 $e^{\sqrt{2}\,t}$

In[84]:= (*solve for intial values*)
Solve[{x[0, c1, c2] == 5, p[0, c1, c2] == p0}, {c1, c2}]

Out[84]= $\left\{\left\{c1 \rightarrow \frac{1}{4}\left(-1-4\sqrt{2}+2\,p0-\sqrt{2}\,p0\right), c2 \rightarrow \frac{1}{4}\left(-1+4\sqrt{2}+2\,p0+\sqrt{2}\,p0\right)\right\}\right\}$

In[85]:= $c1 = \dfrac{-8 - \sqrt{2} - 2\,p\theta + 2\sqrt{2}\,p\theta}{4\sqrt{2}}$;

$c2 = -\dfrac{1}{4} + \sqrt{2} + \dfrac{p\theta}{2} + \dfrac{p\theta}{2\sqrt{2}}$;

In[87]:= x1[t_, pθ_] = x[t, c1, c2]
p1[t_, pθ_] = p[t, c1, c2]

Out[87]= $\dfrac{1}{2} + \left(-1 + \sqrt{2}\right) e^{\sqrt{2}\,t} \left(-\dfrac{1}{4} + \sqrt{2} + \dfrac{p\theta}{2} + \dfrac{p\theta}{2\sqrt{2}}\right) + \dfrac{\left(-1 - \sqrt{2}\right) e^{-\sqrt{2}\,t} \left(-8 - \sqrt{2} - 2\,p\theta + 2\sqrt{2}\,p\theta\right)}{4\sqrt{2}}$

Out[88]= $\dfrac{1}{2} + e^{\sqrt{2}\,t} \left(-\dfrac{1}{4} + \sqrt{2} + \dfrac{p\theta}{2} + \dfrac{p\theta}{2\sqrt{2}}\right) + \dfrac{e^{-\sqrt{2}\,t} \left(-8 - \sqrt{2} - 2\,p\theta + 2\sqrt{2}\,p\theta\right)}{4\sqrt{2}}$

In[89]:= (* x(3)=1, p[3] free*)
Solve[x1[3, pθ] == 1, pθ]

Out[89]= $\left\{\left\{p\theta \to \dfrac{-9 - 5\sqrt{2} + 2\,e^{3\sqrt{2}} - 9\,e^{6\sqrt{2}} + 5\sqrt{2}\,e^{6\sqrt{2}}}{\sqrt{2}\,\left(-1 + e^{6\sqrt{2}}\right)}\right\}\right\}$

In[90]:= $p\theta = \dfrac{-9 - 5\sqrt{2} + 2\,e^{3\sqrt{2}} - 9\,e^{6\sqrt{2}} + 5\sqrt{2}\,e^{6\sqrt{2}}}{\sqrt{2}\,\left(-1 + e^{6\sqrt{2}}\right)}$;

c1
c2

Out[91]= $\dfrac{-8 - \sqrt{2} + \dfrac{2\left(-9 - 5\sqrt{2} + 2\,e^{3\sqrt{2}} - 9\,e^{6\sqrt{2}} + 5\sqrt{2}\,e^{6\sqrt{2}}\right)}{-1 + e^{6\sqrt{2}}} - \dfrac{\sqrt{2}\left(-9 - 5\sqrt{2} + 2\,e^{3\sqrt{2}} - 9\,e^{6\sqrt{2}} + 5\sqrt{2}\,e^{6\sqrt{2}}\right)}{-1 + e^{6\sqrt{2}}}}{4\sqrt{2}}$

Out[92]= $-\dfrac{1}{4} + \sqrt{2} + \dfrac{-9 - 5\sqrt{2} + 2\,e^{3\sqrt{2}} - 9\,e^{6\sqrt{2}} + 5\sqrt{2}\,e^{6\sqrt{2}}}{4\left(-1 + e^{6\sqrt{2}}\right)} +$

$\dfrac{-9 - 5\sqrt{2} + 2\,e^{3\sqrt{2}} - 9\,e^{6\sqrt{2}} + 5\sqrt{2}\,e^{6\sqrt{2}}}{2\sqrt{2}\,\left(-1 + e^{6\sqrt{2}}\right)}$

In[93]:= c1 = $\dfrac{-8 - \sqrt{2} + \dfrac{2\left(-9 - 5\sqrt{2} + 2 e^{3\sqrt{2}} - 9 e^{6\sqrt{2}} + 5\sqrt{2}\, e^{6\sqrt{2}}\right)}{-1 + e^{6\sqrt{2}}} - \dfrac{\sqrt{2}\left(-9 - 5\sqrt{2} + 2 e^{3\sqrt{2}} - 9 e^{6\sqrt{2}} + 5\sqrt{2}\, e^{6\sqrt{2}}\right)}{-1 + e^{6\sqrt{2}}}}{4\sqrt{2}}$;

c2 $= -\dfrac{1}{4} + \sqrt{2} + \dfrac{-9 - 5\sqrt{2} + 2 e^{3\sqrt{2}} - 9 e^{6\sqrt{2}} + 5\sqrt{2}\, e^{6\sqrt{2}}}{4\left(-1 + e^{6\sqrt{2}}\right)} +$

$\dfrac{-9 - 5\sqrt{2} + 2 e^{3\sqrt{2}} - 9 e^{6\sqrt{2}} + 5\sqrt{2}\, e^{6\sqrt{2}}}{2\sqrt{2}\left(-1 + e^{6\sqrt{2}}\right)}$;

x1[t, p0]

p1[t, p0]

Out[95]= $\dfrac{1}{2} + \left(-1 + \sqrt{2}\right) e^{\sqrt{2}\, t}\left(-\dfrac{1}{4} + \sqrt{2} + \dfrac{-9 - 5\sqrt{2} + 2 e^{3\sqrt{2}} - 9 e^{6\sqrt{2}} + 5\sqrt{2}\, e^{6\sqrt{2}}}{4\left(-1 + e^{6\sqrt{2}}\right)} +\right.$

$\left.\dfrac{-9 - 5\sqrt{2} + 2 e^{3\sqrt{2}} - 9 e^{6\sqrt{2}} + 5\sqrt{2}\, e^{6\sqrt{2}}}{2\sqrt{2}\left(-1 + e^{6\sqrt{2}}\right)}\right) + \dfrac{1}{4\sqrt{2}}$

$\left(-1 - \sqrt{2}\right) e^{-\sqrt{2}\, t}\left(-8 - \sqrt{2} + \dfrac{2\left(-9 - 5\sqrt{2} + 2 e^{3\sqrt{2}} - 9 e^{6\sqrt{2}} + 5\sqrt{2}\, e^{6\sqrt{2}}\right)}{-1 + e^{6\sqrt{2}}} -\right.$

$\left.\dfrac{\sqrt{2}\left(-9 - 5\sqrt{2} + 2 e^{3\sqrt{2}} - 9 e^{6\sqrt{2}} + 5\sqrt{2}\, e^{6\sqrt{2}}\right)}{-1 + e^{6\sqrt{2}}}\right)$

Out[96]= $\dfrac{1}{2} + e^{\sqrt{2}\, t}\left(-\dfrac{1}{4} + \sqrt{2} + \dfrac{-9 - 5\sqrt{2} + 2 e^{3\sqrt{2}} - 9 e^{6\sqrt{2}} + 5\sqrt{2}\, e^{6\sqrt{2}}}{4\left(-1 + e^{6\sqrt{2}}\right)} +\right.$

$\left.\dfrac{-9 - 5\sqrt{2} + 2 e^{3\sqrt{2}} - 9 e^{6\sqrt{2}} + 5\sqrt{2}\, e^{6\sqrt{2}}}{2\sqrt{2}\left(-1 + e^{6\sqrt{2}}\right)}\right) +$

$\dfrac{e^{-\sqrt{2}\, t}\left(-8 - \sqrt{2} + \dfrac{2\left(-9 - 5\sqrt{2} + 2 e^{3\sqrt{2}} - 9 e^{6\sqrt{2}} + 5\sqrt{2}\, e^{6\sqrt{2}}\right)}{-1 + e^{6\sqrt{2}}} - \dfrac{\sqrt{2}\left(-9 - 5\sqrt{2} + 2 e^{3\sqrt{2}} - 9 e^{6\sqrt{2}} + 5\sqrt{2}\, e^{6\sqrt{2}}\right)}{-1 + e^{6\sqrt{2}}}\right)}{4\sqrt{2}}$

In[97]:= FullSimplify[x1[0, p0]]

Out[97]= 5

In[98]:= N[x1[3, p0]]

Out[98]= 1.

In[99]:= `Plot[{x1[t, p0], p1[t, p0]}, {t, 0, 3}]`

Out[99]=

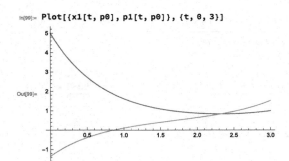

In[100]:= `(* optimal control*)`
`u1[t_] = 1 + p1[t, p0]`
`Plot[u1[t], {t, 0, 3}, PlotRange → {-1, 3}]`

Out[100]= $\frac{3}{2} + e^{\sqrt{2}\,t}\left(-\frac{1}{4} + \sqrt{2} + \frac{-9 - 5\sqrt{2} + 2\,e^{3\sqrt{2}} - 9\,e^{6\sqrt{2}} + 5\sqrt{2}\,e^{6\sqrt{2}}}{4\left(-1 + e^{6\sqrt{2}}\right)} + \right.$

$\left. \frac{-9 - 5\sqrt{2} + 2\,e^{3\sqrt{2}} - 9\,e^{6\sqrt{2}} + 5\sqrt{2}\,e^{6\sqrt{2}}}{2\sqrt{2}\left(-1 + e^{6\sqrt{2}}\right)}\right) +$

$$\frac{e^{-\sqrt{2}\,t}\left(-8 - \sqrt{2} + \frac{2\left(-9 - 5\sqrt{2} + 2\,e^{3\sqrt{2}} - 9\,e^{6\sqrt{2}} + 5\sqrt{2}\,e^{6\sqrt{2}}\right)}{-1 + e^{6\sqrt{2}}} - \frac{\sqrt{2}\left(-9 - 5\sqrt{2} + 2\,e^{3\sqrt{2}} - 9\,e^{6\sqrt{2}} + 5\sqrt{2}\,e^{6\sqrt{2}}\right)}{-1 + e^{6\sqrt{2}}}\right)}{4\sqrt{2}}$$

Out[101]=

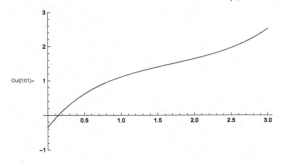

In[102]:=

In[103]:= `(* x(3) free, p[3]=0 *)`

In[104]:= `p0 = .`
`Solve[p1[3, p0] == 0, p0]`

Out[105]= $\left\{\left\{p0 \to -\frac{\left(-1 + e^{3\sqrt{2}}\right)\left(1 + 4\sqrt{2} - e^{3\sqrt{2}} + 4\sqrt{2}\,e^{3\sqrt{2}}\right)}{2 - \sqrt{2} + 2\,e^{6\sqrt{2}} + \sqrt{2}\,e^{6\sqrt{2}}}\right\}\right\}$

In[106]:= $\mathbf{p\theta} = -\dfrac{\left(-1+e^{3\sqrt{2}}\right)\left(1+4\sqrt{2}-e^{3\sqrt{2}}+4\sqrt{2}\,e^{3\sqrt{2}}\right)}{2-\sqrt{2}+2\,e^{6\sqrt{2}}+\sqrt{2}\,e^{6\sqrt{2}}}$;

c1

c2

Out[107]= $\dfrac{-8-\sqrt{2}+\dfrac{2\left(-9-5\sqrt{2}+2\,e^{3\sqrt{2}}-9\,e^{6\sqrt{2}}+5\sqrt{2}\,e^{6\sqrt{2}}\right)}{-1+e^{6\sqrt{2}}}-\dfrac{\sqrt{2}\left(-9-5\sqrt{2}+2\,e^{3\sqrt{2}}-9\,e^{6\sqrt{2}}+5\sqrt{2}\,e^{6\sqrt{2}}\right)}{-1+e^{6\sqrt{2}}}}{4\sqrt{2}}$

Out[108]= $-\dfrac{1}{4}+\sqrt{2}+\dfrac{-9-5\sqrt{2}+2\,e^{3\sqrt{2}}-9\,e^{6\sqrt{2}}+5\sqrt{2}\,e^{6\sqrt{2}}}{4\left(-1+e^{6\sqrt{2}}\right)}+$

$\dfrac{-9-5\sqrt{2}+2\,e^{3\sqrt{2}}-9\,e^{6\sqrt{2}}+5\sqrt{2}\,e^{6\sqrt{2}}}{2\sqrt{2}\left(-1+e^{6\sqrt{2}}\right)}$

In[109]:= $c1 = \dfrac{-8 - \sqrt{2} + \dfrac{2\left(-9 - 5\sqrt{2} + 2e^{3\sqrt{2}} - 9e^{6\sqrt{2}} + 5\sqrt{2}\,e^{6\sqrt{2}}\right)}{-1 + e^{6\sqrt{2}}} - \dfrac{\sqrt{2}\left(-9 - 5\sqrt{2} + 2e^{3\sqrt{2}} - 9e^{6\sqrt{2}} + 5\sqrt{2}\,e^{6\sqrt{2}}\right)}{-1 + e^{6\sqrt{2}}}}{4\sqrt{2}};$

$c2 = -\dfrac{1}{4} + \sqrt{2} + \dfrac{-9 - 5\sqrt{2} + 2e^{3\sqrt{2}} - 9e^{6\sqrt{2}} + 5\sqrt{2}\,e^{6\sqrt{2}}}{4\left(-1 + e^{6\sqrt{2}}\right)} +$

$\dfrac{-9 - 5\sqrt{2} + 2e^{3\sqrt{2}} - 9e^{6\sqrt{2}} + 5\sqrt{2}\,e^{6\sqrt{2}}}{2\sqrt{2}\left(-1 + e^{6\sqrt{2}}\right)};$

x1[t, p0]
p1[t, p0]

Out[111]= $\dfrac{1}{2} + \left(-1 + \sqrt{2}\right)e^{\sqrt{2}\,t}\left(-\dfrac{1}{4} + \sqrt{2} - \dfrac{\left(-1 + e^{3\sqrt{2}}\right)\left(1 + 4\sqrt{2} - e^{3\sqrt{2}} + 4\sqrt{2}\,e^{3\sqrt{2}}\right)}{2\left(2 - \sqrt{2} + 2e^{6\sqrt{2}} + \sqrt{2}\,e^{6\sqrt{2}}\right)} - \right.$

$\left. \dfrac{\left(-1 + e^{3\sqrt{2}}\right)\left(1 + 4\sqrt{2} - e^{3\sqrt{2}} + 4\sqrt{2}\,e^{3\sqrt{2}}\right)}{2\sqrt{2}\left(2 - \sqrt{2} + 2e^{6\sqrt{2}} + \sqrt{2}\,e^{6\sqrt{2}}\right)}\right) + \dfrac{1}{4\sqrt{2}}$

$\left(-1 - \sqrt{2}\right)e^{-\sqrt{2}\,t}\left(-8 - \sqrt{2} + \dfrac{2\left(-1 + e^{3\sqrt{2}}\right)\left(1 + 4\sqrt{2} - e^{3\sqrt{2}} + 4\sqrt{2}\,e^{3\sqrt{2}}\right)}{2 - \sqrt{2} + 2e^{6\sqrt{2}} + \sqrt{2}\,e^{6\sqrt{2}}} - \right.$

$\left. \dfrac{2\sqrt{2}\left(-1 + e^{3\sqrt{2}}\right)\left(1 + 4\sqrt{2} - e^{3\sqrt{2}} + 4\sqrt{2}\,e^{3\sqrt{2}}\right)}{2 - \sqrt{2} + 2e^{6\sqrt{2}} + \sqrt{2}\,e^{6\sqrt{2}}}\right)$

Out[112]= $\dfrac{1}{2} + e^{\sqrt{2}\,t}\left(-\dfrac{1}{4} + \sqrt{2} - \dfrac{\left(-1 + e^{3\sqrt{2}}\right)\left(1 + 4\sqrt{2} - e^{3\sqrt{2}} + 4\sqrt{2}\,e^{3\sqrt{2}}\right)}{2\left(2 - \sqrt{2} + 2e^{6\sqrt{2}} + \sqrt{2}\,e^{6\sqrt{2}}\right)} - \right.$

$\left. \dfrac{\left(-1 + e^{3\sqrt{2}}\right)\left(1 + 4\sqrt{2} - e^{3\sqrt{2}} + 4\sqrt{2}\,e^{3\sqrt{2}}\right)}{2\sqrt{2}\left(2 - \sqrt{2} + 2e^{6\sqrt{2}} + \sqrt{2}\,e^{6\sqrt{2}}\right)}\right) +$

$\dfrac{e^{-\sqrt{2}\,t}\left(-8 - \sqrt{2} + \dfrac{2\left(-1 + e^{3\sqrt{2}}\right)\left(1 + 4\sqrt{2} - e^{3\sqrt{2}} + 4\sqrt{2}\,e^{3\sqrt{2}}\right)}{2 - \sqrt{2} + 2e^{6\sqrt{2}} + \sqrt{2}\,e^{6\sqrt{2}}} - \dfrac{2\sqrt{2}\left(-1 + e^{3\sqrt{2}}\right)\left(1 + 4\sqrt{2} - e^{3\sqrt{2}} + 4\sqrt{2}\,e^{3\sqrt{2}}\right)}{2 - \sqrt{2} + 2e^{6\sqrt{2}} + \sqrt{2}\,e^{6\sqrt{2}}}\right)}{4\sqrt{2}}$

In[113]:= N[x1[0, p0]]
Out[113]= 5.

In[114]:= N[x1[3, p0]]
Out[114]= 0.368698

In[115]:= N[p1[3, p0]]
Out[115]= 7.79585×10^{-15}

In[116]:= **Plot[{x1[t, p0], p1[t, p0]}, {t, 0, 3}]**

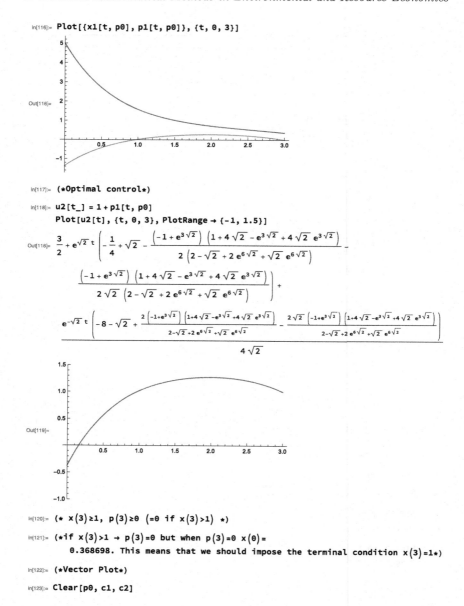

In[117]:= **(*Optimal control*)**

In[118]:= **u2[t_] = 1 + p1[t, p0]**
Plot[u2[t], {t, 0, 3}, PlotRange → {-1, 1.5}]

In[120]:= **(* x(3)≥1, p(3)≥0 (=0 if x(3)>1) *)**

In[121]:= **(*if x(3)>1 → p(3)=0 but when p(3)=0 x(0)=**
0.368698. This means that we should impose the terminal condition x(3)=1*)

In[122]:= **(*Vector Plot*)**

In[123]:= **Clear[p0, c1, c2]**

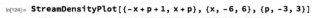

In[124]:= **StreamDensityPlot[{-x + p + 1, x + p}, {x, -6, 6}, {p, -3, 3}]**

Out[124]=

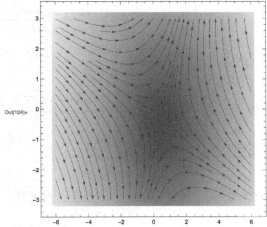

In[125]:= **(*parametric plots*)**

$$x11[t\_] = \frac{1}{2} + \left(-1+\sqrt{2}\right) e^{\sqrt{2}\,t} \left(-\frac{1}{4} + \sqrt{2} + \frac{-9-5\sqrt{2}+2\,e^{3\sqrt{2}}-9\,e^{6\sqrt{2}}+5\sqrt{2}\,e^{6\sqrt{2}}}{4\left(-1+e^{6\sqrt{2}}\right)} + \right.$$

$$\left. \frac{-9-5\sqrt{2}+2\,e^{3\sqrt{2}}-9\,e^{6\sqrt{2}}+5\sqrt{2}\,e^{6\sqrt{2}}}{2\sqrt{2}\left(-1+e^{6\sqrt{2}}\right)}\right) + \frac{1}{4\sqrt{2}}$$

$$\left(-1-\sqrt{2}\right) e^{-\sqrt{2}\,t} \left(-8-\sqrt{2} + \frac{2\left(-9-5\sqrt{2}+2\,e^{3\sqrt{2}}-9\,e^{6\sqrt{2}}+5\sqrt{2}\,e^{6\sqrt{2}}\right)}{-1+e^{6\sqrt{2}}} - \right.$$

$$\left. \frac{\sqrt{2}\left(-9-5\sqrt{2}+2\,e^{3\sqrt{2}}-9\,e^{6\sqrt{2}}+5\sqrt{2}\,e^{6\sqrt{2}}\right)}{-1+e^{6\sqrt{2}}}\right);$$

$$p11[t\_] = \frac{1}{2} + e^{\sqrt{2}\,t} \left(-\frac{1}{4} + \sqrt{2} + \frac{-9-5\sqrt{2}+2\,e^{3\sqrt{2}}-9\,e^{6\sqrt{2}}+5\sqrt{2}\,e^{6\sqrt{2}}}{4\left(-1+e^{6\sqrt{2}}\right)} + \right.$$

$$\left. \frac{-9-5\sqrt{2}+2\,e^{3\sqrt{2}}-9\,e^{6\sqrt{2}}+5\sqrt{2}\,e^{6\sqrt{2}}}{2\sqrt{2}\left(-1+e^{6\sqrt{2}}\right)}\right) + \frac{1}{4\sqrt{2}}$$

$$e^{-\sqrt{2}\,t} \left(-8-\sqrt{2} + \frac{2\left(-9-5\sqrt{2}+2\,e^{3\sqrt{2}}-9\,e^{6\sqrt{2}}+5\sqrt{2}\,e^{6\sqrt{2}}\right)}{-1+e^{6\sqrt{2}}} - \right.$$

$$\left. \frac{\sqrt{2}\left(-9-5\sqrt{2}+2\,e^{3\sqrt{2}}-9\,e^{6\sqrt{2}}+5\sqrt{2}\,e^{6\sqrt{2}}\right)}{-1+e^{6\sqrt{2}}}\right);$$

In[127]:= **N[x11[0]]**
N[x11[3]]
N[p11[0]]
N[p11[3]]

Out[127]= 5.

Out[128]= 1.

Out[129]= -1.34626

Out[130]= 1.52447

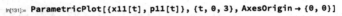

In[131]:= **ParametricPlot[{x11[t], p11[t]}, {t, 0, 3}, AxesOrigin → {0, 0}]**

Out[131]=

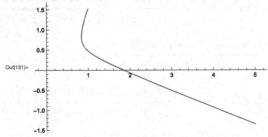

In[132]:= $x22[t\_] = \frac{1}{2} + \left(-1 + \sqrt{2}\right) e^{\sqrt{2}\, t} \left(-\frac{1}{4} + \sqrt{2} - \frac{\left(-1 + e^{3\sqrt{2}}\right)\left(1 + 4\sqrt{2} - e^{3\sqrt{2}} + 4\sqrt{2}\, e^{3\sqrt{2}}\right)}{2\left(2 - \sqrt{2} + 2\, e^{6\sqrt{2}} + \sqrt{2}\, e^{6\sqrt{2}}\right)} \right. -$

$$\left. \frac{\left(-1 + e^{3\sqrt{2}}\right)\left(1 + 4\sqrt{2} - e^{3\sqrt{2}} + 4\sqrt{2}\, e^{3\sqrt{2}}\right)}{2\sqrt{2}\left(2 - \sqrt{2} + 2\, e^{6\sqrt{2}} + \sqrt{2}\, e^{6\sqrt{2}}\right)}\right) + \frac{1}{4\sqrt{2}}$$

$$\left(-1 - \sqrt{2}\right) e^{-\sqrt{2}\, t} \left(-8 - \sqrt{2} + \frac{2\left(-1 + e^{3\sqrt{2}}\right)\left(1 + 4\sqrt{2} - e^{3\sqrt{2}} + 4\sqrt{2}\, e^{3\sqrt{2}}\right)}{2 - \sqrt{2} + 2\, e^{6\sqrt{2}} + \sqrt{2}\, e^{6\sqrt{2}}}\right. -$$

$$\left. \frac{2\sqrt{2}\left(-1 + e^{3\sqrt{2}}\right)\left(1 + 4\sqrt{2} - e^{3\sqrt{2}} + 4\sqrt{2}\, e^{3\sqrt{2}}\right)}{2 - \sqrt{2} + 2\, e^{6\sqrt{2}} + \sqrt{2}\, e^{6\sqrt{2}}}\right);$$

$p22[t\_] = \frac{1}{2} + e^{\sqrt{2}\, t}\left(-\frac{1}{4} + \sqrt{2} - \frac{\left(-1 + e^{3\sqrt{2}}\right)\left(1 + 4\sqrt{2} - e^{3\sqrt{2}} + 4\sqrt{2}\, e^{3\sqrt{2}}\right)}{2\left(2 - \sqrt{2} + 2\, e^{6\sqrt{2}} + \sqrt{2}\, e^{6\sqrt{2}}\right)}\right. -$

$$\left. \frac{\left(-1 + e^{3\sqrt{2}}\right)\left(1 + 4\sqrt{2} - e^{3\sqrt{2}} + 4\sqrt{2}\, e^{3\sqrt{2}}\right)}{2\sqrt{2}\left(2 - \sqrt{2} + 2\, e^{6\sqrt{2}} + \sqrt{2}\, e^{6\sqrt{2}}\right)}\right) + \frac{1}{4\sqrt{2}}$$

$$e^{-\sqrt{2}\, t}\left(-8 - \sqrt{2} + \frac{2\left(-1 + e^{3\sqrt{2}}\right)\left(1 + 4\sqrt{2} - e^{3\sqrt{2}} + 4\sqrt{2}\, e^{3\sqrt{2}}\right)}{2 - \sqrt{2} + 2\, e^{6\sqrt{2}} + \sqrt{2}\, e^{6\sqrt{2}}}\right. -$$

$$\left. \frac{2\sqrt{2}\left(-1 + e^{3\sqrt{2}}\right)\left(1 + 4\sqrt{2} - e^{3\sqrt{2}} + 4\sqrt{2}\, e^{3\sqrt{2}}\right)}{2 - \sqrt{2} + 2\, e^{6\sqrt{2}} + \sqrt{2}\, e^{6\sqrt{2}}}\right);$$

```
N[x22[0]]
N[x22[3]]
N[p22[0]]
N[p22[3]]
```

Out[134]= 5.

Out[135]= 0.368698

Out[136]= -1.37193

Out[137]= 7.79585×10^{-15}

In[138]:= `ParametricPlot[{x22[t], p22[t]}, {t, 0, 3}, AxesOrigin → {0, 0}]`

Out[138]=

In[139]:= **(*Which terminal condition is better?*)**

In[140]:= **(*x$\left(3\right)$=1*)**

In[141]:= $u11[t\_] = \dfrac{3}{2} + e^{\sqrt{2}\,t}\left(-\dfrac{1}{4} + \sqrt{2} + \dfrac{-9 - 5\sqrt{2} + 2\,e^{3\sqrt{2}} - 9\,e^{6\sqrt{2}} + 5\sqrt{2}\,e^{6\sqrt{2}}}{4\left(-1 + e^{6\sqrt{2}}\right)} + \dfrac{-9 - 5\sqrt{2} + 2\,e^{3\sqrt{2}} - 9\,e^{6\sqrt{2}} + 5\sqrt{2}\,e^{6\sqrt{2}}}{2\sqrt{2}\left(-1 + e^{6\sqrt{2}}\right)}\right) +$

$\dfrac{e^{-\sqrt{2}\,t}\left(-8 - \sqrt{2} + \dfrac{2\left(-9-5\sqrt{2}+2e^{3\sqrt{2}}-9e^{6\sqrt{2}}+5\sqrt{2}\,e^{6\sqrt{2}}\right)}{-1+e^{6\sqrt{2}}} - \dfrac{\sqrt{2}\left(-9-5\sqrt{2}+2e^{3\sqrt{2}}-9e^{6\sqrt{2}}+5\sqrt{2}\,e^{6\sqrt{2}}\right)}{-1+e^{6\sqrt{2}}}\right)}{4\sqrt{2}}$

;

In[142]:=

In[143]:= **(*Optimal value*)**

In[144]:= $\displaystyle\int_0^3 \left(u11[t] - 0.5\,(u11[t])\verb|^|2 - 0.5\,(x11[t])\verb|^|2\right)\,dt$

Out[144]= -5.09558

In[145]:= **(*x$\left(3\right)$ free *)**
(*Optimal value*)

$u22[t\_] = \dfrac{3}{2} + e^{\sqrt{2}\,t}\left(-\dfrac{1}{4} + \sqrt{2} - \dfrac{\left(-1+e^{3\sqrt{2}}\right)\left(1+4\sqrt{2}-e^{3\sqrt{2}}+4\sqrt{2}\,e^{3\sqrt{2}}\right)}{2\left(2-\sqrt{2}+2e^{6\sqrt{2}}+\sqrt{2}\,e^{6\sqrt{2}}\right)} -$

$\dfrac{\left(-1+e^{3\sqrt{2}}\right)\left(1+4\sqrt{2}-e^{3\sqrt{2}}+4\sqrt{2}\,e^{3\sqrt{2}}\right)}{2\sqrt{2}\left(2-\sqrt{2}+2e^{6\sqrt{2}}+\sqrt{2}\,e^{6\sqrt{2}}\right)}\right) + \dfrac{1}{4\sqrt{2}}$

$e^{-\sqrt{2}\,t}\left(-8-\sqrt{2}+\dfrac{2\left(-1+e^{3\sqrt{2}}\right)\left(1+4\sqrt{2}-e^{3\sqrt{2}}+4\sqrt{2}\,e^{3\sqrt{2}}\right)}{2-\sqrt{2}+2e^{6\sqrt{2}}+\sqrt{2}\,e^{6\sqrt{2}}} -$

$\dfrac{2\sqrt{2}\left(-1+e^{3\sqrt{2}}\right)\left(1+4\sqrt{2}-e^{3\sqrt{2}}+4\sqrt{2}\,e^{3\sqrt{2}}\right)}{2-\sqrt{2}+2e^{6\sqrt{2}}+\sqrt{2}\,e^{6\sqrt{2}}}\right)$;

$\displaystyle\int_0^3 \left(u22[t] - 0.5\,(u22[t])\verb|^|2 - 0.5\,(x22[t])\verb|^|2\right)\,dt$

Out[146]= -4.18063

```
(*Linear Quadratic Optimal Control, Infinite Time Horizon*)

In[654]:= ClearAll[u, x, u, ustar, λ, λdot ]
          ClearAll[a1, a2, b1, b2, c, g, m, r, C1, C2]

In[656]:= (*Problem set up*)
          U[x_, u_] = a0 + a1 * u - 0.5 * a2 * u^2 - (b1 * x + 0.5 * b2 * x^2) - c * u * x;
          (* Objective:
             max_u ∫_0^∞ e^{-r*t} U[x,u]dt subject to dx/dt=g*u-m*x, x(0)=2*)

In[657]:= (*Hamiltonian Function*)

In[658]:= h[x_, u_, λ_] = U[x, u] + λ * (g * u - m * x)

Out[658]= a0 + a1 u - 0.5 a2 u² - b1 x - c u x - 0.5 b2 x² + (g u - m x) λ

In[659]:= (*FONC*)
          sol1 = Solve[D[h[x, u, λ], u] == 0, u];
          sol = FullSimplify[sol1]
```

$$Out[660]= \left\{\left\{u \to \frac{1.\ a1 - 1.\ c\,x + 1.\ g\,\lambda}{a2}\right\}\right\}$$

```
In[661]:= {u} = {u} /. sol
          ustar[x_, λ_] = u[[1]];
          ustar[x, λ]
```

$$Out[661]= \left\{\left\{\frac{1.\ a1 - 1.\ c\,x + 1.\ g\,\lambda}{a2}\right\}\right\}$$

$$Out[663]= \frac{1.\ a1 - 1.\ c\,x + 1.\ g\,\lambda}{a2}$$

```
In[664]:= ClearAll[u, xdot, λdot]

In[665]:= (*Modified Hamiltonian Dynamic System*)

In[666]:= λdot = r * λ - D[h[x, u, λ], x]

Out[666]= b1 + c u + 1. b2 x + m λ + r λ

In[667]:= (*Substitute ustar[x[t],λ[t]],x[t],
          λ[t] in λdot and xdot to optain the MHDS in terms of x[t],
          λ[t] as shown below*)

In[668]:= xdot = g * ustar[x[t], λ[t]] - m * x[t]
          λdot = b1 + c ustar[x[t], λ[t]] - 1.` b2 x[t] + m λ[t] + r λ[t]
```

$$Out[668]= -m\,x[t] + \frac{g\,(1.\ a1 - 1.\ c\,x[t] + 1.\ g\,\lambda[t])}{a2}$$

$$Out[669]= b1 - 1.\ b2\,x[t] + m\,\lambda[t] + r\,\lambda[t] + \frac{c\,(1.\ a1 - 1.\ c\,x[t] + 1.\ g\,\lambda[t])}{a2}$$

```
In[670]:= (*Steady State Analysis*)
          ClearAll[xdot, λdot]
          ClearAll[a1, a2, b1, b2, c, g, m, r]
```

In[672]:= **xdot[x_, λ_] = g * ustar[x, λ] - m * x;**
λdot[x_, λ_] = -b1 - c * ustar[x, λ] + 1.` b2 * x + m * λ + r * λ;
(*Jacobian*)
J[x_, λ_] = {{∂ₓ xdot[x, λ], ∂_λ xdot[x, λ]}, {∂ₓ λdot[x, λ], ∂_λ λdot[x, λ]}}

Out[674]= $\left\{\left\{\dfrac{(0. - 1. c) g}{a2} - m, \dfrac{g (0. + 1. g)}{a2}\right\}, \left\{1. b2 - \dfrac{(0. - 1. c) c}{a2}, -\dfrac{c (0. + 1. g)}{a2} + m + r\right\}\right\}$

In[675]:= **a1 = 1; a2 = 0.8; b1 = 1.2; b2 = 0.9; c = 0.2; g = 0.9; m = 0.01; r = 0.03;**
Det[J[x, λ]]
{e, v} = Eigensystem[J[x, λ]]

Out[676]= -0.9184

Out[677]= $\{\{-1.19107, 0.771071\}, \{\{-0.727077, 0.686556\}, \{-0.709355, -0.704851\}\}\}$

In[678]:= **(*Steady State*)**
ss = Solve[{xdot[x, λ] == 0, λdot[x, λ] == 0}, {x, λ}]

Out[678]= $\{\{x \to 1.37195, \lambda \to -0.792683\}\}$

In[679]:= **ss1 = {x, λ} /. ss;**

In[680]:= **xstar = ss1[[1, 1]];**
λstar = ss1[[1, 2]];

In[682]:= **(*Solution Construction*)**

In[683]:= **ClearAll[C1, C2]**

In[684]:= **x[t_] = xstar + C1 * v[[1, 1]] Exp[e[[1]] * t] + C2 * v[[2, 1]] Exp[e[[2]] * t]**
λ[t_] = λstar + C1 * v[[1, 2]] Exp[e[[1]] * t] + C2 * v[[2, 2]] Exp[e[[2]] * t]

Out[684]= $1.37195 - 0.727077 \, C1 \, e^{-1.19107 \, t} - 0.709355 \, C2 \, e^{0.771071 \, t}$

Out[685]= $-0.792683 + 0.686556 \, C1 \, e^{-1.19107 \, t} - 0.704851 \, C2 \, e^{0.771071 \, t}$

In[697]:= **(*To approach the steady state we set C2=0*)**
C1 = .; C2 = 0;
x[t]
λ[t]

Out[698]= $1.37195 - 0.727077 \, C1 \, e^{-1.19107 \, t}$

Out[699]= $-0.792683 + 0.686556 \, C1 \, e^{-1.19107 \, t}$

In[627]:= **(*Initial condition x(0)=2*)**

In[700]:= **Solve[x[0] == 2, C1]**

Out[700]= $\{\{C1 \to -0.863799\}\}$

In[705]:= **C1 = -0.863799;**
(*Determine Initial value for λ*)
λ[0]
x[0]

Out[706]= -1.38573

Out[707]= $2.$

In[631]:= **(*The solutions for the state and the costate**
variables that stay on the invariant (stable) manifold*)

In[708]:= **x[t]**
λ[t]

Out[708]= $1.37195 + 0.628049 \, e^{-1.19107 \, t}$

Out[709]= $-0.792683 - 0.593046 \, e^{-1.19107 \, t}$

In[711]:= **Plot[{x[t], λ[t]}, {t, 0, 8}, AxesLabel → {"t", "x,λ"},**
PlotStyle → {{RGBColor[1, 0, 0]}, {RGBColor[0, 1, 0]}}]

Out[711]=

(* The turnpike approach*)

In[720]:= **xFinite[t_] = 1.371951219512195`+ 0.611316921865196` $e^{-1.1910708435174293` \, t}$ +**
0.016917088301285337` $e^{0.7710708435174293` \, t}$;

xF2[t_] = 1.371951219512195`+ 0.6571236939143115` $e^{-1.1910708435174293` \, t}$ −
0.02907491342650652` $e^{0.7710708435174293` \, t}$;

In[724]:= **Plot[{x[t], xFinite[t], xF2[t]}, {t, 0, 5},**
AxesLabel → {"t", "x,xF"}, PlotRange → {0, 2}]

Out[724]=

In[635]:= **(*Stable Manifold, Policy Function obtained by x[t]/λ[t]*)**

In[636]:= `ParametricPlot[{x[t], λ[t]}, {t, 0, 5}, AxesLabel → {"x", "λ"},`
`    PlotRange → {-4, 5}, Background → RGBColor[1, 1, 0]]`

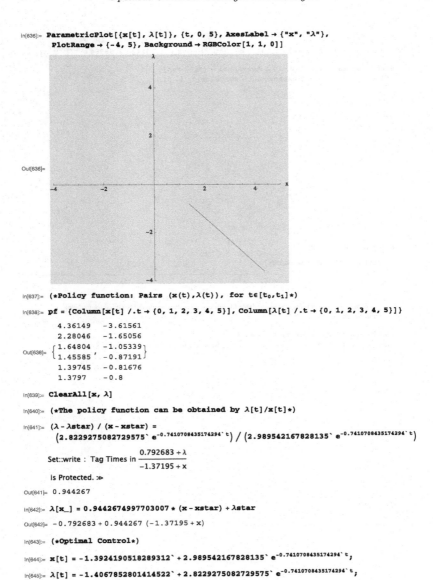

Out[636]=

In[637]:= `(*Policy function: Pairs (x(t),λ(t)), for t∈[t₀,t₁]*)`

In[638]:= `pf = {Column[x[t] /.t → {0, 1, 2, 3, 4, 5}], Column[λ[t] /.t → {0, 1, 2, 3, 4, 5}]}`

Out[638]=
$$\begin{pmatrix} 4.36149 & -3.61561 \\ 2.28046 & -1.65056 \\ 1.64804 & -1.05339 \\ 1.45585 & -0.87191 \\ 1.39745 & -0.81676 \\ 1.3797 & -0.8 \end{pmatrix}$$

In[639]:= `ClearAll[x, λ]`

In[640]:= `(*The policy function can be obtained by λ[t]/x[t]*)`

In[641]:= `(λ - λstar) / (x - xstar) =`
`    (2.829275082729575` e^{-0.7410708435174294` t}) / (2.989542167828135` e^{-0.7410708435174294` t})`

Set::write : Tag Times in $\dfrac{0.792683 + λ}{-1.37195 + x}$
is Protected. ≫

Out[641]= 0.944267

In[642]:= `λ[x_] = 0.9442674997703007 * (x - xstar) + λstar`

Out[642]= $-0.792683 + 0.944267 (-1.37195 + x)$

In[643]:= `(*Optimal Control*)`

In[644]:= `x[t] = -1.3924190518289312` + 2.989542167828135` e^{-0.7410708435174294` t};`

In[645]:= `λ[t] = -1.4067852801414522` + 2.829275082729575` e^{-0.7410708435174294` t};`

In[646]:= **uoptimal[t_] = ustar[x[t], λ[t]]**

Out[646]= $1.25 \left(1. + 0.9 \left(-1.40679 + 2.82293\ e^{-0.741071\ t}\right) - 0.2 \left(-1.39242 + 2.98954\ e^{-0.741071\ t}\right)\right)$

In[853]:= **Plot[uoptimal[t], {t, 0, 10}, AxesLabel → {"t", "u"},**
 PlotRange → {-1, 3}, Background → RGBColor[1, 1, 0]]

Out[853]=

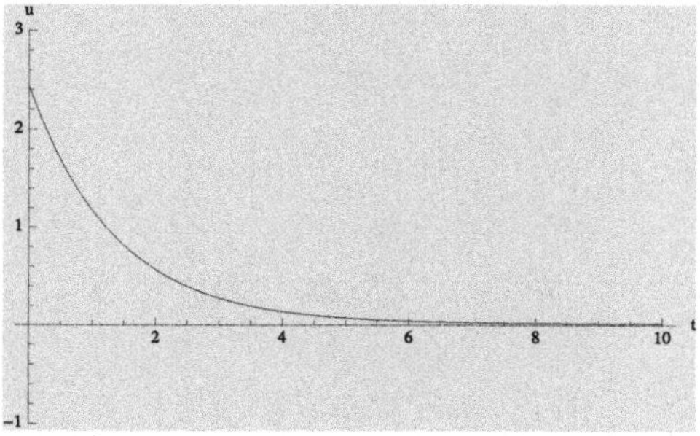

In[648]:= **x[t] =.; λ[t] =.;**

In[649]:= **(*Vector Field of the MHDS*)**

COMPATIBILITY ISSUE

Automatic translation rules are not available for this case. See the Compatibility Guide for updating
information. ≫

In[650]:= **xdot[x_, λ_] = g * ustar[x, λ] - m * x**
 λdot[x_, λ_] = -b1 - c * ustar[x, λ] + 1.` b2 * x + m * λ + r * λ

Out[650]= $-0.01\ x + 1.125\ (1. - 0.2\ x + 0.9\ λ)$

Out[651]= $-1.2 + 0.9\ x - 0.25\ (1. - 0.2\ x + 0.9\ λ) + 0.04\ λ$

In[652]:=

```
StreamPlot[{xdot[x, λ], λdot[x, λ]}, {x, -5, 5}, {λ, -5, 5},
 Axes → True, AxesLabel → {"x", "λ"}, Background → RGBColor[1, 1, 0]]
```

Out[652]=

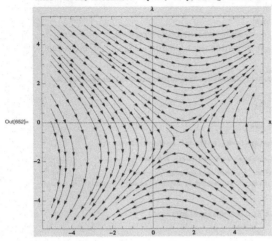

(*Optimal Growth*)

(*The system of differential equations for the Cass-Shell optimal growth model is:

$$\frac{\dot{c}}{c} = \frac{1}{\theta}[f'(k) - \delta - \rho - \theta g],$$

$$\dot{k} = [f(k) - c - (n + \delta + g)k],$$

$f(k) = k^a$, $u(c) = \frac{c^{1-\theta}}{1-\theta}$, $\tilde{c}$ is measured in per effective worker terms, $h = n + \delta + g$

$a = 0.33$, $n = 0.01$, $\delta = 0.02$, $g = 0.03$, $\theta = 2$, $\rho = 0.01$, $w = [\rho - n - (1 - \theta)g] = 0.03$*)

```
a=.;h=.;s=.;theta=.;
a=0.33;h=0.06;s=0.2;theta=2;w=0.03;g=0.03;rho=0.01;delta=0.02;
```

(*Finding the steady state*)

```
ClearAll[k,c,t,z]

kdot[k_,c_]=k^a-c-h*k;

cdot[k_,c_]=(1/theta)*(a*k^(a-1)-delta-rho-g*theta)*c;

Solve[a*k^(a-1)-delta-rho-g*theta==0,k]
```

Solve ::ifun : Inverse functions are being used by Solve , so some
    solutions may not be found ; use Reduce for complete solution information . ≫

```
{{k → 6.95338}}

Evaluate[k^a-h*k /. k → 6.953383214071221`]

1.47917

sol1=FindRoot[{kdot[k,c]==0,cdot[k,c]==0},{k,6},{c,2}]

{k → 6.95338, c → 1.47917}

z = {k, c} /. sol1

{6.95338, 1.47917}

ClearAll[c, k]

c[k_] = k^a - h*k
k = z[[1]]
z[[2]]

k^0.33 - 0.06 k

6.95338

1.47917
```

kisocline = Plot[c[k], {k, 0, 70}]

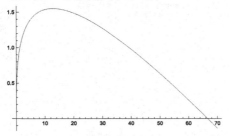

cisocline = Graphics[Line[{{z[[1]], 0}, {z[[1]], 2}}]];

Show[{kisocline, cisocline}, Axes -> True,
 AxesLabel → {"k", "c"}, PlotRange → {{0, 70}, {0, 2}}]

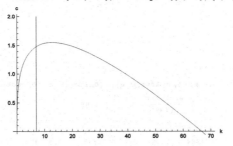

```
ClearAll[c, k]
StreamPlot[{kdot[k, c], cdot[k, k]}, {k, 0.1, 15},
  {c, 0.1, 3}, Axes → True, AxesLabel → {"k", "c"}]
```

```
(*Stability Analysis*)

J[k_, c_] = {{∂ₖ kdot[k, c], ∂_c kdot[k, c]}, {∂ₖ cdot[k, c], ∂_c cdot[k, c]}}
```

$$\left\{\left\{-0.06 + \frac{0.33}{k^{0.67}}, -1.\right\}, \left\{-\frac{0.11055\,c}{k^{1.67}}, 0. + \frac{1}{2}\left(-0.09 + \frac{0.33}{k^{0.67}}\right)\right\}\right\}$$

```
Eigensystem[J[z[[1]], z[[2]]]]
```

{{0.0964784, -0.0664784}, {{0.997798, -0.066332}, {0.995378, 0.0960325}}}

```
(*We have saddle point stability*)

kdot[k, c]
cdot[k, c]
```

$-c + k^{0.33} - 0.06\,k$

$\dfrac{1}{2}\,c\left(-0.09 + \dfrac{0.33}{k^{0.67}}\right)$

```
(*The stable manifold*)

(*Linearization of the stable manifold near the steady state*)

ClearAll[k, c]
clin[k_] = z[[2]] + (0.09603248157889405 / 0.9953782007266381) * (k - z[[1]])
```

$1.47917 + 0.0964784\,(-6.95338 + k)$

```
linearmanifold = Plot[clin[k], {k, 0, 20}]
```

```
clin[6.955]
```

1.47933

(*Contstruction of the non linear manifold*)

(*Solution of the $\frac{dc}{dk}=$

c'(k) = $\frac{dc/dt}{dk/dt}$ with initial condions defined on the linearization of the
    stable manifold to the left and to the right of the steady state*)

(*Solution to the right of the steady state*)

```
ClearAll[k, c]
sol2 = NDSolve[
```
$$\Big\{c'[k] == \Big(\frac{1}{2} * (c[k]) * \Big(-0.09\grave{\ } + \frac{0.33\grave{\ }}{k^{0.6699999999999999\grave{\ }}}\Big)\Big)\Big/ (-c[k] + k^{0.33\grave{\ }} - 0.06\grave{\ } k),$$
$$c[6.955] = 1.479330232252769\Big\}, c[k], \{k, 6.653, 10\}\Big]$$

{{c[k] → InterpolatingFunction[{{6.653, 10.}}, <>][k]}}

```
c[k_] = c[k] /. sol2[[1]]
manifold1 = Plot[c[k], {k, 6.953, 10},
  PlotStyle -> {{RGBColor[1, 0, 0]}}]
```

InterpolatingFunction[{{6.653, 10.}}, <>][k]

```
clin[9]
c[9]
```

1.67663

1.66437

```
(* Solution to the left of the steady state*)
```

```
clin[6.952]
```

1.47904

```
ClearAll[k, c]
sol3 = NDSolve[
```

$$\left\{ c\,'[k] == \left(\frac{1}{2} \ast (c[k]) \ast \left(-0.09\grave{} + \frac{0.33\grave{}}{k^{0.6699999999999999\grave{}}} \right) \right) \middle/ \left(-c[k] + k^{0.33\grave{}} - 0.06\grave{}\, k \right), \right.$$

$$\left. c[6.952] == 1.4790407970968389\grave{} \right\}, c[k], \{k, 0.1, 6.952\} \right]$$

```
c[k_] = c[k] /. sol3[[1]]
manifold2 = Plot[c[k], {k, 0.1, 6.95}, PlotStyle → {{RGBColor[1, 0, 0]}}]
{{c[k] → InterpolatingFunction[{{0.1, 6.952}}, <>][k]}}
```

```
InterpolatingFunction[{{0.1, 6.952}}, <>][k]
```

```
clin[6]
c[6]
```

1.38719

1.3839

```
Show[{linearmanifold, manifold1, manifold2, kisocline, cisocline}, Axes -> True,
 AxesOrigin → Automatic, AxesLabel → {"k", "c"}, PlotRange → {{0, 70}, {0, 2}}]
```

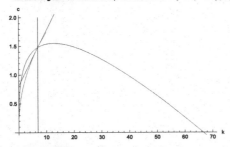

```
Show[{manifold1, manifold2, kisocline, cisocline}, Axes -> True,
 AxesOrigin → Automatic, AxesLabel → {"k", "c"}, PlotRange → {{0, 70}, {0, 2}}]
```

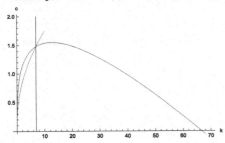

Chapter 7

Linear Optimal Control and Bang-Bang Solutions, Most Rapid Approach Paths

Linear Optimal Control

$$\max_{u(t)} \int_0^T [Px - Qu]\, dt \tag{1}$$

subject to $\dot{x} = Fx + Gu, \ x(0) = x_0$ (2)

$a \le u \le b, \quad x(T) = \text{free}$ (3)

$$H = Px - Qu + p\left(Fx + Gu\right) = Px + pFx + \left(pG - Q\right)u \tag{4}$$

Maximum principle

$$u^* = \begin{cases} a & \text{if } pG - Q < 0 \\ \in [a, b] & \text{if } pG - Q = 0 \\ b & \text{if } pG - Q > 0 \end{cases} \tag{5}$$

$$\dot{p} = -P - pF, p(T) = 0 \tag{6}$$

$$\dot{x} = Fx + Gu^* \tag{7}$$

- The optimal control u switches between a, b which is the **Bang-bang solution**.

- $pG - Q = 0$ determines the switch. $pG - Q$ is the **switching function**.

From $\dot{p} = -P - pF \Rightarrow p(t) = c_0 \exp{(Ft)} - \frac{P}{F}$. The TVC $p(T) = 0$ determines the constant c_0. The optimal control becomes

$$u^* = \begin{cases} a & \text{if } p(t) < Q/G \\ \in [a, b] & \text{if } p(t) = Q/G \\ b & \text{if } p(t) > Q/G \end{cases} \tag{8}$$

The **switch time** τ is determined as

$$\tau \colon c_0 \exp{(F\tau)} - \frac{P}{F} = Q/G, \quad \tau \in [0, T] \tag{9}$$

Then

$$u^*(t) = \begin{cases} a & \text{for } t \in [0, \tau] \\ \in [a, b] & \text{for } t = \tau \\ b & \text{for } t \in [\tau, T] \end{cases} \tag{10}$$

Any admissible value for the control is optimal at $t = \tau$. The state equation evolves as

$$\dot{x}(t) = \begin{cases} Fx + Ga & \text{for } t \in [0, \tau] \\ Fx + Gb & \text{for } t \in [\tau, T] \end{cases} \tag{11}$$

or

$$x^*(t) = \begin{cases} x_1^*(t) = c_1 \exp{(Ft)} + \frac{Ga}{F} & \text{for } t \in [0, \tau] \\ x_2^*(t) = c_2 \exp{(Ft)} + \frac{Gb}{F} & \text{for } t \in [\tau, T] \end{cases} \tag{12}$$

c_1 is determined by the initial condition $x(0) = x_0$. To determine c_2, we use the requirement that the time path for the state variable is to be a continuous path. Thus, $x_1^*(\tau) = x_2^*(\tau)$, and $x_2^*(\tau)$ can be used as an initial condition to determine c_2.

Solve the linear control problem for $(T, P, Q, F, G, a, b, x(0)) = (5, 3, -2, 1, 1, 1, 0, 2)$.

The problem can be extended to many state and control variables in a straightforward way.

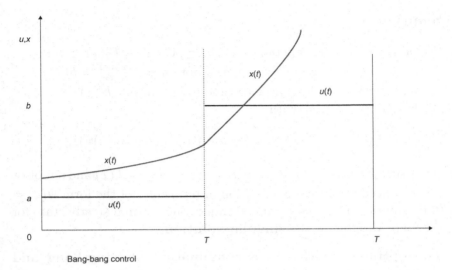

Bang-bang control

A More General Linear Problem

$$\max_{u(t)} \int_0^\infty e^{-\rho t} \left[F_1(x) - F_2(x)u \right] dt \tag{13}$$

subject to $\dot{x} = G_1(x) + G_2(x)u, \ x(0) = x_0$

$a \le u \le b$

$$H = F_1(x) - F_2(x)u + p \left(G_1(x) + G_2(x)u \right)$$
$$= F_1(x) + pG_1(x) + \left(pG_2(x) - F_2(x) \right) u \tag{14}$$

Maximum principle

$$u^* = \begin{cases} a & \text{if } pG_2(x) - F_2(x) < 0 \\ \in [a,b] & \text{if } pG_2(x) - F_2(x) = 0 \\ b & \text{if } pG_2(x) - F_2(x) > 0 \end{cases} \tag{15}$$

$$\dot{p} = \rho p - \left[F_1'(x) - F_2'(x)u + p \left(G_1'(x) + G_2'(x)u \right) \right],$$

TVC at infinity

$$\dot{x} = G_1(x) + G_2(x)u^*$$

Solution Steps

Define the switching function: $\sigma\left(x, p\right) = pG_2(x) - F_2(x)$

Set $\sigma\left(x, p\right) = 0$ and solve for p to obtain $p = \frac{F_2(x)}{G_2(x)} = h(x)$

Differentiate with respect to time to obtain $\dot{p} = h'(x)\dot{x}$

Equate $\dot{p} = h'(x)\dot{x}$ with

$$\dot{p} = \rho p - \left[F_1'(x) - F_2'\left(x\right)u + p\left(G_1'(x) + G_2'(x)u\right)\right],$$

substitute $\dot{x}$ with $G_1(x) + G_2\left(x\right)u$, use $p = \frac{F_2(x)}{G_2(x)} = h(x)$ and simplify.

You need to obtain an equation in terms of x of the form $\Psi(x) = 0$. Its solution x^*: $\Psi\left(x^*\right) = 0$ determines the optimal steady state for the state variable or the **singular solution**.

The optimal solution is a combination of bang-bang and singular control. It is the Most Rapid Approach Path (MRAP) solution

$$u^*(t) = \begin{cases} b & \text{if } x < x^* \\ -\dfrac{G_1(x^*)}{G_2(x^*)} & \text{if } x = x^* (\dot{x} = 0) \\ a & \text{if } x > x^* \end{cases} \qquad (16)$$

The control $u^*(t) = -\frac{G_1(x^*)}{G_2(x^*)}$ is called the **singular control**.

The Fishery Problem

Solve the optimal management problem of a renewable resource (fishery):

$$\max_{h(t)} \int_0^\infty e^{-\rho t}\left[Ph - cE\right]dt, \quad h = qEx, \quad E = \frac{h}{qx} \qquad (17)$$

subject to $\dot{x} = F(x) - h, \quad x\left(0\right) = x_0$ \qquad (18)

$$0 \le h(t) \le h^{\max} \qquad (19)$$

h refers to harvesting, x is biomass, E is effort, $F(x)$ is the resource growth function, $F(0) = 0$, $F(\hat{x}) = 0$, $\hat{x} > 0$, $\bar{x} \in (0, \hat{x})$

maximizes F, $F''(x) < 0$, P, c, q are positive constants (p: price of harvested resource, c: cost per unit effort, q: catchability coefficient.

The Optimal Investment Problem (No Adjustment Costs)

Determine the optimal investment policy for a competitive profit maximizing firm

$$\max_{I(t)} \int_0^\infty e^{-\rho t} \left[pf(k) - qI \right] dt \tag{20}$$

$$\text{subject to } \dot{k} = I - \delta k, \quad k(0) = k_0 \tag{21}$$

$$0 \le I(t) \le I^{\max} \tag{22}$$

where k is capital stock, I is gross investment, p is output price and q is the price of capital good.

Most Rapid Approach Paths

$$\max_{u(t)} \int_0^\infty e^{-\rho t} \left[P(x) + Q(x) f(x, u) \right] dt \tag{23}$$

$$\text{subject to } \dot{x} = F(x) + G(x) f(x, u), \quad x(0) = x_0 \tag{24}$$

$$a(x) \le u \le b(x) \tag{25}$$

From the state dynamics

$$f(x, u) = \frac{\dot{x}}{G(x)} - \frac{F(x)}{G(x)} \tag{26}$$

$$\max \int_0^\infty e^{-\rho t} \left[P(x) - \frac{Q(x)F(x)}{G(x)} + \frac{Q(x)}{G(x)} \dot{x} \right] dt \tag{27}$$

$$= \max \int_0^\infty e^{-\rho t} \left[M(x) + N(x) \dot{x} \right] dt \tag{28}$$

$$\text{subject to } A(x) \le \dot{x} \le B(x) \tag{29}$$

Define $S(x) = \int_{x_0}^{x} N(v)\, dv$, then $S'(x) = N(x)$ and

$$\int_0^\infty e^{-\rho t} \left[M(x) + N(x)\dot{x} \right] dt = \int_0^\infty e^{-\rho t} \left[M(x) + S'(x)\dot{x} \right] dt$$

(30)

Integrate by parts the term $\int_0^\infty e^{-\rho t} S'(x)\dot{x}\, dt$ with $u = e^{-\rho t}$, $dv = S'(x)\dot{x}\, dt$, $v = \int S'(x)\frac{dx}{dt} dt = S(x)$

$$\int_0^\infty u\, dv = uv - \int_0^\infty v\, du = e^{-\rho t} S(x)\big|_0^\infty + \rho S(x) \int_0^\infty e^{-\rho t} dt \quad (31)$$

$$\lim_{t\to\infty} e^{-\rho t} S(x) - S(x_0) + \rho S(x) \int_0^\infty e^{-\rho t} dt \quad (32)$$

$$\text{assuming } \lim_{t\to\infty} e^{-\rho t} S(x) = 0 \quad (33)$$

the objective depends on x and not on $\dot{x}$, and becomes

$$\int_0^\infty e^{-\rho t} \left[M(x) + \rho S(x) \right] dt \quad (34)$$

The objective is to determine the most desirable state of the state variable which is the one that maximizes $\int_0^\infty e^{-\rho t} \left[M(x) + \rho S(x) \right] dt$ as soon a possible.

Determining the Most Rapid Approach Path

Let x^* be the unique maximizer. The first-order conditions for determining x^* is

$$M'(x) + \rho S'(x) = M'(x) + \rho N(x) = 0 \quad (35)$$

where

$$M'(x) + \rho N(x) = 0 \quad (36)$$

is the Euler equation for problem

$$\max \int_0^\infty e^{-\rho t} \left[M(x) + N(x)\dot{x} \right] dt \quad (37)$$

$$\text{subject to } A(x) \leq \dot{x} \leq B(x) \quad (38)$$

Euler equation is of the form $F_x = \frac{d}{dt} F_{\dot{x}}$

$$F_x = e^{-\rho t} M'(x) + e^{-\rho t} N'(x)\dot{x} \tag{39}$$

$$F_{\dot{x}} = e^{-\rho t} N(x) \tag{40}$$

$$\frac{d}{dt} F_{\dot{x}} = -\rho e^{-\rho t} N(x) + e^{-\rho t} N'(x)\dot{x} \tag{41}$$

then

$$F_x = \frac{d}{dt} F_{\dot{x}} \Rightarrow M'(x) + \rho N(x) = 0 \tag{42}$$

Assume

$$\begin{aligned} M'(x) + \rho N(x) > 0 \quad \text{if } x < x^* \\ M'(x) + \rho N(x) < 0 \quad \text{if } x > x^* \end{aligned} \tag{43}$$

then

$$\begin{aligned} \text{if } x < x^* \ \dot{x} = B(x) \ u = a(x) \\ \text{if } x > x^* \ \dot{x} = A(x) \ u = b(x) \end{aligned} \tag{44}$$

assuming that setting $u = b(x)$ provides the highest growth rate for x and setting it at $u = a(x)$ provides the lowest growth rate.

Growth with Linear Utility

$$\max_{c(t)} \int_0^\infty e^{-\rho t} c(t) \, dt \tag{45}$$

$$\text{subject to } \dot{k} = f(k) - c - \delta k \tag{46}$$

$$a \le c(t) \le b \tag{47}$$

write the objective as

$$\max \int_0^\infty e^{-\rho t} \left[f(k) - \delta k - \dot{k} \right] dt \tag{48}$$

Then $M(x) = f(k) - \delta k$, $N(x) = 1$, $S(x) = k$, and the MRAP transformation results in

$$\max_k \int_0^\infty e^{-\rho t} \left[f(k) - \delta k - \rho k \right] dt \tag{49}$$

The optimal steady state state stock of capital is determined by the first-order condition as

$$k^*: f(k^*) = \delta + \rho \tag{50}$$

The Optimal MRAP Policy

$$
\begin{aligned}
&\text{if } k_0 < k^* \quad c^* = a \\
&\text{if } k_0 = k^* \quad c^* = f(k^*) - \delta k^* \\
&\text{if } k_0 > k^* \quad c^* = b
\end{aligned}
\tag{51}
$$

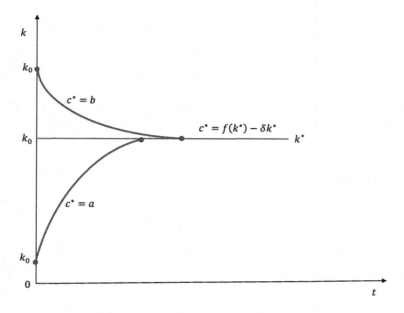

Most rapid approach path.

Chapter 8

Constrained Optimal Control

Mixed Control and State Constraints

$$\max_{x(t)} \int_{t_0}^{t_1} F(t, x(t), u(t)) dt \qquad (1)$$

subject to $\dot{x}(t) = g(x(t), u(t), t), \ x(t_0) = x_0$

$$h_l(x(t), u(t), t) \geq 0, \quad l = 1, \ldots, L \qquad (2)$$

$$x(t) = (x_1(t), \ldots, x_n(t))$$

$$\dot{x}(t) = (\dot{x}_1(t), \ldots, \dot{x}_n(t)) \qquad (3)$$

$$u(t) = (u_1(t), \ldots, u_J(t)), \quad u \in \mathcal{U} \subset \mathbb{R}^J$$

$$x(t_0) = (x_{10}, \ldots, x_{n0})$$

$$x_i(t_1) = x_{i1}, \quad i = 1, \ldots, l$$

$$x_i(t_1) > x_{i1}, \quad i = l+1, \ldots, m$$

$$x_i(t_1) \text{ free}, \quad i = m+1, \ldots, n$$

Introduce the Lagrangean function

$$\mathcal{L} = H(t, x, u, p) + \sum_{l=1}^{L} \mu_l(t) h_l(x(t), u(t), t) \qquad (4)$$

$$H(t, x, u, p) = F(t, x, u) + \sum_{i=1}^{n} p_i(t) g(x, u, t) \qquad (5)$$

The Kuhn–Tucker theorem is used in maximizing the Hamiltonian so the relevant constraint qualification is needed.

Maximum Principle under Mixed Constraints

Let $(x^*(t), u^*(t))$ solve the problem, then

$$\frac{\partial \mathcal{L}}{\partial u_j} = 0, \quad j = 1, \ldots, J \tag{6}$$

$$\dot{p}_i = -\frac{\partial \mathcal{L}^*}{\partial x_i}, \quad i = 1, \ldots, n \tag{7}$$

$$\frac{\partial \mathcal{L}^*}{\partial x_i} \text{ means that } \frac{\partial \mathcal{L}}{\partial x_i} \text{ is evaluated at } u^*(x, p, \mu) \tag{8}$$

$$\mu_l \geq 0, \quad \mu_l h_l(x^*(t), \quad u^*(t), t) = 0, \quad l = 1, \ldots, L \tag{9}$$

The usual TVCs at t_1 are also satisfied.

Sufficiency: Concavity of $H(t, x, u, p)$ and quasi-concavity of $h(x, u, t)$ in (x, u) are required.

- If the problem is discounted, the differential equation for the costate variable λ becomes in terms of the current value Lagrangean

$$\dot{\lambda}_i = \rho \lambda_i - \frac{\partial \mathcal{L}^*}{\partial x_i}, \quad i = 1, \ldots, n \tag{10}$$

Pure State Constraints

$$\max_{x(t)} \int_{t_0}^{t_1} F(t, x(t), u(t)) dt \tag{11}$$

subject to $\dot{x}(t) = g(x(t), u(t), t), \quad x(t_0) = x_0$

$$h_l(x(t), t) \geq 0, \quad l = 1, \ldots, L \tag{12}$$

$$x(t) = (x_1(t), \ldots, x_n(t))$$

$$\dot{x}(t) = (\dot{x}_1(t), \ldots, \dot{x}_n(t)) \tag{13}$$

$$u(t) = (u_1(t), \ldots, u_J(t)), \quad u \in \mathcal{U} \subset \mathbb{R}^J$$

$$x(t_0) = (x_{10}, \ldots, x_{n0})$$

$$x_i(t_1) = x_{i1}, \quad i = 1, \ldots, l$$
$$x_i(t_1) > x_{i1}, \quad i = l+1, \ldots, m$$
$$x_i(t_1) \ free, \quad i = m+1, \ldots, n$$

Introduce the Lagrangean function

$$\mathcal{L} = H(t, x, u, p) + \sum_{l=1}^{L} \mu_l(t) h_l(x(t), t) \tag{14}$$

$$H(t, x, u, p) = F(t, x, u) + \sum_{i=1}^{n} p_i(t) g(x, u, t) \tag{15}$$

Maximum Principle under Pure State Constraints

Let $(x^*(t), u^*(t))$ solve the problem, then there exist functions $\mu_l(t)$ and numbers $\beta_s, s = 1, \ldots, S$ such that

$$\frac{\partial \mathcal{L}}{\partial u_j} = 0, \quad j = 1, \ldots, J$$

$$\dot{p}_i = -\frac{\partial \mathcal{L}^*}{\partial x_i}, \quad i = 1, \ldots, n$$

$\dfrac{\partial \mathcal{L}^*}{\partial x_i}$ means that $\dfrac{\partial \mathcal{L}}{\partial x_i}$ is evaluated at $u^*(x, p, \mu)$

$$\mu_l \geq 0, \quad \mu_l h_l(x^*(t), t) = 0, \quad l = 1, \ldots, L$$

$$p_i(\tau_\gamma^-) - p_i(\tau_\gamma^+)$$

$$= \sum_{s=1}^{S} \beta_s \frac{\partial h_l(x^*(\tau_\gamma), \tau_\gamma)}{\partial x_i}, \quad i = 1, \ldots, n, \quad s = 1, \ldots, S$$

$$\beta_s \geq 0, \quad \beta_s = 0 \ if \ h_l(x^*(\tau_\gamma), \tau_\gamma) > 0, \beta_s h_l(x^*(\tau_\gamma), \tau_\gamma) = 0$$

τ_γ are points of jump discontinuities of $p_i(t)$, $t_0 < \tau_1 < \cdots < \tau_\gamma < \cdots < \tau_\Gamma < t_1$.

Optimal Investment with Adjustment Costs and Pure State Constraints

Determine the optimal investment policy for a competitive profit maximizing firm

$$\max_{I(t)} \int_0^\infty e^{-\rho t} \left[pf(k) - q(I) \right] dt \tag{16}$$

$$\text{subject to } \dot{k} = I - \delta k, \ k(0) = k_0 \tag{17}$$

$$0 \leq k(t) \leq K^{\max} \tag{18}$$

$$I(t) \geq 0 \tag{19}$$

where k is capital stock, I is gross investment, p is the output price, $q(I)$ is the cost of capital goods, $q(0) = 0, q' \geq 0, q'(0) = 0$ and $q'' > 0$.

The Lagrangean for this problem is defined as

$$H = pf(k) - q(I) + \lambda(I - \delta k) \tag{20}$$

$$L = H + \mu_1 k + \mu_2(K^{\max} - k) + \mu_3 I \tag{21}$$

Chapter 9

Dynamic Programming,
Continuous Time

9.1 The Optimal Value Function

Consider the Optimal Control Problem

$$\max_{u(t)} \int_0^T F(t, x(t), u(t))dt + \phi(x(T), T) \tag{1}$$

subject to

$$\dot{x}(t) = g(x(t), u(t), t), \quad x(t_0) = a \tag{2}$$

Define the **optimal value function** $J(t_0, x_0)$ as the best value that can be obtained starting at time t_0 in state x_0. This function is defined for all $t_0 \in [0, T]$ and for any feasible state x_0 that may arise. Thus,

$$J(t_0, x_0) = \max_{u(t)} \int_{t_0}^T F(t, x(t), u(t))dt + \phi(x(T), T) \tag{3}$$

subject to

$$\dot{x}(t) = g(x(t), u(t), t), \quad x(t_0) = x_0 \tag{4}$$

$$J(T, x(T)) = \phi(x(T), T) \tag{5}$$

Derivation of the Hamilton–Jacobi–Bellman (HJB) or Dynamic Programming Equation

$$J(t_0, x_0) = \max_{u(t)} \left(\int_{t_0}^{t_0+\Delta t} F dt + \int_{t_0+\Delta t}^{T} F dt + \phi \right)$$

By the principle of optimality, the control $u(t), t \in [t_0, t_0 + \Delta t]$ should be optimal for the problem beginning at $t_0 + \Delta t$ with initial state $x(t_0 + \Delta t) = x_0 + \Delta x$

$$J(t_0, x_0) = \max_{u(t), t \in [t_0, t_0 \Delta t]} \left[\int_{t_0}^{t_0+\Delta t} F dt \right. \tag{6}$$

$$+ \max_{u(t), t \in [t_0+\Delta t, T]} \left. \left(\int_{t_0+\Delta t}^{T} F dt + \phi \right) \right] \tag{7}$$

subject to $\dot{x} = g(x, u, t), x(t_0 + \Delta t) = x_0 + \Delta x$ (8)

$$J(t_0, x_0) = \max_{u(t), t \in [t_0, t_0+\Delta t]} \left[\int_{t_0}^{t_0+\Delta t} F dt + J(t_0 + \Delta t, x_0 + \Delta x) \right] \tag{9}$$

Approximate

$$\int_{t_0}^{t_0+\Delta t} F dt \simeq F(t_0, x_0, u) \Delta t \tag{10}$$

Assume J is twice continuously differentiable; make a Taylor expansion of the term $J(t_0 + \Delta t, x_0 + \Delta x)$ around (t_0, x_0)

$$J(t_0 + \Delta t, x_0 + \Delta x) = J(t_0, x_0) + J_t \Delta t + J_x \Delta x + h.o.t, \text{ then} \tag{11}$$

$$J(t_0, x_0) = \max_u [F(t_0, x_0, u) \Delta t + J(t_0, x_0)$$
$$+ J_t(t_0, x_0) \Delta t + J_x(t_0, x_0) \Delta x + h.o.t] \tag{12}$$

Subtract $J(t_0, x_0)$ from each side, divide by Δt, take the limit as $\Delta t \to 0$ and note the equation above holds for any t_0 and any feasible state x_0 that may arise, we obtain

$$0 = \max_u [F(t, x, u) + J_t + J_x \dot{x}] \tag{13}$$

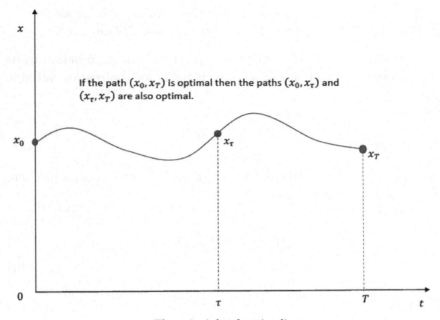

The principle of optimality.

Using $\dot{x} = g(t, x, u)$, we obtain the **HJB or Dynamic programming equation** as follows:

$$-J_t(t, x) = \max_u \left[F(t, x, u) + J_x(t, x)g(t, x, u) \right] \quad \text{or} \quad (14)$$

$$-J_t(t, x) = H(t, x, DJ(t, x)), \quad D_x J(t, x) \equiv J_x(t, x) \quad (15)$$

$$H(t, x, D_x J(t, x)) = \max_u [F(t, x, u) + D_x J(t, x)g(t, x, u)] \quad (16)$$

The HJB equations are a fundamental partial differential equation (PDE) obeyed by the value function $J(t, x)$. Performing the maximization on RHS, we obtain the optimal control in feedback form $u^* = h(x, t)$. Substituting back into the HJB equation, we obtain the PDE as

$$-J_t(t, x) = F(t, x, h(x, t)) + D_x(t, x)g\left(t, x, h\left(x, t\right)\right) \quad (17)$$

which needs to be solved with the boundary condition $J(T, x(T)) = \phi(x(T), T)$.

- If $\phi(x(T), T) = 0$ and $x(T)$ is free then $J(T, x) = 0$ for all x.
- If $\phi(x(T), T) = 0$ and $x(T) = x_T$ fixed, then $J(T, x_T) = 0$.

The RHS of the HJB equation is the Hamiltonian function to be maximized by the choice of u, since it holds for the costate variable $p(t) = J_x(t, x)$.

Verification

The solution of the HJB equation is connected to the control problem (1) by a verification theorem.

Let $W \in C^1$ satisfy

$$-J_t(t, x) = H(t, x, D_x J(t, x)) \tag{18}$$

$$J(T, x(T)) = \phi(x(T), T) \tag{19}$$

Then

$$W(t, x) \leq J(t, x) \tag{20}$$

If controls u^* exist such that

$$F(s, x^*(s), u^*(s)) + g(s, x^*(s), u^*(s))D_x W(s, x^*(s)) = \tag{21}$$

$$H(s, x^*(s), D_x W(s, x^*(s))) \tag{22}$$

for almost all $s \in [0, T]$ then u^* is optimal for the initial data $(0, a)$ and $W(t, x) = J(t, x)$.

The solution of the HJB equation is the value function of the control problem.

Specific Forms of the HJB Equation

(1) **Autonomous problems:** If the problem is autonomous, then the HJB equation becomes

$$0 = \max_u [F(x, u) + J_x(x)g(x, u)] \tag{23}$$

(2) **Problems with discounting**

$$\max_{u(t)} \int_0^T e^{-\rho t} F(t, x(t), u(t)) dt + e^{-\rho T} \phi(x(T)) \qquad (24)$$

subject to

$$\dot{x}(t) = g(x(t), \quad u(t), t), \quad x(0) = a \qquad (25)$$

The HJB equation becomes

$$\rho J(t, x) - J_t(t, x) = \max_u [F(t, x, u) + J_x(t, x) g(t, x, u)] \quad (26)$$

$$J(T, x) = \phi(x) \quad \text{for all } x \qquad (27)$$

The HJB Equation for Infinite Horizon Time Autonomous Problems

$$\max_{u(t)} \int_0^\infty e^{-\rho t} F(x, u) dt \qquad (28)$$

subject to

$$\dot{x}(t) = g(x, u), \quad x(0) = a \qquad (29)$$

$$J(t_0, x_0) = e^{-\rho t_0} \max_u \int_{t_0}^\infty e^{-\rho(t-t_0)} F(x, u) dt \qquad (30)$$

The term $\int_{t_0}^\infty e^{-\rho(t-t_0)} F(x, u) dt$ depends on initial state x_0 but not on initial time. It depends only on elapsed time.

$$\text{Let } V(x_0) = \max_u \int_{t_0}^\infty e^{-\rho(t-t_0)} F(x, u) dt \qquad (31)$$

Then

$$J(t, x) = e^{-\rho t} V(x), \quad J_t(t, x) = -\rho e^{-\rho t} V(x), \quad J_x(t, x) = e^{-\rho t} V'(x)$$

Substituting J, J_t, J_x, into the HJB equation

$$-J_t(t, x) = \max_u [F(t, x, u) + J_x(t, x) g(t, x, u)] \qquad (32)$$

and multiplying through by $e^{\rho t}$, we obtain the fundamental ODE

$$\rho V(x) = \max_u [F(t, x, u) + V'(x)g(t, x, u)] \qquad (33)$$

which is obeyed by the optimal current value function $V(x)$.

Dynamic Programming and Maximum Principle

$$\text{Let} - J_t(t, x) = \max_u [F(t, x, u) + J_x(t, x)g(t, x, u)] \qquad (34)$$

Since u maximizes the RHS, we have

$$\frac{\partial F}{\partial u} + J_x \frac{\partial g}{\partial u} = 0 \qquad (35)$$

Furthermore, using the envelope theorem

$$-J_{tx}(t, x) = F_x(t, x, u^*) + J_{xx}(t, x)g + J_x(t, x)g_x \quad \text{and} \quad (36)$$

$$\frac{d}{dt} J_x(t, x) = J_{xt} + J_{xx}g = F_x(t, x, u^*) + J_x(t, x)g_x \qquad (37)$$

Setting $p = J_x \Rightarrow \dot{p} = \frac{d}{dt} J_x(t, x)$, we obtain the fundamental ODE of the maximum principle

$$\dot{p} = -[F_x(t, x, u^*) + J_x(t, x)g_x] = -H_x^* \qquad (38)$$

Solve

$$\max_{u(t)} \int_0^\infty e^{-\rho t} \left[-\frac{\alpha}{2} u^2 - \frac{\beta}{2} x^2 \right] dt \qquad (39)$$

subject to

$$\dot{x}(t) = u - mx, \quad x(0) = x_0 \qquad (40)$$

The HJB equation becomes

$$\rho V(x) = \max_u \left[\left(-\frac{\alpha}{2} u^2 - \frac{\beta}{2} x^2 \right) + V'(x) [u - mx] \right] \qquad (41)$$

Maximizing the RHS, we obtain

$$u^* = \frac{V'(x)}{\alpha} \tag{42}$$

We consider the trial solution for the value function $V(x) = \frac{A}{2}x^2$. Then $V'(x) = Ax$ and $u^* = \frac{Ax}{\alpha}$

Substituting into the HJB equation, we obtain

$$\rho \frac{A}{2}x^2 = -\frac{\alpha}{2}\left(\frac{Ax}{\alpha}\right)^2 - \frac{\beta}{2}x^2 + Ax\left(\frac{Ax}{\alpha}\right) - Amx^2 \quad \text{or} \quad (43)$$

$$\left[\frac{A^2}{2\alpha} - \left(\frac{\rho}{2} + m\right)A - \frac{\beta}{2}\right]x^2 = 0 \tag{44}$$

since this must be satisfied for all x, the unknown parameter A of the value function must satisfy

$$\frac{A^2}{2\alpha} - \left(\frac{\rho}{2} + m\right)A - \frac{\beta}{2} = 0 \tag{45}$$

Let A^+, A^- be the positive and the negative roots of the quadratic. We choose the negative root. The optimal control in the **feedback form** is

$$u^* = \frac{A^-}{\alpha}x \tag{46}$$

The optimal path for the state equation is

$$\dot{x} = \left(\frac{A^- x}{\alpha} - m\right)x \text{ with } x(0) = x_0 \tag{47}$$

with solution

$$x(t) = x_0 \exp\left(-\left(\frac{A^- x}{\alpha} - m\right)\right)t \tag{48}$$

The **open loop control** is

$$u^*(t) = \frac{A^-}{\alpha}x_0 \exp\left(-\left(\frac{A^- x}{\alpha} - m\right)\right)t \tag{49}$$

Optimal Growth

$$\max_c \int_0^\infty e^{-\rho t} u(c(t)) dt \tag{50}$$

$$\text{subject to } \dot{k} = f(k) - c - \delta k, \ k(0) = k_0 \tag{51}$$

The HJB equation is

$$\rho V(k) = \max_c \left[u(c) + V'(k) \left[f(k) - c - \delta k \right] \right] \tag{52}$$

Maximization of the RHS implies

$$u'(c) = V'(k) \tag{53}$$

Assume differentiability of V and differentiate (52) with respect to k to obtain, after using $u'(c) = V'(k)$,

$$\rho V'(k) = V''(k) \left[f(k) - c - \delta k \right] + V'(k) \left[f'(k) - \delta \right] \Rightarrow \tag{54}$$

$$\rho u'(c) = u''(c) \left[f(k) - c - \delta \right] + u'(c) \left[f'(k) - \delta \right] \tag{55}$$

This is the **envelope or the Benveniste–Scheinkman condition.** At a steady state $f(k^*) - c^* - \delta k^* = 0$, therefore,

$$u'(c^*) \left[f'(k^*) - \delta - \rho \right] = 0 \tag{56}$$

Since $u'(c^*) > 0$,

$$f'(k^*) = \delta + \rho \tag{57}$$

which is the usual long-run equilibrium condition.

Chapter 10

Dynamic Optimization, Discrete Time

Lagrange Multipliers Methods

Discrete time dynamic optimization problems can be solved using Lagrange multiplier methods or dynamic programming methods.

Consider the problem

$$\max_{u_t} \sum_{t=0}^{T} F(x_t, u_t) + \phi(x_{T+1}) \tag{1}$$

$$x_{t+1} = g(x_t, u_t), \quad x_0 = \bar{x}_0, \quad x_{T+1} \geq 0 \tag{2}$$

$$\mathcal{L} = \sum_{t=0}^{T} F(x_t, u_t) + \phi(x_{T+1}) + \sum_{t=0}^{T} \Lambda_t \left[g(x_t, u_t) - x_{t+1} \right] \tag{3}$$

First-order conditions

$$\frac{\partial \mathcal{L}}{\partial u_t} = \frac{\partial F}{\partial u_t} + \Lambda_t \frac{\partial g}{\partial u_t} = 0, \quad t = 0, \ldots, T \tag{4}$$

$$\frac{\partial \mathcal{L}}{\partial x_t} = \frac{\partial F}{\partial x_t} + \Lambda_t \frac{\partial g}{\partial x_t} - \Lambda_{t-1} = 0, \quad t = 0, \ldots, T \tag{5}$$

$$\frac{\partial \mathcal{L}}{\partial x_{T+1}} = \frac{\partial \phi}{\partial x_{T+1}} - \Lambda_T = 0 \tag{6}$$

Given that x_T is fixed at period T, the first-order conditions can be solved recursively starting from period T to obtain feedback rules:

$$x_{t+1} = f(x_t), \qquad t = 0, \ldots, T \tag{7}$$

$$u_{t+1} = h(x_t), \qquad t = 0, \ldots, T \tag{8}$$

$$\Lambda_{t+1} = l(x_t), \qquad t = 0, \ldots, T \tag{9}$$

At period T,

$$\frac{\partial F(x_T, u_T)}{\partial u_T} + \Lambda_T \frac{\partial g(x_T, u_T)}{\partial u_T} = 0 \tag{10}$$

$$\frac{\partial \phi(x_{T+1})}{\partial x_{T+1}} - \Lambda_T = 0 \tag{11}$$

$$x_{T+1} = g(x_T, u_T) \tag{12}$$

For fixed x_T, at period T, we have three equations with three unknowns $(x_{T+1}, u_T, \Lambda_T)$ which can be solved to obtain

$$x_{T+1} = f(x_T) \tag{13}$$

$$u_T = h(x_T) \tag{14}$$

$$\Lambda_T = l(x_T) \tag{15}$$

and so on.

For period $T - 1$, we have

$$\frac{\partial F(x_{T-1}, u_{T-1})}{\partial u_{T-1}} + \Lambda_{T-1} \frac{\partial g(x_{T-1}, u_{T-1})}{\partial u_{T-1}} = 0 \tag{16}$$

$$\frac{\partial F(x_{T-1}, u_{T-1})}{\partial x_{T-1}} + \Lambda_T \frac{\partial g(x_{T-1}, u_{T-1})}{\partial x_{T-1}} - \Lambda_{T-1} = 0 \tag{17}$$

$$x_T = g(x_{T-1}, u_{T-1}) \tag{18}$$

we have three equations with three unknowns $(x_{T-1}, u_{T-1}, \Lambda_{T-1})$ which can be solved given (x_T, u_T, Λ_T) from the previous step and so on.

Dynamic Programming

Consider the infinite horizon optimal control problem

$$\max_{\{u_t\}_{t=0}^{\infty}} \sum_{t=0}^{\infty} \beta^t F(x_t, u_t) \tag{19}$$

$$\text{subject to } x_{t+1} = g(x_t, u_t), \quad x_0 = \bar{x}_0 \tag{20}$$

$\beta \in (0, 1)$ is the discount factor. We assume that $F(x_t, u_t)$ is a concave function and the set $\{(x_{t+1}, x_t) : x_{t+1} \leq g(x_t, u_t), u_t \in \mathbb{R}^m\}$ is convex and compact.

We are seeking a time invariant **feedback rule or policy function** $u_t = h(x_t)$ such that the sequence $\{u_t\}_{t=0}^{\infty}$ generated by

$$u_t = h(x_t) \tag{21}$$

$$x_{t+1} = g(x_t, u_t), \quad x_0 = \bar{x}_0 \tag{22}$$

solves the optimal control problem.

The Value Function

Define the value function

$$V(x_0) = \max_{\{u_t\}_{t=0}^{\infty}} \sum_{t=0}^{\infty} \beta^t F(x_t, u_t) \tag{23}$$

$$\text{subject to } x_{t+1} = g(x_t, u_t), \quad x_0 = \bar{x}_0 \tag{24}$$

As before, this is the optimal value of the original problem starting from any arbitrary initial condition $x \in X$.

If we knew the value function $V(x_0)$, we would determine the policy function h by solving for each $x \in X$ the problem

$$\max_{u} \left[F(x, u) + \beta V(x') \right] \tag{25}$$

$$\text{subject to } x' = g(x, u), \ x \text{ given} \tag{26}$$

where x' denotes the next period state.

The HJB or Dynamic Programming Equation

The HJB equation for the problem is

$$V(x) = \max_{u} \left[F(x, u) + \beta V(g(x, u)) \right] \tag{27}$$

We need to solve for the unknown functions $V(x)$, $h(x)$. The maximizer $u = h(x)$ of the RHS is the policy function that satisfies

$$V(x) = [F(x, h(x)) + \beta V(g(x, h(x)))] \tag{28}$$

Properties of the Value Function

- Under various assumptions about F and g, it turns out that the HJB (27) has a unique strictly concave solution $V(x)$.
- The solution $V(x)$ can be approached by iterations as $j \to \infty$ on

$$V_{j+1}(x) = \max_{u} \left[F(x, u) + \beta V_j(g(x, u)) \right] \tag{29}$$

$$\text{subject to } x' = g(x, u), \quad x \text{ given} \tag{30}$$

starting from any bounded and continuous initial $V_0(x)$.
- The envelope condition or Benveniste–Scheinkman condition: Apart from points of non-differentiability, the limiting function is differentiable

$$V'(x) = \frac{\partial}{\partial x} F(x, u) + \beta \frac{\partial}{\partial x} g(x, u) V'(x') \tag{31}$$

$$u = h(x) \tag{32}$$

Methods for Solving the Optimal Control Problem

1. **First-order conditions and envelope condition:** Start with HJB equation

$$V(x) = \max_{u} \left[F(x, u) + \beta V(x') \right] \tag{33}$$

$$x' = g(x, u), \quad x_0 \text{ given} \tag{34}$$

Find the FOC

$$\frac{\partial}{\partial u}F(x,u)+\beta\frac{\partial}{\partial u}g(x,u)V'(x')=0 \Rightarrow u_t=h(x_t) \quad (35)$$

Use the envelope condition

$$V'(x)=\frac{\partial}{\partial x}F(x,u)+\beta\frac{\partial}{\partial x}g(x,u)V'(x'), \quad u=h(x) \quad (36)$$

Use the FOC and the envelope condition to write the Euler equation, which can be used to uncover the policy function $u=h(x)$.

If the transition law $x'=g(x,u)$ can be reformulated so that the state x does not appear in it, $\frac{\partial}{\partial x}g(x,u)=0$ and the envelope condition becomes

$$V'(x)=\frac{\partial}{\partial x}F(x,u), \quad u=h(x) \quad (37)$$

2. Undetermined coefficients (Guess and verify the value function): Start with the HJB equation

$$V(x)=\max_u[F(x,u)+\beta V(x')] \quad (38)$$

$$x'=g(x,u), \quad x_0 \text{ given} \quad (39)$$

Guess a form for the value function $V(x)=V^G(x)$ and substitute the guess into the HJB equation

$$V(x)=\max_u[F(x,u)+\beta V^G(x')] \quad (40)$$

Perform the optimization on the RHS, obtain the policy function $h^G(x)$, and substitute into the HJB

$$V(x)=[F(x,h^G(x))+\beta V^G(g(x,h^G(x)))] \quad (41)$$

Verify that the form of $V(x)$ is the same as $V^G(x')$

$$V^G(x)=[F(x,h^G(x))+\beta V^G(g(x,h^G(x)))] \quad (42)$$

In practice, you try to obtain the coefficients of the guess value function (see linear quadratic problems).

3. **Iterations:** Start with the HJB equation

$$V_1(x) = \max_u [F(x,u) + \beta V_0(x')] \tag{43}$$

$$x' = g(x,u), \quad x_0 \text{ given} \tag{44}$$

Set $V_0 = \psi(x)$ for a starting function $\psi(\cdot)$. Solve

$$V_1(x) = \max_u [F(x,u) + \beta \psi(x')] \tag{45}$$

to obtain a policy function $u = h_1(x)$. Use the policy function to obtain

$$V_1(x) = [F(x, h_1(x)) + \beta \psi (g(x, h_1(x)))] \tag{46}$$

Write the new HJB equation

$$V_2(x) = \max_u \left[F(x, h_1(x)) + \beta V_1'(x') \right] \tag{47}$$

solve to obtain a policy function $u = h_2(x)$.
    Use the policy function to obtain

$$V_2(x) = \left[F(x, h_2(x)) + \beta V_2' (g(x, h_2(x))) \right] \tag{48}$$

Write the new HJB equation

$$V_3(x) = \max_u [F(x, h_1(x)) + \beta V_2'(x')] \tag{49}$$

continue the iterations until $V_j(x)$ converges to $V(x.)$.

The Savings Problem

$$\max_{c_t, A_{t+1}} \sum_{t=0}^{\infty} \beta^t u(c_t) \tag{50}$$

$$\text{subject to } A_{t+1} = R_{t+1}(A_t + y_t - c_t) \tag{51}$$

A_{t+1}: consumer's holdings of an asset at the beginning of the period $t+1$, y_t: endowment sequence, c_t: consumption of a single good, R_{t+1}: gross return of the asset between t and $t+1$.

Solution by Lagrange Multipliers

$$\mathcal{L} = \sum_{t=0}^{\infty} \beta^t u\left(c_t\right) + \sum_{t=0}^{\infty} \beta^t \lambda_t \left[A_{t+1} - R_{t+1}\left(A_t + y_t - c_t\right)\right] \quad (52)$$

$$= \sum_{t=0}^{\infty} \beta^t u\left(c_t\right) + \lambda_0 \left[A_1 - R_1\left(A_0 + y_0 - c_0\right)\right] \quad (53)$$

$$+ \cdots \beta^t \lambda_t \left[A_{t+1} - R_{t+1}\left(A_t + y_t - c_t\right)\right] \quad (54)$$

$$+ \beta^{t+1}\lambda_{t+1} \left[A_{t+2} - R_{t+2}\left(A_{t+1} + y_{t+1} - c_{t+1}\right)\right] \quad (55)$$

$$+ \cdots$$

First-order conditions:

$$\frac{\partial \mathcal{L}}{\partial c_t} = \beta^t u'\left(c_t\right) + \beta^t \lambda_t R_{t+1} = 0 \quad (56)$$

$$\frac{\partial \mathcal{L}}{\partial c_{t+1}} = \beta^{t+1} u'\left(c_{t+1}\right) + \lambda_{t+1}\beta^{t+1} R_{t+2} = 0, \quad \text{or} \quad (57)$$

$$\frac{u'\left(c_{t+1}\right)}{u'\left(c_t\right)} = \frac{\lambda_{t+1}R_{t+2}}{\lambda_t R_{t+1}} \quad (58)$$

$$\frac{\partial \mathcal{L}}{\partial A_{t+1}} = \beta^t \lambda_t - \beta^{t+1}\lambda_{t+1}R_{t+2} = 0, \quad \text{or} \quad (59)$$

$$\lambda_t = \beta \lambda_{t+1} R_{t+2} \quad (60)$$

Then

$$\beta R_{t+1} \frac{u'\left(c_{t+1}\right)}{u'\left(c_t\right)} = 1 \quad (61)$$

Lars Ljungqvist and Thomas J. Sargent, *Recursive Macroeconomic Theory*, second edition (The savings problem).

Solution by Dynamic Programming

State of the system: A_t, with $A_{t+1} = R_{t+1}\left(A_t + y_t - c_t\right) \Rightarrow c_t = A_t + y_t - R_{t+1}^{-1}A_{t+1}$ control is A_{t+1} and $u\left(c_t\right) = u\left(\left(A_t + y_t\right) - R_{t+1}^{-1}A_{t+1}\right)$.

The HJB equation is

$$v(A_t) = \max_{A_{t+1}} \left[u\left(A_t + y_t - R_{t+1}^{-1}A_{t+1}\right) + \beta v\left(A_{t+1}\right) \right] \qquad (62)$$

First-order conditions

$$R_{t+1}^{-1}u'\left(c_t\right) = \beta v'\left(A_{t+1}\right) \qquad (63)$$

By the envelope condition

$$v'\left(A_t\right) = u'\left(c_t\right) \qquad (64)$$

$$v'\left(A_{t+1}\right) = u'\left(c_{t+1}\right) \qquad (65)$$

Therefore,

$$R_{t+1}^{-1}u'\left(c_t\right) = \beta u'\left(c_{t+1}\right) \quad \text{or} \qquad (66)$$

$$\beta R_{t+1}\frac{u'\left(c_{t+1}\right)}{u'\left(c_t\right)} = 1 \qquad (67)$$

The Ramsey Problem

$$\max_{\{c_t\}_{t=0}^{\infty}} \sum_{t=0}^{\infty} \beta^t u\left(c_t\right) \qquad (68)$$

$$\text{subject to } c_t + k_{t+1} = f(k_t) \qquad (69)$$

Let k' denote next period's capital stock. Then $c = f(k) - k'$ and $u(c) = u(f(k) - k')$. Control is k' and state is k. The HJB equation is

$$V(k) = \max_{k'} \left[u\left(f(k) - k'\right) + \beta V\left(k'\right) \right] \qquad (70)$$

FOC

$$u'(c) = \beta V'(k')$$

The envelope condition is

$$V'(k) = u'\left(f(k) - k'\right) f'(k) \qquad (71)$$

$$V'(k') = u'\left(f(k') - \hat{k}\right) f'(k') \qquad (72)$$

where $\hat{k}$ denotes capital stock two periods ahead of k. Then $f(k) - k' = c_t$ and $f(k') - \hat{k} = c_{t+1}$ and the FOC implies

$$u'\left(f(k) - k'\right) = \beta'\left(f(k') - \hat{k}\right)f'(k') \tag{73}$$

$$u'(c_t) = \beta u'(c_{t+1})f'(k_{t+1}) \tag{74}$$

$$1 = \beta\frac{u'(c_{t+1})}{u'(c_t)}f'(k_{t+1}) \tag{75}$$

which is the Euler equation.

The Linear Quadratic Regulator (LQR)

Solve

$$\max_{\{u_t\}_{t=0}^{\infty}} (-1)\sum_{t=0}^{\infty}\beta^t\left[x_t'Rx_t + u_t'Qu_t\right], \quad 0 < \beta < 1 \tag{76}$$

$$\text{subject to } x_{t+1} = Ax_t + Bu_t \quad x_0 \text{ given} \tag{77}$$

x_t: $(n \times 1)$ vector of state variables, u_t: $(k \times 1)$ vector of control variables, R, Q are symmetric positive semidefine matrices, A, B are $(n \times n)$ and $(n \times k)$ matrices, respectively,$'$ denotes transpose.

The HJB equation for this problem is

$$V(x_t) = \max_u\left[-x_t'Rx_t - u_t'Qu_t - \beta V(x_{t+1})\right] \tag{78}$$

Guess a quadratic value function

$$V(x_t) = -x_t'Px_t \tag{79}$$

P is a symmetric positive semidefine matrix of undetermined coefficients.

The HJB becomes

$$-x_t'Px_t = \max_u\left[-x_t'Rx_t - u_t'Qu_t - \beta x_{t+1}'Px_{t+1}\right] \tag{80}$$

$$-x'Px = \max_u\left[-x'Rx - u'Qu - \beta(Ax + Bu)'P(Ax + Bu)\right] \tag{81}$$

Performing the optimization on the RHS, the FOC results in:

$$\left(Q + \beta B'PB\right) u = -\beta B'PAx$$

Differentiation rules $\dfrac{\partial x' Ax}{\partial x} = \left(A + A'\right) x;\quad \dfrac{\partial y' Bz}{\partial y} = Bz;$

$$\frac{\partial y' Bz}{\partial z} = B'y$$

$A' = A$ by symmetry

the feedback rule is linear in the state

$$u_t = -Fx_t, \quad F = \beta \left(Q + \beta B'PB\right)^{-1} B'PAx \tag{82}$$

F is a matrix that depends on P. Substituting the feedback rule into the HJB equation and rearranging, we obtain the algebraic matrix Riccati equation.

The Matrix Riccati Equation

$$P = R + \beta A'PA - \beta^2 A'PB \left(Q + \beta B'PB\right)^{-1} B'PA \tag{83}$$

Solution of the matrix Ricatti equation provides the parameters P of the value function. The optimal feedback rule becomes

$$u_t = -\hat{F}x_t \tag{84}$$

where $\hat{F}$ is the matrix resulting from the estimates of P. The state dynamics under the optimal feedback rule are

$$x_{t+1} = \left(A - B\hat{F}\right) x_t \tag{85}$$

For stability, the eigenvalues λ_i of the matrix $\Omega = \left(A - B\hat{F}\right)$ need to be within the unit circle, $|\lambda_i| < 1$ for all i.

In this case,

$$\lim_{t \to \infty} x_t = 0 \text{ starting from } x \in \mathbb{R}^n \tag{86}$$

The solution of the matrix Riccati equation can be obtained under certain conditions related to stability by iterations of the matrix Riccati difference equation

$$P_{j+1} = R + \beta A' P_j A - \beta^2 A' P_j B \left(Q + \beta B' P_j B \right)^{-1} B' P_j A \qquad (87)$$

The solution is approached in the limit as $j \to \infty$, starting from $P_0 = 0$.

The Stochastic Linear Quadratic Regulator (S-LQR)

$$\max_{\{u_t\}_{t=0}^{\infty}} (-1) E_0 \sum_{t=0}^{\infty} \beta^t \left[x_t' R x_t + u_t' Q u_t \right], \quad 0 < \beta < 1 \qquad (88)$$

$$\text{subject to } x_{t+1} = A x_t + B u_t + C \varepsilon_{t+1}, \quad x_0 \text{ given} \qquad (89)$$

ε_{t+1} is an $(n \times 1)$ vector of random variables which are i.i.d. according to the normal distribution with mean vector zero and covariance matrix

$$E \varepsilon_t \varepsilon_t' = I \qquad (90)$$

The value function for this problem is

$$v(x) = -x' P x - d \qquad (91)$$

$$d = \beta (1 - \beta)^{-1} \quad \text{trace } PCC' \qquad (92)$$

Certainty Equivalence Principle (CEP)

The optimal policy is given by

$$u_t = -F x_t, \quad F = \beta \left(Q + \beta B' P B \right)^{-1} B' P A x \qquad (93)$$

The CEP states that the feedback rule that solves the S-LQR is identical with the feedback rule that solves the corresponding nonstochastic LQR.

Chapter 11

Stochastic Control: Stochastic Processes and Stochastic Calculus

Sigma — Algebras and Probability Measures

An experiment $\mathcal{E}$ is the operation through which several possible outcomes or results can be produced. A *probability space* is a triplet $(\Omega, \mathcal{F}, P)$ which can be associated with an experiment. Ω is an arbitrary set of points $\omega \in \Omega$. Each point ω is called a *sample point* or *outcome* of the experiment, for example head (H) or tail (T) in a single toss of a coin where $\Omega = \{H, T\}$, or a set of objects with detectable characteristics and/or properties. The set Ω is called the *sample space*, while a subset of Ω is called an *event*. Thus, an event is a collection of some of the possible outcomes of an experiment. The set of all events is the power set of Ω which contains 2^{Ω} events. For example, if we toss two coins $\Omega = \{HH, TT, HT, TH\}$ and its power set contains $2^4 = 16$ events.

$\mathcal{F}$ is a class of subsets (or events) of Ω, that is, $\mathcal{F} \subset 2^{\Omega}$. It is called a *$\sigma$-algebra* and has the following properties:

(1) The sample space Ω belongs to $\mathcal{F}$, or $\Omega \in \mathcal{F}$ (equivalently $\varnothing \in \mathcal{F}$).
(2) If $A \in \mathcal{F}$, then the complement of A also belongs to $\mathcal{F}$, or $A^c = \{\omega \in \Omega : \omega \notin A\} \in \mathcal{F}$.
(3) For any sequence $A_i \in \mathcal{F}, i = 1, 2, \ldots$ the union of all A_i belongs to $\mathcal{F}$, or $\cup_{i=1}^{\infty} A_i \in \mathcal{F}$.

The pair $(\Omega, \mathcal{F})$ is called a measurable space. Let P a set function $P : \mathcal{F} \to \mathbb{R}$. This function is called a *probability measure* if it satisfies the following:

(1) $P(\varnothing) = 0$ and $P(\Omega) = 1$. ($\varnothing$ is usually called the 'impossible event').
(2) $0 \le P(A) \le 1$ for all $A \in \mathcal{F}$.
(3) If $A_i \in \mathcal{F}$ and the A_i's are mutually disjoint, that is, $A_i \cap A_j = \varnothing$ if $i \ne j$, then $P(\cup_{i=1}^{\infty}) = \sum_{i=1}^{\infty} P(A_i)$.

The real number $P(A)$ which is assigned to the event A is interpreted as

$$P(A) = \text{'the probability that event } A \text{ occurs'}.$$

Random Variables

Let $(\Omega, \mathcal{F})$, $(\Omega', \mathcal{F}')$ denote two measurable spaces. A mapping $X : \Omega \to \Omega'$ is $(\mathcal{F}, \mathcal{F}')$ measurable, if for every meaningful event $\omega' \in \Omega'$, there exists a meaningful event $\omega \in \Omega$, or for each $A' \in \mathcal{F}'$, $X^{-1}(A') = \{\omega \colon X(\omega) \in A'\} \in \mathcal{F}$.

If the image space Ω' is the real line $\mathbb{R}$, then the measurable real function $X : \Omega \to \mathbb{R}$ is called a **random variable**. That is, a random variable is a measurable function from the sample space Ω to the real line $\mathbb{R}$ such that for each event $\omega \in \Omega$ there corresponds a unique real number $X(\omega)$. If $X : \Omega \to \mathbb{R}^m$ and it is measurable, then it is called a **random vector**, $\mathbf{X}(\omega) = (X_1(\omega), \dots, X_m(\omega))$.

Distribution Functions

Let X be a random variable, its *distribution function* which is denoted by $F(X)$ is defined as

$$F(x) = P(\{\omega \in \Omega : X(\omega) \le x\}) = P[X \le x]$$

All distribution functions satisfy the following:

(1) $0 \le F(x) \le 1$.
(2) $\lim_{x \to -\infty} F(x) = 0, \quad \lim_{x \to \infty} F(x) = 1$.

(3) $F(x)$ is a non-decreasing function. That is, for any $h \geq 0$, $F(x+h) \geq F(x)$.

Distribution functions could be discrete, continuous or mixed. We will focus on the purely continuous case. In this case, $F(x)$ is assumed continuous and differentiable for almost all x. X is called a *continuous random variable*.

Probability Density Functions

The *probability density function* of a continuous random variable X is the derivative $f(x)$ of the distribution function $F(x)$, or

$$F(x) = \int_{-\infty}^{x} f(u) \, du, \quad f(x) = \frac{dF(x)}{dx}$$

with the following properties:

(1) $f(x) \geq 0$.
(2) $\int_{-\infty}^{\infty} f(x) \, dx = 1$.
(3) For any a, b $(a \leq b)$, $P[a < X \leq b] = \int_{a}^{b} f(x) \, dx$.

Let X be a continuous random variable X with probability density function $f(x)$. The mean μ and the variance σ of $f(x)$ are defined as

$$\mu = \int_{-\infty}^{\infty} x f(x) \, dx$$

$$\sigma^2 = \int_{-\infty}^{\infty} (x - \mu)^2 f(x) \, dx = \int_{-\infty}^{\infty} x^2 f(x) \, dx - \mu^2$$

Stochastic Processes

A **stochastic (or random)** *process* $\{X(t) : t \in T\}$ is a family of random variables indexed by t, where t belongs to a given index set T that denotes time. If T is such that $t = 0, 1, 2, \ldots$ then $\{X(t)\}$ is said to be a **discrete time (or discrete parameter) stochastic process**. If $T = [0, \infty)$ or $T = [0, 1]$, then $\{X(t)\}$ is said to be a **continuous time (or continuous parameter) stochastic process**. Since $X(t)$ is a random variable, each time the experiment is performed, a different value of X will in general be observed. An observed record of a stochastic process is a collection of observed outcomes at different points in time which is called a **realization, sample path, or trajectory** of the stochastic process. The collection of all possible records is called the **ensemble** of the stochastic process.

A stochastic process can be regarded as a function defined on $T \times \Omega$, or $X : T \times \Omega \to \mathbb{R}$. For a given $t \in T$, $X_t(\cdot) : \Omega \to \mathbb{R}$ is a random variable. For a given $\omega \in \Omega$, $X(\cdot, \omega) : \Omega \to \mathbb{R}$ is a function from T to $\mathbb{R}$. This function is the **sample path**. The range of X is the **state space**, while the value $X(t, \omega)$ is the *state* at time t, and X is the **state variable**.

Stationary Processes

For each t, $X(t)$ will have a probability distribution and, when $X(t)$ is a continuous random variable, a probability density function $f_t(x)$. The mean and the variance of $X(t)$ will be given by

$$\text{mean } X(t) = EX(t) = \int_{-\infty}^{\infty} x f_t(x) dx = \mu(t)$$

$$\text{variance } X(t) = E(X(t) - \mu(t))^2 = \sigma^2(t)$$

A stochastic process is called *stationary* up to order 2 (or simply stationary) if

(1) it has the same mean μ at all points in time, or $E[X(t)] = \mu$.
(2) it has the same variance σ^2 at all points in time, or $\text{var}[X(t)] = \sigma^2$.
(3) the covariance between the values of X at any two points of time t and s, defined as $\text{cov}\{X(t)X(s)\} = E[X(t)X(s)] - \mu^2$, depends only on the difference $t - s$.

White Noise

A stochastic process $\{X(t)\}$ is called **Gaussian or normal**, if for any n and a subset $\{t_1, t_2, \ldots, t_n\} \in T$, the joint probability distribution of $\{X(t_1), X(t_2), \ldots, X(t_n)\}$ is *multivariate normal* and is completely determined by its mean value function $E\left[X(t)\right]$, and covariance function $cov\left\{X(t)X(s)\right\}$.

A discrete parameter stochastic process $\{X_t\}, t = 0, \pm 1, \pm 2, \ldots$, is called a **purely random process or white noise** if it is a sequence of uncorrelated random variables. That is, $cov\left\{X_t, X_s\right\} = 0$ for all $t \neq s$. A white noise process will be denoted by $\{\varepsilon_t\}$.

A continuous parameter white noise $\{\varepsilon(t)\}$ is a process such that for any subset of times $t_1, t_2, \ldots, t_n$, the sequence $\varepsilon(t_1), \varepsilon(t_2), \ldots, \varepsilon(t_n)$ form a set of uncorrelated random variables. If $E\left[\varepsilon(t)\right] = 0$ and $var\left\{\varepsilon(t)\right\} = \sigma_\varepsilon^2$, the autocovariance and autocorrelation functions are

$$R_\varepsilon(\tau) = \begin{cases} \sigma_\varepsilon^2 & \tau = 0 \\ 0 & \tau \neq 0 \end{cases}, \quad \rho_\varepsilon(\tau) = \begin{cases} 1 & \tau = 0 \\ 0 & \tau \neq 0 \end{cases}$$

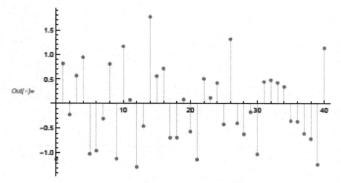

White noise $\mu = 0$, $\sigma = 1$.

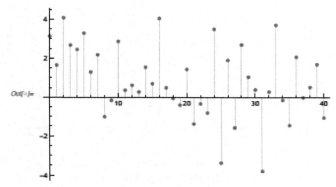

White noise $\mu = 0$, $\sigma = 2$.

The Random Walk

The simplest random walk may be described as a particle that moves along a line by steps; each step takes it one unit to the right or to the left with probabilities p and $q = 1 - p$, respectively, where $0 < p < 1$. Each step is taken in a unit of time so that the tth step is made instantaneously at time t.

Let ξ_t be the tth step taken or displacement, so that

$$\xi_t = \begin{cases} +1 \text{ with probability } p \\ -1 \text{ with probability } q \end{cases}$$

and the ξ_t's are independent random variables. If we denote the initial state by X_0, then the position at time t (or after t steps) is

$$X_t = X_0 + \xi_1 + \cdots + \xi_t.$$

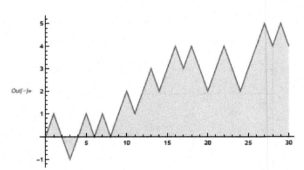

Random walk $p = 0.5$.

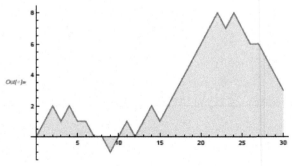

Random walk $p = 0.4$, $q = 0.5$
probability of zero step 0.1.

   Thus, the random walk is represented by the sequence of random variables $\{X_t, t \geq 0\}$ which is a stochastic process in discrete time.

The Wiener Process

A stochastic process $W(t)$, $t \in [0, \infty)$ is a *Wiener process* or a *Brownian motion process*, if it satisfies the following properties:

(1) $W(0) = 0$ with probability 1 (w.p.1), that is, the process starts at zero.
(2) For any two points of time t and s ($0 \leq s < t$), the increment $W(t) - W(s)$ is not influenced by the increment $W(s) - W(0)$.

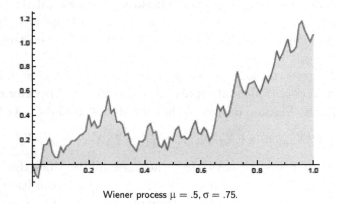

Wiener process $\mu = .5, \sigma = .75$.

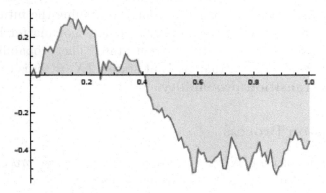

Wiener process $\mu = -.25, \sigma = .5$.

Thus, the increment $\{\Delta W_t\} = \{W(t) - W(t-1)\}$ for an integer t is *identically and independently distributed (i.i.d)*. This is the **independent increment property**.

(3) The increments of the process between any two points of time t and s ($0 \leq s < t$) are distributed normally, or

$$W(t) - W(s) \sim N\left(\mu(t-s), \sigma^2(t-s)\right)$$

if we standardize the process, that is, $\mu = 0, \sigma^2 = 1$, then $W(t) - W(s) \sim N(0, t-s)$.

The Markov Process

A stochastic process satisfies the **Markov property,** if the probable future state at any time $t > s$ is independent of the past behavior of the state variable at time $t < s$, and depends only on the current state s.

A discrete parameter stochastic process $\{X_t : t = 0, 1, 2, \ldots\}$ defined on a countable state space B is said to be a **Markov chain** if it satisfies the Markov property, that for all $x \in B$ and $t = 0, 1, 2, \ldots,$

$$P[X_{t+1} = x \mid X_0, X_1, \ldots, X_t] = P[X_{t+1} = x \mid X_t]$$

The Markov property says that the probability that the random variable X will be at state x at time $t + 1$ is conditioned only on current (or present) information provided by X_t. The Markov property implies that what matters for determining the future state of the system is only its current state. It does not matter how the stochastic process reached the current state. The probability that X_{t+1} is at state x, given that X_t is at state z ($X_t = z$), is called the **one-step transition probability**.

The Poisson Process

A stochastic process $X(t)$, $t \in [0, \infty)$ is a *Poisson process* with parameter λ if it satisfies the following properties:

(1) $X(0) = 0$ w.p.1, that is, the process starts at zero.

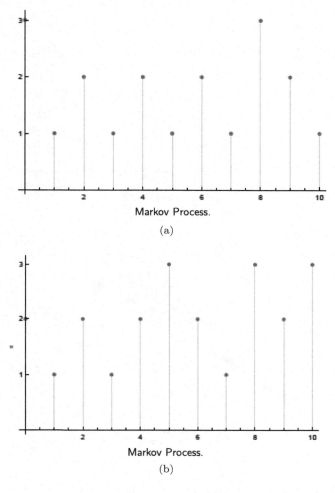

Markov Process.

(a)

Markov Process.

(b)

(2) For $0 < t_1 < t_2 < \ldots < t_n$, the increments $\{\Delta X_{t_i}\} = \{X(t_i) - X(t_{i-1})\}$, $i = 1, \ldots, n$, $t_0 = 0$ are independent.

(3) The increments of the process between any two points of time t and s $(0 \leq s < t)$ have a Poisson distribution, or

$$P[N(t+s) - W(t) = k] = \frac{[\lambda s]^k}{k!} e^{[-\lambda s]}, \quad k \in N = \{0, 1, 2, \ldots\}$$

(4) $N(t+s) - W(t) = k$ is the number of events in the interval $(t, t+s)$.

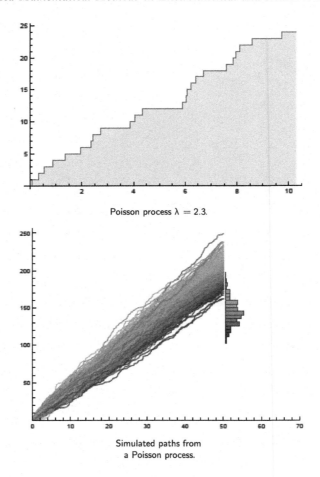

Poisson process $\lambda = 2.3$.

Simulated paths from
a Poisson process.

Stochastic Differential Equations

Deterministic differential equations

$$\frac{dX}{dt} = \mu(t, X), \quad \text{or} \quad dX = \mu(t, X)dt$$

can be extended to a stochastic differential equation as

$$dX(t) = \mu\left(X(t), t\right) dt + \sigma\left(X(t), t\right) dW(t), \ X(0) = X_0 \text{ given} \quad (1)$$

or $dX_t = \mu(t, X_t)dt + \sigma(X_t, t) \ dW_t, X_0$ given where W_t is a Wiener process. In (1), the stochastic process $X\left(t,\omega\right)$ and the Wiener process $W\left(t,\omega\right)$ are defined for $\omega \in \Omega$ and $t \in T$ where $(\Omega, \mathcal{F}, P)$ a probability space. The stochastic differential equation (1) is called an **Itô stochastic differential equation**.

Itô Stochastic Differential Equation

The Itô stochastic differential equation (1) can be interpreted heuristically showing that in a small time interval Δt, the change in X_t is an amount which is normally distributed with expectation $\mu(X_t, t)\Delta t$ and variance $\sigma^2(X_t, t)\Delta t$.

The change in X_t is independent of the past behavior of the process since the increments of a Wiener process are i.i.d. The function μ is referred to as the **drift coefficient**, while σ is called the **diffusion coefficient**. The stochastic process X_t is called a **diffusion process**.

The stochastic differential equation (1) can be associated with the stochastic integral equation

$$X_t - X_0 = \int_0^t \mu\left(t, X_t\right) dt + \int_0^t \sigma\left(t, X_t\right) dW_t \qquad (2)$$

The integral $\int_0^t \sigma\left(t, X_t\right) dW_t$ is an *Itô integral*.

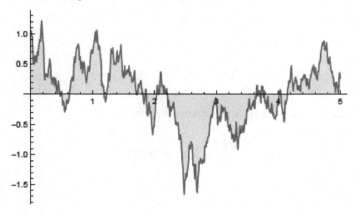

Ito process.

(a)

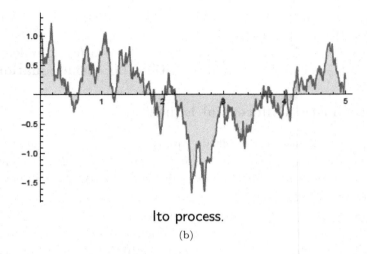

Ito process.

(b)

Geometric Brownian Motion

$$dX_t = \mu X_t dt + \sigma X_t \, dW_t, \; X_0 \text{ given} \tag{3}$$

Closed form solution is

$$X_t = X_0 \exp\left[\left(\mu - \frac{\sigma^2}{2}\right) t + \sigma W_t\right] \tag{4}$$

$$E\left(X_t\right) = X_0 e^{\mu t} \tag{5}$$

$$V\left(X_t\right) = X_0^2 e^{2\mu t} \left(e^{\sigma^2 t} - 1\right) \tag{6}$$

Stochastic population in optimal growth is

$$\frac{dL}{L} = n \, dt + \sigma \, dW \tag{7}$$

Stock price X is

$$dX = \mu X dt + \sigma X dW \tag{8}$$

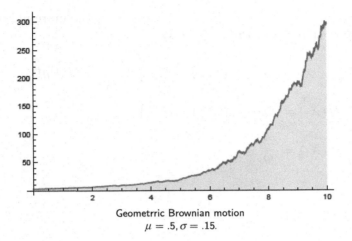

Geometrric Brownian motion
$\mu = .5, \sigma = .15.$

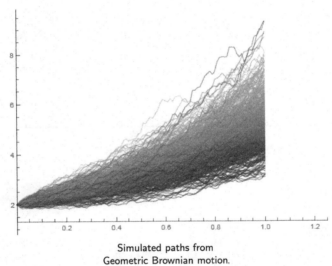

Simulated paths from
Geometric Brownian motion.

The Ornstein–Uhlenbeck Process Mean Reversing Process)

$$dX_t = \theta \left(\mu - x_t \right) dt + \sigma dW_t, \quad X_0 \text{ given} \tag{9}$$

Long run oil prices should be drawn back to the marginal cost of production (Dixit and Pindyck, 1994).

$$X_t = X_0 e^{-\theta t} + \mu \left(1 - e^{-\theta t}\right) + \int_0^t \sigma e^{\theta(s-t)} dW_s \qquad (10)$$

$$E\left(X_t\right) = X_0 e^{-\theta t} + \mu \left(1 - e^{-\theta t}\right) \qquad (11)$$

$$V\left(X_t\right) = \frac{\sigma^2}{2\theta} \qquad (12)$$

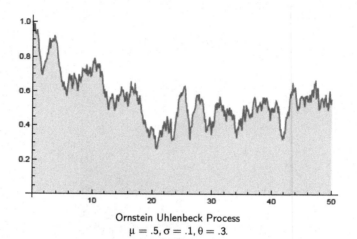

Ornstein Uhlenbeck Process
$\mu = .5, \sigma = .1, \theta = .3.$

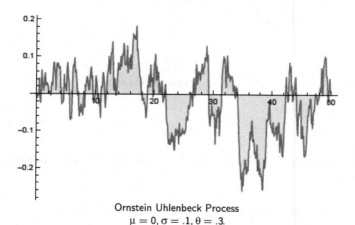

Ornstein Uhlenbeck Process
$\mu = 0, \sigma = .1, \theta = .3.$

Itô's Lemma

Consider the integral equation

$$X(t) = X_0 + \int_0^t \mu(s)ds + \int_0^t \sigma(s)dW_s$$

It is said that the process $X(t)$ possesses a stochastic differential on $t \in [0, T]$, defined as

$$dX(t) = \mu(t)dt + \sigma(t)dW(t)$$

Itô's lemma is the basic stochastic calculus rule for computing stochastic differentials of composite stochastic (or random) functions.

Itô's lemma: *Let $Y(t) = u(t, X(t))$. Then the process $Y(t)$ also has a differential on $t \in [0, T]$ given by*

$$dY(t) = \left[\frac{\partial u\,(t, X)}{\partial t} + \frac{\partial u\,(t, X)}{\partial X}\mu(t) + \frac{1}{2}\frac{\partial^2 u\,(t, X)}{\partial X^2}\sigma^2(t)\right]dt$$
$$+ \frac{\partial u\,(t, X)}{\partial X}\sigma(t)dW(t) \tag{13}$$

If $Y(t) = u(X(t))$, then $\frac{\partial u(t,X)}{\partial t} = 0$ in (13).

If the stochastic differential of $X(t)$ is given by

$$dX = \mu(X)dt + \sigma(X)dW(t)$$

and $Y = u(X)$, Itô's lemma implies that

$$dY = \left[u'(X)\mu(X) + \frac{1}{2}u''(X)\sigma^2(X)\right]dt + u'(X)\sigma(X)dW(t) \tag{14}$$

Itô's lemma can be obtained by direct computation using a second-order Taylor expansion of the function $Y = u(X)$. For the case leading to (14) we have, using the second-order Taylor expansion,

$$dY = u'(X)dX + \frac{1}{2}u''(X)(dX)^2$$
$$= u'(X)\left[\mu(X)dt + \sigma(X)dW(t)\right]$$
$$+ \frac{1}{2}u''(X)\left[\mu(X)dt + \sigma(X)dW(t)\right]^2$$

Differential (14) is obtained by using the 'multiplication table':

$\times$	dW	dt
dW	dt	0
dt	0	0

The Black–Scholes Formula

A European (call) option gives the right to by one share of common stock at the time of maturity. The stock price X follows a geometric Brownian motion

$$dX = \mu X dt + \sigma X dW \tag{15}$$

Let $V(t, X(t))$ be the value of the option at time t when the stock price is $X(t)$. For each share of stock long the investor has n units of option short. The value of portfolio at any point of time is $J = X - nV$, and the change in the value from t to $t + dt$ is $dJ = dX - n\,dV$. By Ito's lemma (second-order Taylor expansion), we have

$$dV = V_t\,dt + V_X\,dX + \frac{1}{2}\left(V_{tt}\,(dt)^2 + 2V_{tX}\,dt\,dX + V_{XX}\,(dX)^2\right)$$

$$V_{tt}\,(dt)^2 = 0, \quad V_{tX}\,dt\,dX = V_{tX}dt\,(\mu X dt + \sigma X dW) = 0$$
$$V_{XX}\,(dX)^2 = V_{XX}\,(\mu X dt + \sigma X dW)^2 = V_{XX}\sigma^2 X^2 dt$$

Therefore,

$$dV = \left(V_t + \frac{1}{2}\sigma^2 X^2 V_{XX}\right)dt + V_X dX \tag{16}$$

and the change in the value of the portfolio becomes

$$dJ = dX - n\,dV = dX - nV_X\,dX - n\left(V_t + \frac{1}{2}\sigma^2 X^2 V_{XX}\right) \quad (17)$$

The term $n\left(V_t + \frac{1}{2}\sigma^2 X^2 V_{XX}\right)$ is risk free because it does not contain dW. If we choose $n\left(t, X_t\right) = \frac{1}{V_X(t,X_t)}$, so that the portfolio consists of holding one unit of X and shorting $\frac{1}{V_X}$ units of V, the adjustment is done continuously risk free, since

$$dJ = dX - n\,dV = -n\left(V_t + \frac{1}{2}\sigma^2 X^2 V_{XX}\right) \quad (18)$$

The return from holding a portfolio consisting of holding one unit of X and shorting $\frac{1}{V_X}$ units of V must be equal to its return from the bond market at a constant short-term interest rate r. Therefore,

$$-\left(V_t + \frac{1}{2}\sigma^2 X^2 V_{XX}\right) = (r\,dt)\left(X - \frac{1}{V_X}V\right), \quad \text{or} \quad (19)$$

$$V_t = rV - rXV_X - \frac{1}{2}\sigma^2 X^2 V_{XX} \quad (20)$$

which is the fundamental PDE for option pricing. The PDE is solved for the unknown function $V\left(t, X\right)$ with the boundary condition

$$V\left(T, X\right) = \max\{X - c, 0\} = \begin{cases} X - c & \text{if } X \geq c \\ 0 & \text{if } X < c \end{cases} \quad (21)$$

where c is the exercise price and T is the maturity date.

Existence and Uniqueness of Solutions, Dependence on Parameters and Initial Conditions

A solution $X(t)$ of the stochastic differential equation is a stochastic process $X(t)$, which has stochastic differential and which satisfies for all $t \in [0, T]$ an integral equation.

Suppose that

(1) the functions $\mu\left(t, x\right)$ and $\sigma\left(t, x\right)$ are measurable with respect to $x \in \mathbb{R}$ and $t \in [0, T]$.

(2) for $x, y \in \mathbb{R}$ and $t \in [0, T]$ there exists a constant K such that

(1) $|\mu(t, x) - \mu(t, y)| + |\sigma(t, x) - \sigma(t, y)| \leq K |x - y|$

(2) $|\mu(t, x)|^2 + |\sigma(t, x)|^2 \leq K \left(1 + |x|^2\right)$

(3) X_0 is given.

Then there is a solution $X(t)$ of the stochastic differential equation (1) defined on $[0, T]$ which is continuous w.p.1, such that

$$\sup_{[0,T]} E\left[X^2(t)\right] < \infty$$

Furthermore, this solution is pathwise unique, that is, if X and Y are two solutions

$$P\left[\sup_{[0,T]} |X(t) - Y(t)| = 0\right] = 1$$

Assume that the stochastic differential equation (1) depends on a parameter α, or

$$dX(\alpha, t) = \mu(\alpha, t, X(t)) \, dt + \sigma(\alpha, t, X(t)) \, dW_t \qquad (22)$$

and that the functions μ and σ satisfy the conditions for existence and uniqueness of a solution, then under certain assumptions about the structure of the functions μ and σ with respect to α, the solution of the stochastic differential equation (1) depends on the parameter α and the initial condition X_0. Furthermore, if the derivatives $\frac{\partial \mu}{\partial \alpha}, \frac{\partial \sigma}{\partial \alpha}$ are continuous and bounded, then the derivative $Y(t) = \frac{\partial X(t, \alpha)}{\partial \alpha}$ exists where $X(t, \alpha)$ is the solution of (22).

Reference
Dixit, R.K. and Pindyck, R.S. 2012. *Investment Under Uncertainty*. Princeton University Press.

Chapter 12

Optimal Stochastic Control

Optimal Stochastic Control: The Problem

Optimal stochastic control studies problems where the evolution of the stochastic process $X(t)$ is influenced by another stochastic processes $u(t)$ called a *control process*, which belongs to an appropriately defined control space U. For the Itô stochastic differential equation (1) the control process can be introduced into the drift and the variance functions as

$$dX(t) = \mu(X(t),\, u(t),\, t)dt + \sigma(X(t),\, u(t),\, t)dW_t,\, X(0)$$

$$= X_0 \text{ given} \tag{1}$$

In this case, (1) is called a **controlled stochastic differential equation,** while the process $X(t)$ which satisfies (1) is said to be a **controlled Markov diffusion process**. Given a finite time interval $t \leq s \leq T$, the optimal stochastic control problem is to choose the control process $u(t)$ to maximize (or minimize), subject to the dynamics imposed by (1), *a criterion or objective* defined as in the following.

The Objective

Finite time horizon

$$J = E_t \left\{ \int_t^T F(X(s),\, u(s),\, s)ds + \phi(T, X_T) \right\} \qquad (2)$$

subject to (1).

Infinite time horizon with discounting

$$J^\infty = E_0 \left\{ \int_0^\infty e^{-\rho s} F(X(s),\, u(s),\, s)ds \right\}, \quad \rho > 0 \qquad (3)$$

subject to (1).

The solution to the optimal stochastic control problem is obtained by using Bellman's *principle of optimality* to obtain the *dynamic programming* equation or the *Hamilton–Jacobi–Bellman* equation.

The Hamilton–Jacobi–Bellman (HJB) or Dynamic Programming Equation

Assume that in the finite time interval $t \leq s \leq T$, the controller observes the states $X(t)$ of the controlled process, and the initial data $X_0 \equiv x$ are known and given. For any initial data,

$$V(X, t) = \sup_{u \in U_C} J(t, X; u)$$

where U_C is the class of controls admitted, V is said to be the **value function**. Bellman's principle of optimality states that

$$V(X, t) = \sup_{u \in U_C} E_t \left\{ \int_t^{t+h} F(X(s), u(s), s)\, ds \right.$$

$$\left. + V(X(t+h), t+h) \right\}$$

HJB Finite Horizon

$$\frac{\partial V(X,t)}{\partial t} = \mathcal{H}\left(t, X, \frac{\partial V}{\partial X}, \frac{\partial^2 V}{\partial X^2}\right) \tag{4}$$

$$\mathcal{H}\left(t, X, \frac{\partial V}{\partial X}, \frac{\partial^2 V}{\partial X^2}\right) \tag{5}$$

$$= \max_{u \in U}\left\{F(X, u, t) + \frac{\partial V}{\partial X}\mu(X, u, t) + \frac{1}{2}\frac{\partial^2 V}{\partial X^2}\sigma^2(X, u, t)\right\}$$

$$V(T, X) = \psi(T, X_T) \tag{6}$$

The HJB equation is a nonlinear PDE of second order (5), with boundary condition (6), satisfied by the value function $V(X, t)$.

The Verification Theorem

Formally, the HJB equation is connected to the optimal stochastic control problem through the *verification theorem* (Fleming and Soner, 1993). *Let $W(t, X)$ be continuously differentiable in t and twice continuously differentiable in X. Let $W(t, X)$ be a solution to* (5)–(6).
   Then:

- $W(t, X) \geq J(t, X)$ *for any admissible control $u \in U$ and initial data (t, X).*
- *If a $u^*(s)$ exists such that* (7) *is satisfied*

$$u^*(s) \in \tag{7}$$

$$\arg\max\left\{F(X^*(s), u, s) + \frac{\partial V}{\partial X}\mu(X^*(s), u, s)\right.$$

$$\left. + \frac{1}{2}\frac{\partial^2 V}{\partial X^2}\sigma^2(X^*(s), u, s)\right\} \tag{8}$$

then $W(t, X) = V(t, X) = J(t, X; u^*)$ and $u^*(s)$ is optimal. $X^*(s)$ is the solution of (1) corresponding to $u^*(\cdot)$ with $X^*(t) = X$.

The value function is a classical (twice continuously differentiable) solution of the HJB equation.

Condition (7) suggests that the *optimal feedback control* should satisfy

$$u^{*}\left(s,X\right) \in \tag{9}$$

$$\arg\max\left\{F\left(X,u,s\right) + \frac{\partial V}{\partial X}\mu\left(X,u,s\right) + \frac{1}{2}\frac{\partial^{2}V}{\partial X^{2}}\sigma^{2}\left(X,u,s\right)\right\}$$

Infinite Time Horizon

The optimal stochastic control problem is written as

$$\max_{u} J^{\infty} = E_{0}\left\{\int_{0}^{\infty} e^{-\rho t}F\left(X(t),u(t)\right)ds\right\}, \quad \rho > 0 \tag{10}$$

$$\text{subject to } dX\left(t\right) = \mu\left(X(t),\,u(t)\right)dt + \sigma\left(X(t),\,u(t)\right)dW_{t} \tag{11}$$

$$X\left(0\right)\text{given} \tag{12}$$

The HJB equation for this problem is

$$\rho V\left(X\right) = \mathcal{H}\left(X,V'(X),V''\left(X\right)\right) \tag{13}$$

$$\mathcal{H}\left(X,V',V''\right) \tag{14}$$

$$= \max_{u\in U}\left\{F\left(X,u\right) + V'\mu\left(X,u\right) + \frac{1}{2}V''\sigma^{2}\left(X,u\right)\right\} \tag{15}$$

$$\lim_{t\to\infty} E\left[e^{-\rho t}V\left(X_{t}\right)\right] = 0 \tag{16}$$

with (16) being a *transversality condition at infinity*.

The value function is a classical solution of the HJB equation The optimal feedback policy satisfies

$$u^{*}\left(X\right) \in \tag{17}$$

$$\arg\max\left\{F\left(X,u\right) + V'\mu\left(X,u\right) + \frac{1}{2}V''\sigma^{2}\left(X,u\right)\right\}$$

Solving the Optimal Stochastic Control Problem

Undetermined coefficients (guess and verify the value function):

- For linear quadratic problems, use a quadratic value function. Solve

$$\max_{\{c_t\}} E_0 \int_0^\infty e^{-\rho t} \left[-\alpha x_t^2 - b u_t^2\right] dt \qquad (18)$$

$$\text{subject to } dx_t = (\beta u_t - m x_t)\, dt + \sigma x_t\, dW_t \qquad (19)$$

with $V(x) = Ax^2$.

Problems in Economics

In economic problems, the objective is determined most of the times by the utility function. In this case, the guess function depends on the form of the utility function. If the state dynamics follow a geometric Brownian motion, then the guess value function to be used as solution of the HJB for infinite time horizon problems with discounting at rate ρ takes the following form.

CRRA (constant relative risk aversion):

$$u(c) = \begin{cases} \frac{c^b}{b} & \text{if } b < 1 \\ \log c & \text{if } b = 0 \end{cases} \qquad (20)$$

Value function for $\frac{c^b}{b}$

$$V(X) = AX^b, \quad A > 0 \text{ to be determined} \qquad (21)$$

Value function for $\log c$

$$V(X) = \left(\frac{1}{A}\log X + B\right), \quad A, B \text{ to be determined} \qquad (22)$$

CARA (constant absolute risk aversion):

$$u\left(c\right) = -\frac{1}{\alpha}e^{-\alpha c}, \quad \alpha > 0 \tag{23}$$

Value function

$$V\left(X\right) = \left(-\frac{A}{\alpha}\right)e^{-\alpha\rho X}, \quad A > 0 \text{ to be determined.} \tag{24}$$

Optimal Portfolio Rules

There are n assets and the price of each assets follows a geometric Brownian motion

$$dP_{it} = \mu_i P_{it} dt + \sigma_i P_{it} dz_t \tag{25}$$

The investor owns N_{it} units of asset i, with total wealth $W(t) = \sum_{i=1}^{n} N_i(t) P_{it}$. Assume that portfolio and consumption remain unchanged in the time interval $[t + dt]$. Then

$$dW = \sum_{i=1}^{n} N_i(t) dP_{it} - c(t) dt \tag{26}$$

Let $s_i(t) = \frac{N_i(t) P_{it}}{W(t)}$ the share of wealth in asset i. Then

$$dW = \sum_{i=1}^{n} N_i(t) \left(\mu_i P_{it} dt + \sigma_i P_{it} dz_{it}\right) - c\left(t\right) dt \tag{27}$$

$$= \sum_{i=1}^{n} s_i\left(t\right) \mu_i W\left(t\right) dt - c\left(t\right) dt + \sum_{i=1}^{n} s_i\left(t\right) \sigma_i W dz_i\left(t\right) \tag{28}$$

If the nth asset is risk free with $\mu_n = r > 0$ and $\sigma_n = 0$, the budget equation becomes

$$dW = \sum_{i=1}^{n-1} s_i(t)\left(\mu_i - r\right) W dt + \left(rW - c\right) dt + \sum_{i=1}^{n} s_i(t)\sigma_i W dz_{it} \tag{29}$$

Assume one risky asset and one riskless asset to simplify. The budget equation becomes the following. s is the fraction of wealth in the risky asset:

$$dW = [s(\mu - r)W + rW - c]\,dt + s\sigma W\,dz, \quad W(0) = W_0 \quad (30)$$

Assuming utility function $u(c) = \frac{c^b}{b}, b < 1$, the problem for the investor is

$$\max_{c,s} \int_0^\infty e^{-\rho t}\left(\frac{c^b}{b}\right) dt \quad (31)$$

$$\text{subject to (30)} \quad (32)$$

The HJB equation for the problem is

$$\rho V(W) = \max_{c,s}\left[\frac{c^b}{b} + V'(W)\left[s(\mu - r)W + rW - c\right]\right. \quad (33)$$

$$\left. + \frac{1}{2}s^2\sigma^2 W^2 V''(W)\right] \quad (34)$$

Performing the maximization on the RHS of the HJB equation, we obtain

$$c = \left[V'(W)\right]^{1/(b-1)}, \quad s = \frac{(r-\mu)V'(W)}{\sigma^2 W V''(W)} \quad (35)$$

A solution for this nonlinear second-order ODE is of the form $V(W) = AW^b$. The undetermined coefficient A can be obtained by substituting the trial solution into the HJB equation and collecting terms.

Viscosity Solutions and Solvability of the HJB Equation

The solvability of HJB equation for general nonlinear problems often encountered in economics is an open issue. To obtain a solution to the control problem, the validity of the dynamic programming principle has to be checked, and then it has to be shown that the dynamic programming principle leads to the HJB equation as a result. Then, even if this is true, usually, the validity of the whole argument requires the existence of classical solutions (i.e., solutions in $C^2(\mathbb{R}^n)$ — twice continuously differentiable functions) for the HJB equation leading to well-posedness of the feedback rules, which are defined through the gradient vector and the Hessian matrix of the value function $D_X V, D_X^2 V$.

However, this is not always true. The HJB equation may not (and this happens quite often) have solutions which are classical, therefore, the whole construction sketched above cannot be justified in a rigorous sense. To remedy this situation, the concept of **viscosity solutions**, which are continuous but not necessarily differentiable functions that solve the HJB equation in a weak sense has been introduced. It can then be shown that the dynamic programming principle may be generalized in terms of this new solution concept, and under certain general conditions, the value function of the problem is given by this viscosity solution.

The Deterministic Problem

Write the HJB equation or dynamic programming equation.

$$\rho v \left(x \right) + \sup_{u \in U} \left\{ -g \left(x, u \right) Dv \left(x \right) - f \left(x, u \right) \right\} = 0 \qquad (36)$$

$$F \left(x, v, Dv \right) = 0 \qquad (37)$$

This is first-order nonlinear ODE satisfied by the value function v of the problem. $Dv \left(x \right)$ is the gradient of v at point x.

- The derivation of HJB requires some smoothness of v. In this case, the HJB holds at all points where v is differentiable.
- It is well known, however, that everywhere differentiability is a too restrictive assumption on v.
- This means that we seek a solution in some weak sense where the value function is continuous and bounded in $\mathbb{R}^n$ but not necessarily differentiable.

Classical and Weak Solutions

Definition: Given an ODE (or PDE) of order $k > 1$, a function $\psi : X \to \mathbb{R}^n$ is called a classical solution if $\psi \in C^k \left(X \right)$ and ψ solves the ODE (or PDE) at any $x \in X$.

Under suitable assumptions, classical solutions are, in general, unique but they might not exist. If the derivatives do not exist at any point but just almost everywhere, a weaker notion of solution is to require that the equations are satisfied at the points where the derivatives exist. Weak solutions are good for existence and uniqueness.

Grandall and Lions (1982) introduced the concept of the **viscosity solution** as a notion of weak solution to first, and second-order ODEs, PDEs that satisfy properties of existence, uniqueness and stability.

Assume a second-order ODE with a classical solution $\psi \in C^2$. Consider a function $\varphi \in C^2$ touching ψ from above at x_0 which means that $\varphi \geq \psi$ and $\varphi(x_0) = \psi(x_0)$. Then $\psi - \varphi$ has a local maximum at x_0, and $\psi - \varphi$ looks concave around x_0. Consider a function φ touching ψ at x_0 from below, then $\psi - \varphi$ has a local minimum at x_0. When ψ is not C^2, we will use the same properties for C^2 **test functions** φ touching from above and from below to state whenever ψ solves the ODE in a weak sense.

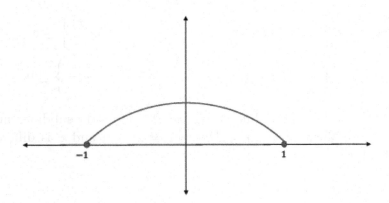

A typical test function is the bump function shown above. It is smooth (infinitely differentiable) and has compact support. It is zero outside an interval the $[-1, 1]$ here.

The following definition applies to the first-order ODE corresponding to the HJB equation (37).

Definition:

(1) $\psi \in C^1$ is a viscosity subsolution of (40) if for any test function $\varphi \in C^1$ such that x is a local maximum of $\psi - \varphi$, $F(x, \psi(x), D\varphi(x)) \leq 0$.

(2) $\psi \in C^1$ is a viscosity supersolution of (40) if for any test function $\varphi \in C^1$ such that x is a local minimum of $\psi - \varphi$, $F(x, \psi(x), D\varphi(x)) \geq 0$.

(3) $\psi \in C^1$ is a viscosity solution of (40) if it is both a viscosity subsolution and a viscosity supersolution.

If the value function v is continuous, then it satisfies the HJB in the viscosity sense. (e.g., Bardi and Capuzzo–Dolcetta, Optimal Control and Viscosity Solutions of Hamilton–Jacobi–Bellman Equations, 2008).

For ODEs of order k, the definition requires a C^k regularity of the test function.

This definition uses subgradients. Assuming that v is continuous in $\mathbb{R}^n$, the HJB can be interpreted in the viscosity sense.

Define the sets

$$D^+v(x) = \left\{ p \in \mathbb{R}^n : \limsup_{y \to x} \frac{v(y) - v(x) - p(y - x)}{|y - x|} \right\} \leq 0 \qquad (38)$$

$$D^-v(x) = \left\{ p \in \mathbb{R}^n : \limsup_{y \to x} \frac{v(y) - v(x) - p(y - x)}{|y - x|} \right\} \geq 0 \qquad (39)$$

$D^+v(x)$ is the superdifferential and $D^-v(x)$ is the subdifferential of v at x. When $D^+v(x) = D^-v(x) = Dv(x)$ and v is differentiable at x.

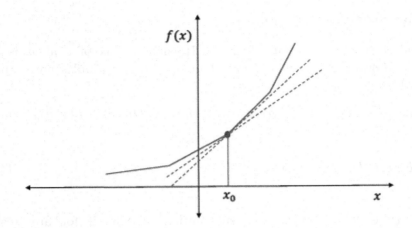

A convex function (solid line) and subdifferentials (dashed lines) at x_0.

A continuous function ψ is a viscosity solution of the nonlinear ODE

$$F\left(x, \psi(x), D\psi\left(x\right)\right) = 0, \quad x \in \mathbb{R}^n \tag{40}$$

If

$$\text{(i)} \ F\left(x, \psi(x), p\right) \le 0 \quad \forall x \in \mathbb{R}^n, \quad \forall p \in D^+ v\left(x\right) \tag{41}$$

$$\text{(ii)} \ F\left(x, \psi(x), q\right) \ge 0 \quad \forall x \in \mathbb{R}^n, \quad \forall q \in D^- v\left(x\right) \tag{42}$$

Any ψ satisfying (i) will be called a viscosity subsolution of (40). Any ψ satisfying (ii) will be called a viscosity supersolution of (40).

The Stochastic Problem

The HJB equation, with D^2v the Hessian matrix of v at x, is a second-order PDE when more than one state variables enter the problem

$$\rho v\left(x\right) + \sup_{u\in U}\left\{-\sigma^2\left(x,u\right)D^2v\left(x\right) - g\left(x,u\right)Dv\left(x\right) - f\left(x,u\right)\right\} = 0,$$

or

$$F\left(x,v,Dv,D^2v\right) = 0 \tag{43}$$

(1) $\psi \in C$ is a viscosity subsolution of (43) if for any test function $\varphi \in C^2$ such that x is a local maximum of $\psi - \varphi$, $F(x,\psi(x),\mathsf{D}\varphi(x),\mathsf{D}^2\varphi(x)) \leq 0$.

(2) $\psi \in C$ is a viscosity supersolution of (43) if for any test function $\varphi \in C^2$ such that x is a local minimum of $\psi - \varphi$, $F(x,\psi(x),\mathsf{D}\varphi(x),\mathsf{D}^2\varphi(x)) \geq 0$.

(3) $\psi \in C$ is a viscosity solution of (43) if it is both a viscosity subsolution and a viscosity supersolution.

If the value function v is continuous, then it satisfies the HJB in the viscosity sense.

Reference

Fleming, W.H. and Soner, H.M. 2006. *Controlled Markov Processes and Viscosity Solutions* (Vol. 25). Springer Science & Business Media.

Chapter 13

Differential Games

Description

A differential game can be defined as a situation of conflict where players choose optimal strategies over time. Thus, in a differential game (or dynamic game), there is **strategic and forward-looking behavior** on the part of the agents (business, firms, communities, regions, nations). Conflicts arise because agents have their own objectives and their own preferred courses of action. Agents act strategically and are aware that other strategically acting agents are part of the problem and that their decisions influence the outcome. Agents take into account the present and future consequences of their own actions and those of other agents.

A dynamic game is a state-space game A state-space game is one which contains a set of state variables that describe the main features of a dynamic system at any instant of time during the game. In a differential game, the state variables evolve in continuous time.

Apart from state variables, a dynamic game model also contains control variables chosen by the players to optimize each player objective. Differential games are related closely with optimal control problems. In an optimal control problem, there is a single control and a single criterion to be optimized. Differential games generalize this to many controls and many criteria, one for each player. Each player attempts to control the state of the system so as to achieve his goal; the system responds to the inputs of all players. Thus, in addition to the characteristics of an optimal control problem, the following concepts are introduced in a differential game.

Control and Strategy Spaces

In a differential game, there exists a set of players indexed by $\alpha = 1, \ldots, N$. Let $N_\alpha = \{1, \ldots, N\}$ be the player's index set. For each player $\alpha \in N_\alpha$, a **control space** $\mathcal{U}^\alpha$ exists with elements $u^\alpha(t)$, $t \in [t_0, t_1]$ the control variables for each player $\alpha = 1, \ldots, N$.

The state dynamics for the differential game describing the state of the game at each point in time depend on the control variables of all players, or

$$\dot{x}_i(t) = f_i\left(x(t), u^1(t), \ldots, u^\alpha(t), \ldots, u^N(t)\right) \tag{1}$$

$$x(t) \in \mathbb{R}^n, x(0) = x_0 \text{ fixed} \tag{2}$$

$$u^\alpha(t) = (u_1^\alpha(t), \ldots, u_l^\alpha(t), \ldots, u_m^\alpha(t)), \quad \alpha = 1, \ldots, N \tag{3}$$

Each player has m controls.

The **strategy** for each player is a function $u^\alpha(t) = \theta^\alpha(x(t), t)$. The set of strategies for player α is his/her **strategy space**.

Information Structures

Crucial to the structure of the differential game is the specification of the information about the state of the game gained and recalled by each player at each point in time $t \in [t_0, t_1]$. There are a number of possible information structures for a differential game (Basar and Olsder, 1982), we defined the two mostly used structures in economic applications.

Definition: The **information structure** of each player is determined by $\eta^\alpha(t) = \{x(s), 0 \leq s \leq \varepsilon_t^\alpha\}$, $0 \leq \varepsilon_t^\alpha \leq t$, where ε_t^α is nondecreasing in t. $\eta^\alpha(t)$ determines the information gained and recalled by player α at time $[t_0, t_1]$. We will say that player's α information structure is as follows:

1. Open loop (OL) pattern if $\eta^\alpha(t) = \{x_0\}, t \in [t_0, t_1]$.
2. Feedback (perfect state) (FB) pattern if $\eta^\alpha(t) = \{x(t)\}, t \in [t_0, t_1]$.

Open Loop and Feedback Strategies

- When the information structure is open loop (OL) each player follows the OL strategy. An OL strategy depends only on the initial state and time

$$u^\alpha(t) = \theta^\alpha(x_0, t) \tag{4}$$

An equilibrium in OL strategies is called an open loop Nash equilibrium (OLNE).
- When the information structure is feedback (FB) each player follows the OL strategy. An FB strategy depends only on the current state

$$u^\alpha(t) = \theta^\alpha(x(t)) \tag{5}$$

In economics, FB strategies are also called **Markov strategies** to emphasize the lack of memory in the information structure. An equilibrium in FB strategies is called feedback Nash equilibrium (FBNE).

Given the above definitions, a fixed time duration differential game is defined as

$$\max_{u^\alpha} J^\alpha \tag{6}$$

$$= \int_{t_0}^{t_1} F\left(x(t), u^1(t), \ldots, u^\alpha(t), \ldots, u^N(t)\right) dt + \phi^\alpha\left(x\left(T\right)\right)$$

subject to

$$\dot{x}_i(t) = f\left(x(t), u^1(t), \ldots, u^\alpha(t), \ldots, u^N(t)\right) \quad x(t) \in \mathbb{R}^n$$

$$\alpha = 1, \ldots, N, \; x(0) = x_0 \text{ fixed}, x\left(T\right) \text{ free}$$

OLNE

An OLNE is defined as the N-tuple of strategies $\left(u^{*1}(t), \ldots, u^{*\alpha}(t), \ldots, u^{*N}(t)\right)$ satisfying

$$J^\alpha\left(u^{*1}, \ldots, u^{*\alpha}, \ldots, u^{*N}\right)$$
$$\geq J^\alpha\left(u^{*1}, \ldots, u^{*\alpha-1}, u^\alpha, u^{*\alpha+1}, \ldots, u^{*N}\right) \text{ for all } \alpha \quad (7)$$

If $u^{*a}(t) = \theta^\alpha(x_0, t)$ for all α provides an OLNE and $x^*(t)$ is the associated optimal trajectory for the state variables, then the costate variables $p^\alpha(t) \in \mathbb{R}^n$, $\alpha = 1, \ldots, N$ exist such that the conditions of Pontryagin's maximum principle are satisfied for all α, or

$$\dot{x}_i^*(t) = f_i\left(x^*(t), u^{*1}(t), \ldots, u^{*\alpha}(t), \ldots, u^{*N}(t)\right),$$
$$\times x^*(t) \in \mathbb{R}^n, \ x^*(0) = x_0 \theta^{*\alpha}(x_0, t) \equiv u^{*a}(t)$$
$$\arg\max_{u^\alpha} H^\alpha\left(t, p^\alpha(t), x^*(t), u^{*1}, \ldots, u^{*\alpha-1}, u^\alpha, u^{*\alpha+1}, \ldots, u^{*N}\right)$$
$$\dot{p}^\alpha(t) = -\frac{\partial}{\partial x} H^\alpha\left(t, p^\alpha(t), x^*(t), u^{*1}, \ldots, u^{*N}\right),$$
$$\times p^\alpha(T) = \frac{\partial}{\partial x} \phi^\alpha(x^*(T))$$
$$H^\alpha\left(t, p, x, u^1, \ldots, u^N\right) = F\left(x(t), u^1(t), \ldots, u^\alpha(t), \ldots, u^N(t)\right)$$
$$+ \sum_{i=1}^{n} p_i^\alpha f_i\left(x, u^1, \ldots, u^\alpha, \ldots, u^N\right)$$

If terminal conditions are different than (6), the transversality conditions are determined as in optimal control problems.

If the problem is of infinite time horizon with discounting

$$\max_{u^\alpha} J^\alpha = \int_0^\infty e^{-\rho t} F(x(t), u^1(t), \ldots, u^\alpha(t), \ldots, u^N(t)) dt \quad (14)$$
$$\text{subject to} \quad (15)$$
$$\dot{x}_i(t) = f_i\left(x(t), u^1(t), \ldots, u^\alpha(t), \ldots, u^N(t)\right) \ x(t) \in \mathbb{R}^n \quad (16)$$
$$\alpha = 1, \ldots, N, \ x(0) = x_0 \text{ fixed} \quad (17)$$

the OLNE is defined using the current value Hamiltonian, with ODEs for the costate variables

$$\dot{\lambda}^\alpha(t) = \rho\lambda^\alpha(t) - \frac{\partial}{\partial x}H^\alpha\left(t, p^\alpha(t), x^*(t), u^{*1}, \ldots, u^{*N}\right) \qquad (18)$$

and transversality conditions at infinity. OLNE can be fully determined using Pontryagin's maximum principle.

FBNE

If $u^{*a}(t) = \theta^\alpha(x(t), t)$ for all α provides an FBNE in Markov Strategies (no memory) or simply FBNE and $x^*(t)$ is the associated optimal trajectory for the state variables, then the costate variables $p^\alpha(t) \in \mathbb{R}^n$, $\alpha = 1, \ldots, N$ exist such that the conditions of Pontryagin's maximum principle are satisfied for all α, or

$$\dot{x}_i^*(t) = f_i\left(x^*(t), u^{*1}(t), \ldots, u^{*\alpha}(t), \ldots, u^{*N}(t)\right), \quad x^*(t) \in \mathbb{R}^n$$

$$x^*(0) = x_0, \; u^{*a}(t) = \theta^\alpha(x(t), t)$$

$$\arg\max_{u^\alpha} H^\alpha\left(t, p^\alpha(t), x^*(t), u^{*1}, \ldots, u^{*\alpha-1}, u^\alpha, u^{*\alpha+1}, \ldots, u^{*N}\right)$$

$$\dot{p}^\alpha(t) = -\frac{\partial}{\partial x}H^\alpha\left(t, p^\alpha(t), x^*, \theta^{*1}(t, x^*, x_0), \ldots, \theta^{*\alpha-1}(t, x^*, x_0), u^{*a},\right.$$

$$\left.\theta^{*\alpha+1}(t, x^*, x_0), \ldots, \theta^{*N}(t, x^*, x_0)\right), \quad p^\alpha(T) = \frac{\partial}{\partial x}\phi^\alpha(x^*(T))$$

$$H^\alpha\left(t, p, x, u^1, \ldots, u^N\right) = F\left(x(t), u^1(t), \ldots, u^\alpha(t), \ldots, u^N(t)\right)$$

$$+ \sum_{i=1}^n p_i^\alpha f_i\left(x, u^1, \ldots, u^\alpha, \ldots, u^N\right)$$

If terminal conditions are different than (6), the transversality conditions are determined as in optimal control problems.

In an infinite time horizon problem with discounting, the ODEs for the costate variables are

$$\dot{\lambda}^\alpha(t) = \rho\lambda(t) - \frac{\partial}{\partial x}\left(H^\alpha t, p^\alpha(t), x^*, \theta^{*1}(t, x^*, x_0), \ldots,\right.$$

$$\times \theta^{*\alpha-1}(t, x^*, x_0), u^{*a}, \theta^{*\alpha+1}(t, x^*, x_0), \ldots, \theta^{*N}(t, x^*, x_0)\right),$$

with transversality conditions at infinity.

The conditions for FBNE in general admit an uncountable number of solutions, which correspond to "informationally nonunique" Nash equilibrium solutions. To eliminate informational nonuniqueness, the Nash solution is constrained to satisfy the following conditions.

The N-tuple of strategies $\theta^{*\alpha}$ constitutes an FBNE solution if there exist functionals $V^\alpha(\cdot, \cdot)$ satisfying for each α

$$
\begin{aligned}
V^\alpha(t, x) \equiv & \int_t^{t_1} F^\alpha\left(s, x^*(s), \theta^{*1}(s, x^*(s), x_0), \ldots, \theta^{*\alpha}\right. \\
& \times (s, x^*(s), x_0), \ldots, \theta^{*N}\left(t, x^*(s), x_0\right)) \, ds + \phi^\alpha\left(x^\alpha(T)\right) \\
\leq & \int_t^{t_1} F^\alpha\left(s, x^*(s), \theta^{*1}(s, x^*(s), x_0), \ldots,\right. \\
& \times \theta^{*\alpha-1}(s, x^*(s), x_0), \ldots, \theta^\alpha(s, x^*(s), x_0) \\
& \times \theta^{*\alpha+1}(s, x^*(s), x_0), \ldots, \theta^{*N}\left(t, x^*(s), x_0\right)) \, ds \\
& + \phi^\alpha\left(x^\alpha(T)\right)
\end{aligned}
$$

where in the interval $[t, t_1]$

$$
\begin{aligned}
\dot{x}^\alpha(s) = & f\left(s, x^{*\alpha}(s), \theta^{*1}(s, x^*(s), x_0), \ldots, \theta^{*\alpha-1}(s, x^*(s), x_0), \ldots,\right. \\
& \theta^\alpha(s, x^*(s), x_0), \theta^{*\alpha+1}(s, x^*(s), x_0), \ldots, \theta^{*N}\left(t, x^*(s), x_0\right)) \\
x^\alpha(t) = & x \\
\dot{x}^\alpha(s) = & f\left(s, x^{*\alpha}(s), \theta^{*1}(s, x^*(s), x_0), \ldots, \theta^\alpha(s, x^*(s), x_0), \ldots,\right. \\
& \theta^{*N}\left(t, x^*(s), x_0\right)), \quad x^*(t) = x
\end{aligned}
$$

Strong and Weak Time Consistency

- An important feature of the FBNE is that if an N-tuple of strategies $\theta^{*\alpha}$ constitutes a FBNE solution for the N-person differential game with duration $[t_0, t_1]$, its restriction to the time interval $[t, t_1]$ provides a FBNE solution for the same differential game defined in the shorter time interval $[t, t_1]$ with initial state $x(t)$ for all $t_0 \leq t \leq t_1$. This feature of the FBNE solutions is referred to as **strong time consistency** and corresponds to subgame perfection. OLNE solution does not have this property. OLNE solutions are referred to as **weak time consistent** solutions. This means that under OLNE, if a player deviates from the equilibrium control for a while and decides to play again "correctly", then the previously defined equilibrium is not an equilibrium any more.

- An FBNE solution is strongly time consistent and depends only on the current value of the state variable (time stationary or autonomous strategies). It will also depend on the time variable for non-autonomous FB strategies.

- When each player **precommits** to a control path from the outset of the game, the outcome is described by OLNE.

- When players **do not precommit** to a control path, the outcome is described by FBNE.

Dynamic Programming Characterization of FBNE Solutions

If the value functions $V^\alpha(t, x)$ are continuously differentiable in both arguments, then the FBNE solutions can be determined by using the HJB equation

$$-\frac{\partial V^\alpha(t, x)}{\partial t} = \max_{u^\alpha} \left[\hat{F}^{*\alpha}(t, x, u^\alpha) + \frac{\partial V^\alpha(t, x)}{\partial t} \hat{f}^{*\alpha}(t, x, u^a) \right] \quad (19)$$

$$V^\alpha(T, x) = q^\alpha(x) \quad (20)$$

$$\hat{F}^{*\alpha}(t, x, u^\alpha) := F^\alpha\left(t, x, \theta^{*1}(x), \ldots, \theta^{*\alpha-1}(t, x), \ldots, \right. \quad (21)$$

$$\times \left. u^\alpha, \theta^{*\alpha+1}(x), \ldots, \theta^{*N}x\right) \quad (22)$$

$$\hat{f}^{*\alpha}(t, x, u^a) := f^\alpha\left(t, x, \theta^{*1}(x), \ldots, \theta^{*\alpha-1}(t, x), \ldots, \right. \quad (23)$$

$$\times \left. u^\alpha, \theta^{*\alpha+1}(x), \ldots, \theta^{*N}x\right) \quad (24)$$

For problem with infinite time horizon, the HJB becomes

$$\rho V^\alpha(t, x) = \max_{u^\alpha} \left[\hat{F}^{*\alpha}(t, x, u^\alpha) + \frac{\partial V^\alpha(t, x)}{\partial t} \hat{f}^{*\alpha}(t, x, u^a) \right] \quad (25)$$

- If the problem is linear quadratic, the dynamic programming approach provides a straightforward way for determining the

FBNE solution through the matrix Ricatti equations. For problems with nonlinear quadratic structure, one needs to deal with the issues of solvability of the HJB equation.

- Pontryagin's maximum principle is not very useful in determining FBNE solutions because the unknown functions θ for the FB strategies should be determined along with the solution and this is not in general possible. The maximum principle can provide, however, important qualitative information about the solution.

A Linear-Quadratic Differential Game

$$\max_{u_i} J^i = \int_0^\infty e^{-\rho t} \left[A u_i(t) - \frac{1}{2} u_i^2(t) - \frac{s}{2} x^2(t) \right] dt, \quad i = 1, 2$$
$$(26)$$

subject to $\dot{x} = u_1(t) + u_2(t) - mx(t), \quad x(0) = x_0, \quad A, s, m > 0$
$$(27)$$

OLNE:

$$H^i = A u_i - \frac{1}{2} u_i^2 - \frac{s}{2} x^2 + \lambda_i \left(u_i + \bar{u}_j - mx \right) \quad i, j = 1, 2 \quad (28)$$

$$\frac{\partial H^i}{\partial u_i} = 0 \Rightarrow u_i = A + \lambda_i \tag{29}$$

$$\text{and} \tag{30}$$

$$\frac{\partial H^j}{\partial u_j} = 0 \Rightarrow u_j = A + \lambda_j \tag{31}$$

$$\dot{\lambda}_i = \rho \lambda_i - \frac{\partial H^i}{\partial x} = (\rho + m) \lambda_i + sx \tag{32}$$

$$\dot{\lambda}_j = \rho \lambda_j - \frac{\partial H^j}{\partial x} = (\rho + m) \lambda_j + sx \tag{33}$$

$$\lambda_i = \lambda_j = \lambda \text{: symmetry} \tag{34}$$

$$\dot{x} = 2 \left(A + \lambda \right) - mx \tag{35}$$

The MHDS for the OLNE becomes

$$\dot{x} = 2 \left(A + \lambda \right) mx, \quad x(0) = x_0 \tag{36}$$

$$\dot{\lambda} = \left(\rho + m \right) \lambda + sx \tag{37}$$

Steady state $(x^*_{OL}, \lambda^*_{OL})$: $\dot{x} = \dot{\lambda} = 0$

$$\lambda^*_{OL} = -\frac{s}{(\rho + m)} x \tag{38}$$

$$x^*_{OL} = \frac{(\rho + m)\lambda^*}{s} \tag{39}$$

$$J = \begin{pmatrix} -m & 2 \\ s & \rho + m \end{pmatrix} \tag{40}$$

trace $J = \rho > 0$, det $J = -m(\rho + m) < 0$. Therefore, $(x^*_{OL}, \lambda^*_{OL})$ is a saddle point.

FBNE

Assume symmetric FB time stationary strategies $u_i = u_j = \theta(x)$

$$H^i = Au_i - \frac{1}{2}u_i^2 - sx^2 + \lambda_i (u_i + \theta(x) - mx) \tag{41}$$

$$\frac{\partial H^i}{\partial u_i} = 0 \Rightarrow u_i = A + \lambda_i \tag{42}$$

$$\frac{\partial H^i}{\partial u_j} = 0 \Rightarrow u_j = A + \lambda_j \tag{43}$$

$$\dot{\lambda}_i = \rho\lambda_i - \frac{\partial H^i}{\partial x} = (\rho + m - \theta'(x))\lambda_i + sx \tag{44}$$

$$\dot{\lambda}_j = \rho\lambda_j - \frac{\partial H^j}{\partial x} = (\rho + m - \theta'(x))\lambda_j + sx \tag{45}$$

$$\lambda_i = \lambda_j = \lambda: \text{symmetry} \tag{46}$$

$$\dot{x} = 2(A + \lambda) - mx \tag{47}$$

The MHDS for the OLNE becomes

$$\dot{x} = 2(A + \lambda) - mx, \quad x(0) = x_0 \tag{48}$$

$$\dot{\lambda} = (\rho + m - \theta'(x))\lambda + sx \tag{49}$$

However, $\theta(x)$ is unknown and should be determined as part of the solution. The FBNE solution cannot be determined in a straightforward way.

There is the possibility of qualitative comparisons with the OLNE. If $\theta'(x) = 0$, then OLNE and FBNE coincide. Thus, OLNE is a special case of FBNE.

Assume $\theta'(x) = -b < 0$. The FB strategy has a negative slope, so player i expects player j to reduce his control u if the state x increases and vise versa. This is typical behavioral assumption in problems of international pollution control. Then

$$\lambda^*_{FB} = -\frac{s}{(\rho + m + b)} x > \lambda^*_{OL} = -\frac{s}{(\rho + m)} \tag{50}$$

$$x^*_{FB} = \frac{(\rho + m)\lambda^*}{s} \tag{51}$$

$$J = \begin{pmatrix} -m & 2 \\ s & \rho + m + b \end{pmatrix} \tag{52}$$

trace $J = \rho + b > 0, \det J = -m(\rho + m + b) < 0$. Therefore $(x^*_{FB}, \lambda^*_{FB})$ is a saddle point.

Dynamic Programming Approach

The HJB equation is

$$\rho V^i(x) = \max_{u_i} \left[Au_i - \frac{1}{2}u_i^2 - \frac{s}{2}x^2 + DV^i(x)(u_i + \theta(x) - mx) \right] \tag{53}$$

$\frac{dV^i(x)}{dx} \equiv DV^i(x)$, maximization of the RHS results in

$$u_i = A - DV^i(x), \quad u_j = A + DV^j(x), \quad i, j = 1, 2 \tag{54}$$

Use a quadratic value function and imposing symmetry

$$V(x) = -\frac{1}{2}\alpha x^2 - \beta x - \gamma \tag{55}$$

$$DV(x) = -ax - \beta \tag{56}$$

The FB strategies for both i and j are linear and take the form

$$u \equiv \theta(x) = (A - \beta) - \alpha x \tag{57}$$

Substituting into the HJB equation, we obtain

$$\rho\left(-\frac{1}{2}\alpha x^2 - \beta x - \gamma\right) = A((A - \beta) - \alpha x) - \frac{1}{2}((A - \beta) - \alpha x)^2$$

$$-\frac{s}{2}x^2 + (-ax - \beta)[2((A - \beta) - \alpha x) - mx] \tag{58}$$

Since the equation holds for any level of admissible x, we equate coefficients of the same power to obtain three equations in the three unknowns (α, β, γ). Let $\left(\hat{\alpha}, \hat{\beta}, \hat{\gamma}\right)$ be the estimates. The optimal path for the state equations will be determined by the ODE

$$\dot{x} = 2\left(\left(A - \hat{\beta}\right) - \hat{\alpha}x\right) - mx(t), \quad x(0) = x_0 \tag{59}$$

we require $\hat{\alpha} > 0$ for stability. The optimal trajectories for the state and the control variables are

$$x^*(t) = Ce^{-(2\alpha+m)t} + \frac{2(A - \beta)}{2\alpha + m}, \quad x(0) = x_0 \tag{60}$$

$$u^*(t) = (A - \beta) - \alpha x^*(t) \tag{61}$$

Cooperative and Noncooperative Solutions

Note that OLNE and FBNE are **noncooperative solutions**. The **cooperative solution** can be obtained by solving the problem

$$\max_{u_1,u_2} \int_0^\infty e^{-\rho t} \sum_{i=1}^2 \left[Au_i(t) - \frac{1}{2}u_i^2(t) - \frac{s}{2}x^2(t)\right] dt \tag{62}$$

subject to $\dot{x} = u_1(t) + u_2(t) - mx(t), \quad x(0) = x_0, \quad A, s, m > 0$ $\tag{63}$

This problem can be easily solved using Pontryagin's maximum principle or dynamic programming.

Dynamic Duopoly

Two firms are denoted by $i = 1, 2$, k_i denotes capacity and I_i is gross investment. Linear capacity accumulation is

$$\dot{k}_i = I_i - \delta k_i, \quad k_i(0) = k_{i0} \tag{64}$$

Investment costs: $C(I_i) = qI_i + \frac{c}{2}I_i^2$.

Net revenue: Sales less production costs for firm i $R^i(y_1, y_2) = y_i(a - y_1 - y_2)$, $a > 0$, $i = 1, 2$, y_i is the output of firm i.

$k = (k_1, k_2)$ pair of capacities, and introduce the reduced form net revenue function (Reynolds, 1987):

$$R^i(k) = k_i(a - k_1 - k_2) \tag{65}$$

Each firm solves

$$\max_{I_i} \int_0^\infty e^{-\rho t}\left[R^i(k) - C(I_i)\right] dt, \quad i = 1, 2 \tag{66}$$

$$\text{subject to } \dot{k}_i = I_i - \delta k_i, \quad k_i(0) = k_{i0} \tag{67}$$

OLNE

The current value Hamiltonian is

$$H^i = ak_i - k_i^2 - k_i k_j - qI_i - \frac{c}{2}I_i^2 + \mu_i(I_i - \delta k_i) \tag{68}$$

Solve using Pontryagin's maximum principle.

FBNE

The HJB equation for the problem is

$$\rho V^i(k) = \max_{I_i} R^i(k) - C(I_i) + D_{k_i}V^i(k)(I_i - \delta k_i) \tag{69}$$

$$+ D_{k_j}V^j(k)(I_j(k_i, k_j) - \delta k_j)], \quad k = (k_1, k_2) \tag{70}$$

maximizing the RHS, we obtain

$$-q - cI_i + D_{k_i}V^i(k) = 0 \tag{71}$$

The FB investment strategy is

$$I_i = \frac{-q + D_{k_i}V^i(k_1, k_2)}{c} \tag{72}$$

The problem can be solved by using a quadratic value function

$$V^i(k) = b_0 + b_1 k_i + b_2 k_j + \frac{b_3}{2}k_i^2 + b_4 k_i k_j + \frac{b_5}{2}k_j^2 \tag{73}$$

Thus,

$$D_{k_i}V^i(k) = b_1 + b_3 k_i + b_4 k_j \tag{74}$$

$$D_{k_j}V^j(k) = b_2 + b_5 k_j + b_4 k_i \tag{75}$$

The b coefficients can be obtained by substituting into the HJB equation and equating coefficients of the same power.

Reference

Reynolds, S.S. 1987. Capacity investment, preemption and commitment in an infinite horizon model. *International Economic Review*, pp. 69–88.

Chapter 14

Nonlinear Differential Games in Environmental and Resource Economics: International Pollution Control (The Lake Problem)

International Pollution Control under Risk

A Model

Two countries are denoted by $i = 1, 2$. Utility in each country is $u_i(F_i(E_i)) - C(P)$ with $C(P)$ being the cost of the global pollutant where

$$u_i\left(F_i\left(E_i\right)\right) = AE_i - \frac{1}{2}E_i^2, \quad A > 0 \tag{1}$$

$$C(P) = \frac{s}{2}P^2, \quad s > 0 \tag{2}$$

Each country's objective is to maximize individual welfare or

$$\max_{E_i \geq 0} \int_0^\infty \mathrm{e}^{-\rho t}\left(AE_i - \frac{1}{2}E_i^2 - \frac{s}{2}P^2\right)dt \tag{3}$$

subject to pollution dynamics.

The stock of the pollutant accumulates according to the stochastic differential equation

$$dP = (E_1 + E_2 - mP)\, dt + \sigma d\hat{z}, \quad P(0) = P_0 \text{ fixed} \qquad (4)$$

where $\{\hat{z}(t) : t \geq 0\}$ is a Brownian motion on an underlying probability space $\{\Omega, \mathcal{F}, G\}$.

The Cooperative Solution

The HJB equation for this problem, where DW and D^2W denote the first and second derivatives of the value function, respectively, is

$$\rho W = \max_{E_1, E_2} \left\{ A\left(E_1 + E_2\right) - \frac{1}{2}\left(E_1^2 + E_2^2\right) - sP^2 \right.$$

$$\left. + DW\left(E_1 + E_2 - mP\right) + \frac{1}{2}\sigma^2 D^2W \right\} \qquad (5)$$

Given the linear quadratic structure of the problem, a quadratic value function

$$W(P) = -\frac{1}{2}\alpha P^2 - \beta P - \gamma \qquad (6)$$

with first and second derivatives

$$DW = -\alpha P - \beta, \quad D^2W = -\alpha \qquad (7)$$

is considered.

Optimality implies

$$E_1 = E_2 = A - \beta - \alpha P \qquad (8)$$

Then

$$\rho\left(-\frac{1}{2}\alpha P^2 - \beta P - \gamma\right)$$

$$= 2A(A - \beta - \alpha P) - (A - \beta - \alpha P)^2 - sP^2$$

$$- (\alpha P + \beta)\left[2\left(A - \beta - \alpha P\right) - mP\right] - \frac{\alpha}{2}\sigma^2 \qquad (9)$$

The parameters of the value function are obtained as usual by equating coefficients of the same power. In this case, the optimal cooperative emissions in a feedback form will be

$$E^* = (A - \beta) - aP \tag{10}$$

Substituting optimal cooperative emissions from (10) into (4), the evolution of the pollutant stock under the cooperative solutions will be determined by the solution of the stochastic differential equation

$$dP = [2(A - \beta) - (2\alpha + m)P]dt + \sigma dz \tag{11}$$

This an Ornstein–Uhlembeck process with solution

$$P(t) = P_0 e^{-r_0 t} + \mu \left(1 - e^{-r_0 t}\right) + \int_0^t \sigma e^{r_0(u-t)} dz_u \tag{12}$$

$$r_0 = 2\alpha + m, \quad \mu = \frac{2(A - \beta)}{2\alpha + m} \tag{13}$$

Mean and variance of the cooperative solution are as follows:

$$\mathcal{E}P(t) = P_0 e^{-r_0 t} + \mu \left(1 - e^{-r_0 t}\right) \tag{14}$$

$$\mathrm{var}P(t) = \frac{\sigma^2}{2r_0} \left(1 - e^{-2r_0 t}\right) \tag{15}$$

with long-run expected value $\mathcal{E}P^* = \mu = \frac{2(A-\beta)}{(2\alpha+m)}$, $\mathrm{var}P^* = \frac{\sigma^2}{2r_0} = \frac{\sigma^2}{2(2\alpha+m)}$. It is obvious that if $\alpha > 0$, this steady state will be stable. For a numerical example where

$$\rho = 0.05, \quad \sigma = 1, \quad A = 100, \quad m = 0.03, \quad s = 1 \tag{16}$$

then $\alpha = 0.972878$, $\beta = 96.0509$, $E^*(t) = 3.94914 - 0.972878P(t)$, and $\mathcal{E}P^* = 3.9976$.

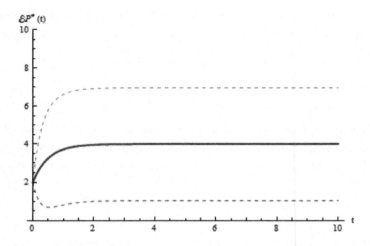

The time path for $\mathcal{E}P^*(t)$ (thick line) along with a belt of $\pm 3\sqrt{\mathrm{var}P^*(t)}$ (dashed lines) from an initial stock accumulation $P_0 = 2$.

Feedback Nash Equilibrium

Linear equilibrium strategies can be represented in a time-stationary feedback form, $E_i(t) = \zeta_0 + \zeta_1 P(t)$, $i = 1, 2$, and the value functions W_i depend only on the state x. Since the problem is symmetric, only symmetric equilibria are considered. The value function for each country is

$$W_i(P) = -\frac{1}{2}\alpha_i P^2 - \beta_i P - \gamma_i \qquad (17)$$

and the corresponding HJB for each country is

$$\rho W_i = \max_{E_i} \left\{ A E_i - \frac{1}{2}E_i^2 - \frac{s}{2}P^2 \right.$$

$$\left. + D W_i \left(E_1 + E_2 - mP\right) + \frac{1}{2}\sigma^2 D^2 W_i \right\} \qquad (18)$$

Optimality implies

$$E_i = A - \beta_i - \alpha_i P = E_1 = E_2 \qquad (19)$$

so individual country strategies are in a feedback or closed loop form. Dropping the index i due to symmetry, the HJB satisfies

$$\rho \left(-\frac{1}{2}\alpha P^2 - \beta P - \gamma \right)$$

$$= A\left(A - \beta - \alpha P\right) - \frac{1}{2}\left(A - \beta - \alpha P\right)^2$$

$$- \frac{s}{2}P^2 + -(\alpha P + \beta)\left[2\left(A - \beta - \alpha P\right) - mP\right] - \frac{\alpha}{2}\sigma^2$$

The feedback equilibrium strategy is defined as $E_i(t) = 36.3672 - 0.55931P(t)$, $i = 1, 2$, $\alpha_1 = \alpha_2 = 0.55931$, while the expected FBNE pollution steady state is $\mathcal{E}P_{FBNE} = 63.3235$. The comparison of the cooperative equilibrium with the FBNE confirms the well-known result that the FBNE results in higher emissions and higher pollution accumulation both in terms of time paths and the steady states than the cooperative equilibrium. The FBNE is stochastically stable since $\alpha_i > 0$.

The Lake Game — Nonlinear Problems

The Lake Model

Nonlinear lake dynamics:

$$\dot{x}(t) = \sum_{i=1}^{n} a_i(t) - bx(t) + f(x(t)), \quad x(0) = x_0 \qquad (20)$$

$$\dot{x}(t) = a(t) - bx(t) + \frac{x^2(t)}{x^2(t) + 1}, \quad x(0) = x_0 \qquad (21)$$

Flow of net benefits accruing to each agent $U(a_i(t)) - D(x(t))$. Each agent is choosing a strategy a_i to maximize the present value of net benefits over an infinite time horizon, or

$$\max_{a_i(.)} \int_0^\infty e^{-\rho t}[U(a_i(t)) - D(x(t))]dt, \quad i = 1, 2, \ldots, n \qquad (22)$$

subject to (20), where $\rho > 0$ is a discount rate, common for all agents.

Cooperative Solution

$$\max_{\{a_1(.),\ldots,a_n(.)\}} \int_0^\infty e^{-\rho t}\left[\sum_{i=1}^n U(a_i(t)) - nD(x(t))\right]dt \qquad (23)$$

subject to (20). The current-value Hamiltonian H for this problem is given by

$$H = \sum_{i=1}^n U(a_i) - nD(x) + \lambda[a - bx + f(x)], \quad a = \sum_{i=1}^n a_i, \qquad (24)$$

and Pontryagin's maximum principle yields the necessary conditions

$$U'(a_i) + \lambda = 0, \quad i = 1, 2, \ldots, n \qquad (25)$$

$$\dot{x}(t) = a(t) - bx(t) + f(x(t)), \quad x(0) = x_0 \qquad (26)$$

$$\dot{\lambda}(t) = \left[\rho + b - f'(x(t))\right]\lambda(t) + nD'(x(t)), \qquad (27)$$

$$\dot{a}(t) = -\left[\rho + b - f'(x(t))\right]a(t) + a^2(t)2cx(t) \qquad (28)$$

$$\dot{x}(t) = a(t) - bx(t) + f(x(t)), \quad x(0) = x_0$$

$$\dot{a}(t) = -(\rho + b - \frac{2x(t)}{(x^2(t) + 1)^2})a(t) + 2ca^2(t)x(t)$$

An example of the solution of this Hamiltonian system, for the parametrization $b = 0.6, c = 1, U = \ln a_i$ and $\rho = 0.03$, is shown in below figure. On the left panel is the steady state which has the saddle point property and on the right panel the stable nonlinear manifold exists.

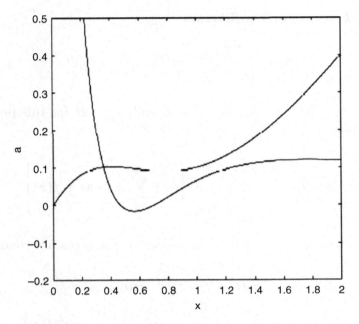

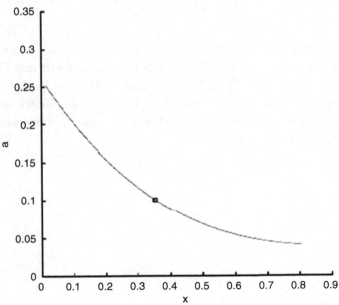

Open Loop Nash Equilibrium

$$\max_{\{a_i(.)\}} \int_0^\infty e^{-\rho t}[U(a_i(t)) - D(x(t))]dt \qquad (29)$$

subject to (20). The current-value Hamiltonian H for this problem is given by

$$H = U(a_i) - D(x) + \lambda_i \left[a_i + \sum_{j \neq i}^n \bar{a}_j - bx + f(x) \right] \qquad (30)$$

and Pontryagin's maximum principle yields the necessary conditions

$$\dot{x}(t) = a(t) - bx(t) + f(x(t)), \quad x(0) = x_0$$

$$\dot{a}(t) = -\left(\rho + b - \frac{2x(t)}{(x^2(t) + 1)^2} \right) a(t) + \frac{1}{n} 2ca^2(t)x(t)$$

The solution is shown in below figure. There are three steady states (left panel). The middle one is an unstable focus and the other two are saddle points. The left is an oligotrophic steady state and the right is a eutrophic steady state. The right panel shows the stable manifolds associated with each saddle point steady state along with the unstable steady state.

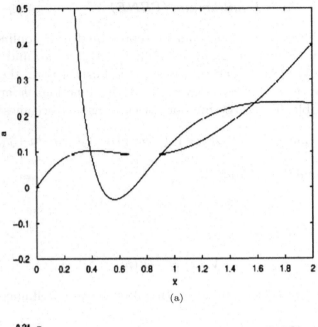

(a)

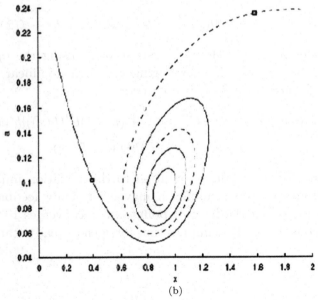

(b)

Feedback Nash Equilibrium (FBNE)

The equilibrium strategies can be represented in a nonlinear time-stationary feedback form $a_i = h_i(x)$, $i = 1, 2, \ldots, n$, and the value functions V_i only depend on the state x. Furthermore, the problem is symmetric and it is assumed that the functions h and V are differentiable. The HJB equation for each agent i becomes

$$\rho V(x) = \max_{a_i}\{U(a_i) - D(x) + V'(x)[a_i + (n-1)h(x) - bx + f(x)]\} \quad (31)$$

The optimality condition is

$$U'(a_i) + V'(x) = 0 \quad (32)$$

In equilibrium $a_i = h(x)$, so

$$V'(x) = -U'(h(x)) \quad (33)$$

The dynamic programming or Hamilton–Jacobi–Bellman equation becomes

$$\rho V(x) = U(h(x)) - D(x) - U'(h(x))[nh(x) - bx + f(x)] \quad (34)$$

By differentiating (34) with respect to x, using the optimality condition (33) again and rearranging terms, a nonlinear ordinary differential equation in $h(x)$ is obtained:

$$[(nh(x) - bx + f(x))U''(h(x)) + (n-1)U'(h(x))]h'(x)$$
$$= (\rho + b - f'(x))U'(h(x)) - D'(x) \quad (35)$$

The absence of a boundary condition to this equation implies that multiple feedback Nash equilibria may exist. Only feedback Nash equilibria for which the level of pollutants x converges to a steady state are considered. This implies that for such a steady state x_f, the equation

$$h(x_f) = \frac{bx_f - f(x_f)}{n} \quad (36)$$

can be used as a boundary condition for the differential equation (35).

The Lake Specification for the FBNE

The specifications for the shallow lake problem ($U(a_i) = \ln a_i$, and $D(x) = cx^2, f(x) = \frac{x^2}{x^2+1}$) turn the nonlinear ordinary differential equation (35) into

$$\left[-h(x) + bx - \frac{x^2}{x^2+1}\right] h'(x) = \left(\rho + b - 2cxh(x) - \frac{2x}{(x^2+1)^2}\right) h(x)$$
$$(37)$$

and the boundary condition (36) into

$$h(x_f) = \frac{1}{n}\left(bx_f - \frac{x_f^2}{x_f^2+1}\right) \tag{38}$$

Equation (37) is an Abel differential equation of the second kind, which cannot be solved analytically.

The values for the feedback Nash equilibria are given by

$$V_f(x_0, x_f) = \int_0^\infty e^{-\rho t}[\ln h(x(t)) - cx^2(t)]dt \tag{39}$$

where $h(x)$ is the solution of the differential equation (37), with boundary condition (38), and $x(t)$ is the solution of the differential equation

$$\dot{x}(t) = nh(x(t)) - bx(t) + \frac{x^2(t)}{x^2(t)+1}, \quad x(0) = x_0 \tag{40}$$

If a number of stable steady states can be reached from some initial state, it is reasonable to assume that the agents will be able to coordinate on the best feedback Nash equilibrium, if it exists. This means that in that case the value will be only a function of the initial state:

$$V_f(x_0) = \max_{x_f} V_f(x_0, x_f) \tag{41}$$

where x_f must be reachable from x_0 and stable.

Numerical algorithm for the best FBNE

- *Step 1.* For each candidate x_f the nonlinear ordinary differential equation (37) with boundary condition (38) is solved, with the ode solver *ode15s* of Matlab, in the intervals $[p, x_f]$ and $[x_f, q]$, where p and q are chosen appropriately.
- *Step 2.* The numerical solution for $h(x)$ is then used to solve the transition equation (40) in the interval $[0, T]$, where T is chosen appropriately.
- *Step 3.* Then the value (39) is computed, using a Matlab *quad* function.
- *Step 4.* Finally, the set of values is maximized over the set of admissible x_f according to (41), to determine the best FBNE.

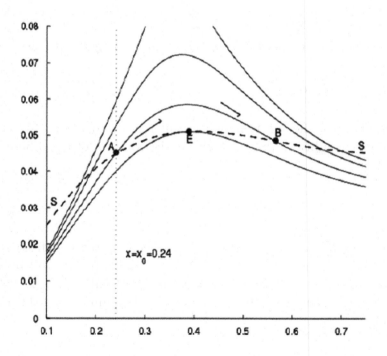

The best FBNE at point is at point E on the curve of the steady states SS determined by $\frac{1}{n}\left(bx - \frac{x^2}{x^2+1}\right)$.

Comparison among the maximized objectives for the cooperative solution, the OLNE and the FBNE. The FBNE is the inferior solution.

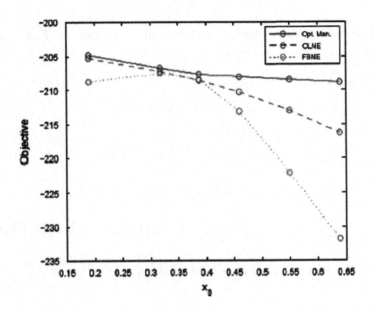

Regulation in Nonlinear Differential Games

Regulated FBNE

Regulation is introduced in the form of a time-stationary tax rate per unit loading a_i which depends on the state of the system. The tax rate is defined as $\tau(x)$. Under the state-dependent tax, the HJB equation becomes

$$\rho V(x) = \max_{a_i}\{U(a_i) - \tau(x)a_i - D(x)$$
$$+ V'(x)[a_i + (n-1)h(x) - bx + f(x)]\} \qquad (42)$$

The optimality condition is

$$U'(a_i) - \tau(x) + V'(x) = 0 \qquad (43)$$

In equilibrium $a_i = h(x)$, so that

$$V'(x) = -U'(h(x)) + \tau(x) \quad \text{and} \tag{44}$$

$$V''(x) = -U''(h)h'(x)) + \tau'(x) \tag{45}$$

The nonlinear ordinary differential equation in $h(x)$, which depends on $\tau(x)$, is obtained:

$$\big[(nh(x) - bx + f(x))U''(h(x))$$
$$- (n-1)\,\tau(x) + (n-1)U'(h(x))]h'(x)$$
$$= (\rho + b - f'(x)) \left[U'(h(x)) - \tau(x)\right]$$
$$+ \left[(n-1)\,h(x) - bx + f(x)\right]\tau'(x) - D'(x)$$
$$[-h(x) - (n-1)\,\tau(x)h^2(x) + bx - \frac{x^2}{x^2 + 1}]h'(x)$$
$$= \left[\left(\rho + b - \frac{2x}{(x^2+1)^2}\right)(1 - \tau(x)\,h(x)) - 2cxh(x)\right]h(x)$$
$$+ \left[(n-1)\,h(x) - bx + \frac{x^2}{x^2 + 1}\right]\tau'(x)h^2(x).$$

Choosing the Tax Function

The parameters of the tax function are chosen such that the steady state of the socially optimal management (SOM) solution is attained as a feedback Nash equilibrium steady state of the regulated system.

We consider polynomial tax functions of the general form

$$\tau(x) = \beta_0 + \beta_1 x + \beta_2 x^2 + \cdots + \beta_p x^p, \quad \beta_j \gtreqless 0, \quad j = 0, 1, \dots, p \tag{46}$$

Let x_0 be a given initial state and let x^* be the optimal steady state which corresponds to the SOM solution, then an optimal steady-state tax function (OSSTF) can be defined as follows.

Definition (OSSTF): Assume that a state-dependent tax function $\tau^*(x)$ exists, for which the corresponding best regulated feedback Nash equilibrium $h^*(x, \beta^*)$ generates a path that converges, starting from x_0, to the FBNE-SS x_f which is equal to x^*.[1] This tax function is called the optimal steady-state tax function.

In this sense the specific tax function $\tau^*(x)$ and the regulated feedback strategies $h^*\left(x, \beta^*\right)$ reproduce the OSS of the SOM solution.

Numerical algorithm for the best FBNE under OSSTF

- *Step 1.* For each candidate x_f and tax parameters $\beta \in \mathcal{B} = [0, \beta^{\max}]$, the nonlinear ordinary differential equation in $h(x)$ is solved with appropriate boundary conditions, with the ode solver *ode15s* of Matlab, in the intervals $[p, x_f]$ and $[x_f, q]$, where p and q are chosen appropriately, and the $h\left(x, \beta\right)$ profile is determined.
- *Step 2.* The numerical solution for $h(x, \beta)$ is used to solve the transition equation (40) in the interval $[0, T]$, where T is chosen appropriately.
- *Step 3.* The value (39) is computed, using a Matlab *quad* function.
- *Step 4.* The value is maximized over the set of admissible x_f.
- *Step5a.* If the tax function corresponds to a fixed tax $\tau_0(x) = \beta_0$ or to a tax that is proportional to the current state $\tau_1(x) = \beta_1 x$ (i.e. the state-dependent tax is determined by a single parameter β_j, $j = 0$ or 1), then we proceed as follows. We construct the relationship $x_f = \phi\left(\beta_j\right)$, $j = 0$ or 1, that determines the FBNE-SS which can be reached from a given initial state x_0 with the best regulated feedback Nash equilibrium when the tax function is $\tau_0(x) = \beta_0$ or $\tau_1(x) = \beta_1 x$. Since we search for a tax function that will steer the regulated system to the SOM steady state x^*, the parameter of the OSSTF should satisfy $x^* = \phi\left(\beta_j^*\right)$, $j = 0$ or 1. If x^* is in the domain of ϕ, the OSSTF will be $\tau_0^*(x) = \beta_0^*$ or $\tau_1^*(x) = \beta_1^* x$.
- *Step5b.* If the tax function corresponds to the quadratic function $\tau_2(x) = \beta_1 x + \beta_2 x^2$ (i.e., the state-dependent tax is determined by the parameter vector (β_1, β_2)), or the cubic tax function $\tau_3\left(x\right) = \beta_1 x + \beta_2 x^2 + \beta_3 x^3$ (i.e. the state-dependent tax is determined by the parameter vector $(\beta_1, \beta_2, \beta_3)$), then we proceed as follows.

---

[1]Note that x^* may depend on x_0.

Provided that the set of x_f in step 4 contains x^*, we construct for the quadratic case the contour $\psi(\beta_1, \beta_2) = x^*$ which describes combinations of the tax-function parameters (β_1, β_2) that attain the SOM steady state x^*, and for the cubic case the corresponding isosurface $\psi(\beta_1, \beta_2, \beta_3) = x^*$. We choose from these isolines as parameters of the OSSTF the pair (β_1^*, β_2^*) or the triplet $(\beta_1^*, \beta_2^*, \beta_3^*)$ that maximizes the social welfare given by

$$W(\beta) = \int_0^\infty e^{-\rho t} \sum_{i=1}^n [\ln h(x(t), \beta) - cx^2(t)]dt \qquad (47)$$

The OSSTF will be $\tau_2^*(x) = \beta_1^* x + \beta_2^* x^2$ or $\tau_3^*(x) = \beta_1^* x + \beta_2^* x^2 + \beta_3^* x^3$.

Social Welfare under Regulation

The following table presents social welfare per individual for the SOM solution.

The second column of this table shows that the difference in social welfare between e.g., "unregulated" and "fixed tax" is 46.6% of the difference between "unregulated" and "social optimum", while the difference between "unregulated" and "quadratic tax" is 55.2% of the difference between "unregulated" and " social optimum" and the difference between "unregulated" and "cubic tax" is 62.2% of the difference between "unregulated" and "social optimum".

Social Welfare		
Socially Optimal Management	−107.227	100.0%
Cubic tax	−107.786645	62.2%
Quadratic tax	−107.891307	55.2%
Proportional tax	−107.993973	48.3%
Fixed tax	−108.018644	46.6%
Unregulated	−108.709334	0.0%

Time paths for the phosphorus stock under different regimes are shown in below figure. The path at the bottom corresponds to SOM while the path at the top corresponds to unregulated equilibrium.

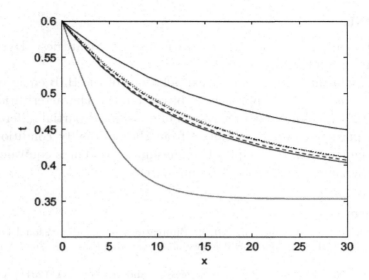

Concluding Remarks

- When do we need differential games?
  - An open question: Can the cooperative solution be attained as a Nash equilibrium of a non-cooperative game?
- Mathematical tools:
  - Maximum Principle
  - Dynamic Programming
  - Stochastic Control
- Information Structures and Nash Equilibria:
  - Open Loop OLNE
  - Feedback FBNE
  - Time Consistency Issues

Solution Approaches:

- Cooperative Solution or OLNE
  - Maximum Principle, Dynamic Programming

- **FBNE**

  - Linear Quadratic Games with Linear Strategies: Dynamic Programming.
  - Nonlinear Games: Numerical Solutions of the HJB equation.
  - An alternative approach is based on the characterization of FBNE as solutions to a system of quasilinear partial differential equations which is obtained from the optimality conditions of the maximum principle. The quasilinear system is equivalent to the Hamilton–Jacobi–Bellman system.

References

Kiseleva, T. and Wagener, F. (2010). Bifurcations of one-dimensional optimal vector fields in the shallow lake system. *Journal of Economic Dynamics and Control*, 34, pp. 825–843.

Kossioris, G., Plexoysakis, M., Xepapadeas, A. and de Zeeuw, A. (2011). On the optimal taxation of common-pool resources. *Journal of Economic Dynamics and Control*, 35, pp. 1868–1879.

Kossioris, G., Plexoysakis, M., Xepapadeas, A., de Zeeuw, A. and Mäler, K.-G. (2008). Feedback nash equilibria for non-linear differential games in pollution control. *Journal of Economic Dynamics and Control*, 32, pp. 1312–1331.

Mäler, K.-G., Xepapadeas, A. and de Zeeuw, A. (2003). The economics of Shallow Lakes. *Environmental and Resource Economics*, 26, pp. 603–624.

Tsutsui, S. and Mino, K. (1990). Nonlinear strategies in dynamic duopolistic competition with sticky prices. *Journal of Economic Theory*, 52, pp. 136–161.

Chapter 15

Robust Control

Expected Utility

- Modeling of uncertainty relies on expected utility as a means of performing cost-benefit analysis and, more broadly, as a normative criterion. Expected utility theory has solid theoretical underpinnings, going back to the ground breaking work of von Neumann and Morgenstern and Savage, and leads to tractable optimization problems.
- However, its attractive qualities often come at a steep price, primarily due to two basic factors: (a) the high structural uncertainty over the processes governing the phenomena which make the assignment of precise probabilistic model structure untenable, and (b) the high sensitivity of model outputs to seemingly ad hoc modeling assumptions (for instance, the functional form for a chosen function).
- As a result, separate models may arrive at different policy recommendations, generating heated debate and much confusion over the magnitude and the timing of a desirable policy.

Knightian Uncertainty

This section discusses attention on the problem of deep and structural uncertainty that is defined by an inability to posit precise probabilistic structure to physical processes. This is close to the concept of uncertainty as introduced by Franc Knight to represent a situation where there is ignorance, or not enough information, to assign probabilities to events. Knight argued that this deeper kind uncertainty is quite common in economic decision making, and thus deserving of systematic study. Knightian uncertainty is contrasted to risk (measurable or probabilistic uncertainty) where probabilities can be assigned to events and are summarized by a subjective probability measure or a *single* Bayesian prior.

Ambiguity

- Based on Knight and consequently Ellsberg, economic theorists have questioned the classical expected utility framework and attempted to formally model preferences in environments in which probabilistic beliefs are not of sufficiently high quality to generate prior distributions.
- Klibanoff *et al.* (2005) developed an axiomatic framework, the so-called "smooth ambiguity" model, in which different degrees of aversion for uncertainty are explicitly parameterized in agents' preferences. An act f is preferred to an act g if and only if $\mathbf{E}_p\phi(\mathbf{E}_\pi u \circ f) > \mathbf{E}_p\phi(\mathbf{E}_\pi u \circ g)$, where u is a von Neumann Morgenstern utility function, ϕ is an increasing function, and p is a subjective second order probability over a set Π of probability measures π that the decision maker is willing to consider ($\mathbf{E}$ denotes the expectation operator). When ϕ is concave, the decision maker is said to be *ambiguity averse*.

Robust Control (Hansen and Sargent)

Ambiguity (or deep uncertainty can) be regarded as a situation where a decision maker does not formulate decisions based on a single probability model but on a set of probability models. Gilboa and Schmeilder (1989) extended decision-making under uncertainty by incorporating ambiguity and by moving away from the framework of expected utility maximization. They adopted a **maxmin expected**

utility framework by arguing that when the underlying uncertainty of the system is not well understood and the decision maker faces a set of prior probability density functions associated with the phenomenon, it is sensible — and axiomatically compelling — to optimize over the worst-case outcome (i.e., the worst-case prior) that may conceivably come to pass. Doing so guards against potentially devastating losses in any possible state of the world, and thus adds an element of robustness to the decision-making process.

Motivated by concerns about model misspecification in macroeconomics, Hansen and Sargent (2001, 2008, 2012) and Hansen *et al.* (2006) extended Gilboa and Schmeidler's insights into dynamic optimization problems, thus introducing the concept of robust control to economic environments. A decision maker characterized by robust preferences takes into account the possibility that the model used to design regulation, call it benchmark or approximating model P, may not be the correct one but only an approximation of the correct one. Other possible models, say $Q_1, \ldots, Q_J$, which surround P, should also be taken into account with the relative differences among these models measured by an entropy measure. Hansen and Sargent (2003) characterize robust control as a theory "... [that] instructs decision makers to investigate the fragility of decision rules by conducting worst-case analyses," and suggest that this type of model uncertainty can be related to ambiguity or deep uncertainty so that robust control can be interpreted as a recursive version of maxmin expected utility theory.

- The agent is concerned about model misspecification and is unsure about his/her model, in the sense that there is a group of approximate models which are also considered as possibly true, given a set of finite data.
- These approximate models are obtained by disturbing a benchmark model, and the admissible disturbances reflect the set of possible probability measures that the decision maker is willing to consider.
- The resulting problem is one of robust dynamic control, where the objective is to choose a rule that will work under a range of different

model specifications. This methodology provides a tractable way to incorporate uncertainty aversion.

Robustness

The decision-maker has concerns about possible misspecification of the benchmark model describing state dynamics. Assume that state dynamics evolve according to the stochastic differential equation

$$dx = \mu\left(x, u\right) dt + \sigma\left(x\right) dW, \quad x\left(0\right) = x_0 \tag{1}$$

where W is a Brownian motion.

If there were no fear of model misspecification, using the benchmark model would be sufficient. As this is not the case under ambiguity aversion, following Hansen and Sargent, model misspecification can be reflected by a family of stochastic perturbations to the Brownian motion so that the probabilistic structure implied by stochastic differential equation (1) is distorted and the probability measure P is replaced by another Q.

The perturbed model is obtained by performing a change of measure and replacing $W(t)$ in (1) by

$$\hat{W}(t) + \int_0^t v(s)ds \tag{2}$$

where $\{\hat{W}(t): t \geq 0\}$ is a Brownian motion and $\{v(t): t \geq 0\}$ is a measurable drift distortion. These changes to the distribution of $W(t)$ are parametrized as drift distortions to a Brownian motion $\{\hat{W}(t): t \geq 0\}$. The measurable process $v(s)$ could correspond to any number of misspecified or omitted dynamics. The distortions will be zero when $v = 0$ and the two measures P and Q coincide. State dynamics under misspecification concerns are given by

$$dx = \left[\mu\left(x, u\right) + \sigma\left(x\right) v(t)\right] dt + \sigma\left(x\right) dW. \tag{3}$$

These concerns can be modelled via alternative probability distributions, expressed as preference shocks that are martingales on the underlying probability space (Ω, F). Let Q denote the set of probability measures $Q = Q_1 \otimes Q_2, \ldots, \otimes Q_n$, which are absolutely continuous with respect to P. To measure the discrepancy between distributions P and Q, define the discounted measure of relative entropy (Hansen *et al.* 2006), $R(Q)$, as

$$R(\mathbf{Q}) = \rho \int_0^\infty e^{-\rho s} \left[\int \log \left(\frac{dQ_s}{d\mathcal{P}_s} \right) dQ_s \right] ds$$

To express the idea that even when the model is misspecified the benchmark model remains a "good" approximation, the misspecification error is constrained so that we only consider distorted probability measures Q such that

$$R(Q) = \int_0^\infty e^{-\rho t} \frac{1}{2} \mathbf{E}_Q[v(t)^2] dt \leq \eta < \infty \qquad (4)$$

Kullback–Leibler Divergence

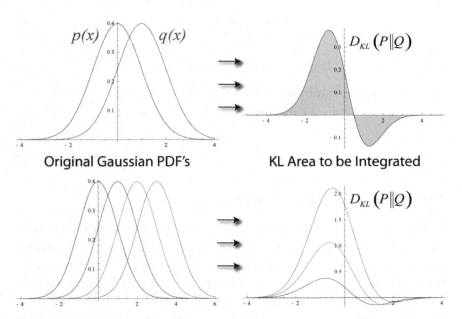

Assume that the regulator has a benchmark or approximate model P surrounded by other possible models, say $Q_1, \ldots, Q_J$, with the difference between P and Qs measured by relative entropy. The worst-case model that the decision maker is willing to consider, given the existing knowledge and information, is the one differing the most from P in terms of entropy. Thus, the size of ambiguity can be regarded as the length of the radius η of the entropy ball that surrounds P.

Let the decision-maker's objective be

$$\max_{u} E \int_0^\infty e^{-\rho s} F\left(x, u\right) dt \tag{5}$$

Two robust control problems can be associated with the solution to the misspecified problem: (a) a **constraint robust control problem** which explicitly models a bound on relative entropy, and (b) a **multiplier robust control problem** which incorporates a Lagrange multiplier to a relative entropy constraint. Using the maxmin expected utility criterion, the constraint robust control problem is given by

$$\max_{u} \min_{v} E \int_0^\infty e^{-\rho s} \left[F\left(x, u\right)\right] dt \tag{6}$$

$$\text{subject to (3), (4)} \tag{7}$$

and the multiplier robust control problem is defined as

$$\max_{u} \min_{v} E \int_0^\infty e^{-\rho s} \left[F\left(x, u\right) + \frac{\theta}{2} v^2\right] dt \tag{8}$$

$$\text{subject to (3)} \tag{9}$$

Preferences for Robustness

In both extremization problems, the distorting process $v(t)$ is such that allowable measures Q have finite entropy. In the constraint problem (6), the parameter η is the maximum expected misspecification error that the decision-maker is willing to consider. In the multiplier problem (8), the parameter θ can be interpreted as a Lagrangean multiplier associated with entropy constraint $R\left(Q\right) \leq \eta$, or a parameter reflecting preferences for robustness or ambiguity aversion. Our choice of θ lies in an interval $(\theta_{\min} + \infty)$, where the lower bound θ is a breakdown point beyond which it is fruitless to seek more robustness.

Regulation Breakdown

This is because if the deviation between the benchmark and the worst-case distribution exceeds a threshold, then robust control regulation is not possible because the impact of the worst-case distribution is so large that regulation using the maxmin expected utility criterion is meaningless. In such a case, the worst case is so far from the benchmark case i.e., η is so large that maximization over the worst case is not possible. This breakdown can be viewed as a situation where an adversarial agent chooses the worst case, trying to minimize the regulator's objective, while the regulator is trying to maximize over this minimizing choice.

Breakdown means that the adversarial agent can choose a worst case which is so "bad" that it will create a very large loss for the regulator or, put differently, it will push the regulator's objective to minus infinity. In such a case, any maximization on the regulator's part would be meaningless. Thus, when $\theta < \theta_{\min}$, robust control rules cannot be attained. On the other hand, when $\theta \to \infty$ or, equivalently $\eta = 0$, there are no concerns about model misspecification and the decision-maker may safely consider just the benchmark model.

Solution

Solution of the robust control problem is equivalent to solving a differential game. Since the variance of the system dynamics does not depend on the controls, and the decisions regarding u and v separate, the time protocol regarding maximization and minimization decisions does not matter, so the min, max operators can be interchanged. This means that the robust control static game has a Nash equilibrium, which is provided by the solution of the Hamilton–Jacobi–Bellman–Isaacs (HJBI) equation which is of the form (Fleming and Souganidis, 1989).

$$\rho V(x) = \max_{u} \min_{v} \left[F(x, u) + \frac{\theta}{2} v^2 + DV \left[\mu(x, u) + \sigma(x) v \right] \right. \quad (10)$$

$$\left. + \frac{1}{2} D^2 V \sigma^2(x) \right]$$

Feedback controls satisfy

$$F_u\left(x, u\right) + DV\mu_u\left(x, u\right) = 0 \tag{11}$$

$$\theta v + DV\sigma\left(x\right) = 0 \tag{12}$$

The problem can be solved following the dynamic programming approaches.

If the problem is linear-quadratic, the solution approach is similar to the standard linear-quadratic problems (For applications in macroeconomics, see Hansen and Sargent, 2011.).

References

Klibanoff, P., Marinacci, M. and Mukerji, S. 2005. A smooth model of decision making under ambiguity. *Econometrica*, 73(6), pp. 1849–1892.

Fleming, W.H. and Souganidis, P.E. 1989. On the existence of value functions of two-player, zero-sum stochastic differential games. *Indiana University Mathematics Journal*, 38(2), pp. 293–314.

Hansen, L.P. and Sargent, T.J. 2011. *Robustness*. Princeton University Press.

Chapter 16

Optimal Control under Spatio-temporal Dynamics: Optimal Control in Infinite Dimensional Spaces

Introduction

These lectures are based on results obtained through joint research with William Brock and Athanasios Yannacopoulos on spatiotemporal dynamics of economic/ecological systems.

Why spatiotemporal dynamics?

Economic and ecological systems evolve in time and space. Interactions take place among units occupying distinct spatial points. Thus, geographical patterns of production activities, urban concentrations or species concentrations occur. My purpose is

- to discuss approaches for modeling, in a meaningful way, economic and ecological processes evolving in space time;
- to examine mechanisms under which a spatially homogenous state — a flat landscape — acquires a spatial pattern;
- to examine how this pattern evolves in space-time.

The spatial dimension has been brought into the picture through the following:

- New economic geography/growth models.
- Models of resource management (e.g., Sanchirico; Wilen; Smith; Brock and Xepapadeas).
- In fields like biology or automatic control systems, spatially distributed parameter aspects in the dynamics have been used to study pattern formation:
  - on biological agents (e.g., Murray),
  - of infinite platoons of vehicles over time,
  - in groundwater management.

Topics to be covered

- Modelling short-range (local) and long-range (nonlocal) spatial movements.
- Modelling coupled economic-environmental models using systems of reaction-diffusion equations or integrodifferential equations.
- Emergence of pattern formation and agglomerations through the classic Turing mechanism.
- Optimal control of spatiotemporal economic/ecological models modelled as distributed parameter systems.
- Emergence of pattern formation in the optimal control of these systems through optimal diffusion induced or spillover induced instabilities.
- Global analysis and persistence of optimal spatial patterns and agglomerations in long run.
- Robust control of spatiotemporal models.

Local Effects

Some definitions

- Let $x(t, z)$ be a scalar quantity that denotes the concentration of a biological or economic variable which evolves in time and depends on the particular point z of the spatial domain $\mathcal{O}$. Thus, $x(t, z)$ is described as a function of time t and space z, i.e., $x\colon I \times \mathcal{O} \to \mathbb{R}$ where $I = (0, T)$ is the time interval over which the temporal evolution of the phenomenon takes place. For an infinite horizon model, $I = \mathbb{R}_+$.

- The spatial behavior of x is modelled by assuming that the functions $x(t, \cdot)$ belong for all t to an appropriately chosen function space $\mathbb{H}$ that describes the spatial properties of the function x. Different choices for $\mathbb{H}$ are possible. A convenient choice is to let $\mathbb{H}$ be a Hilbert space, e.g., $\mathbb{H} = L^2(\mathcal{O})$, the space of square integrable functions on $\mathcal{O}$, or an appropriately chosen subspace, e.g., $L^2_{per}(\mathcal{O})$, the space of square integrable functions on $\mathcal{O} = [-L, L]$ satisfying periodic boundary conditions (this would model a circular economy).

- Thus, spatial concentration or size is defined such that $(x(t))(z) := x(t, z)$. Therefore, by $x(t)$, we denote an element of $\mathbb{H}$, which is in fact a function $x(t)\colon \mathcal{O} \to \mathbb{R}$ which describes the spatial structure of x at time t. Examples are shown in what follows.

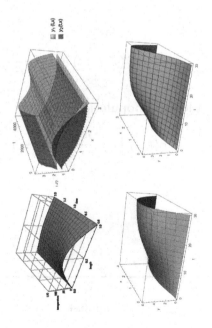

Fickian diffusion

- Let $\phi(t, z)$ denote the flow of 'material' such as animals, commodities, or capital, past z at time t. The flux is proportional to the gradient of the concentration

$$\phi(t, z) = -D\frac{\partial}{\partial z}x(t, z) \tag{1}$$

- D is the diffusion coefficient and the minus sign indicates that the material moves from high levels of concentration to low levels of concentration. In a small interval, Δz,

$$\frac{d}{dt}\int_z^{z+\Delta z} x(t, s)\, ds = \phi(t, z) - \phi(t, z + \Delta z) \tag{2}$$

$$+ \int_z^{z+\Delta z} Fx((t, s))\, ds \tag{3}$$

where $F(t, s)$ is a source or growth function.
- Dividing by Δz and taking limits as $\Delta z \to 0$, we obtain

$$\frac{\partial x(t, z)}{\partial t} = -\frac{\partial \phi(t, z)}{\partial z} + F(t, z) \tag{4}$$

$$\frac{\partial x(t, z)}{\partial t} = F(x(t, z)) + D\frac{\partial x^2(t, z)}{\partial z^2} \tag{5}$$

- For $F(x(t, z))$, a logistic population growth

$$\frac{\partial x(t, z)}{\partial t} = sx(t, z)\left[1 - \frac{rx(t, z)}{s}\right] + D\frac{\partial x^2(t, z)}{\partial z^2} \tag{6}$$

$$\times r/s \text{ carrying capacity} \tag{7}$$

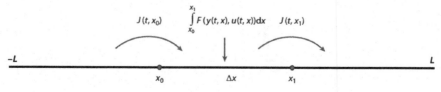

Fickian diffusion.

Reaction–Diffusion systems

Two interacting species $x(t, z), y(t, z)$, without cross diffusion, are

$$\frac{\partial x}{\partial t} = F_1(x, y) + D_x \nabla^2 x \tag{8}$$

$$\frac{\partial y}{\partial t} = F_2(x, y) + D_y \nabla^2 y \tag{9}$$

$$\nabla^2 = \frac{\partial^2}{\partial z^2} \tag{10}$$

Nonlocal Effects

Long-range effects can be modelled by integral equations. The evolution of $x(t, z)$ can be represented by

$$\frac{\partial x(t, z)}{\partial t} = F(x(t, z)) + \int_{-L}^{L} w(z, z') x(t, z') \, dz' \tag{11}$$

where $w : \mathcal{O} \times \mathcal{O} \to \mathbb{R}$ is an integrable kernel function modelling the effect that position s has on position z. This introduces nonlocal (spatial) effects, and may be understood as defining a mapping which takes an element $x(t, \cdot) \in \mathbb{H}$ and maps it to a new element $X(t, \cdot) \in \mathbb{H}$ such that (48) holds for every $z \in \mathcal{O}$. This mapping is understood as an operator $\mathsf{T} : \mathbb{H} \to \mathbb{H}$.

Exponential symmetric kernels

Kernel	$w_1(\zeta) = b_1 \exp\left[-(\zeta/d_1)^2\right], b_1, d_1 > 0, \zeta = z - z'$
Kernel	$w_2(\zeta) = b_1 \exp\left[-(\zeta/d_1)^2\right] - b_2 \exp\left[-(\zeta/d_2)^2\right]$ $b_1 > b_2, d_1 < d_2$

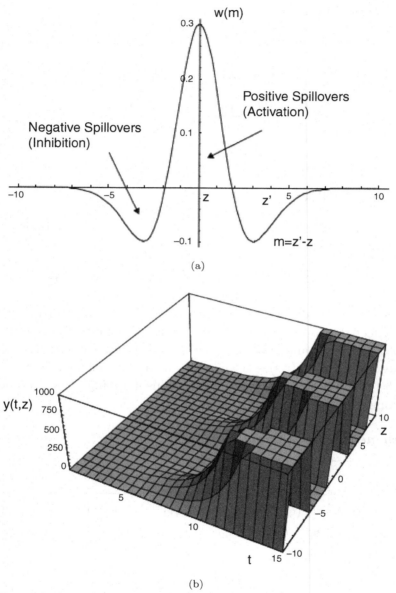

(a) Kernel function with positive short-range and negative long-range geographical spillovers. (b) A spatially heterogeneous distribution.

Discrete spatial domain

- Consider a discrete finite lattice $\mathfrak{L}$, e.g., $\mathfrak{L} = (\mathbb{Z}_N)^d$. The quantity that denotes the concentration of a biological or economic variable which evolves in time and depends on the particular point n of the spatial domain $\mathfrak{L}$ is described by a function $\breve{x} : I \to \mathbb{R}^N$ such that $\breve{x}(t) = \{x_n(t)\}$, $n \in \mathfrak{L}$, where $x_n(t)$ is the state of the system at site n at time t.

- We therefore consider the state variable x as taking values on a (finite dimensional) sequence space $\ell^2 := \ell^2(\mathbb{Z}_N) = \{\{x_n\}, \sum_{n \in \mathbb{Z}_N} x_n^2 < \infty\}$. This space is a Hilbert space with a norm derivable from the inner product $\langle x, y \rangle = \sum_{n \in \mathbb{Z}_N} x_n y_n$ and is in fact equivalent to $\mathbb{R}^N$.

Kernels in discrete space

- Spatial effects such that the state of the system at point m has an effect on the state of the system at point n are quantified through an discretized version of an influence kernel which can be represented in terms of a matrix $\mathsf{A} = (a_{nm})$. The entry a_{nm} provides a measure of the influence of the state of the system at point m to the state of the system at point n. Network effects' knowledge spillovers can be modelled, for example, through a proper choice of A.

$$\mathsf{A}x = \sum_m a_{nm} x_m \tag{12}$$

$\mathsf{A} : \mathbb{R}^N \to \mathbb{R}^N$ is a linear operator, representable by a finite matrix with elements a_{nm}.

- With no spatial interactions at all, then $\mathsf{A} = a_{nm} = \delta_{n,m}$ where $\delta_{n,m}$ is the Kronecker delta. If only next neighborhood effects are possible, then a_{nm} is non-zero only if m is a neighbor of n. Such an example is the discrete Laplacian.

The discrete Laplacian

$$D \frac{\partial^2 x(t, z)}{\partial z^2} \approx D \left[x_{n+1}(t) - 2x_n(t) + x_{n-1}(t) \right] \tag{13}$$

Matrix A, in this case, has a general form

$$A = D \begin{pmatrix} 1 & -2 & 1 & 0 & 0 & 0 \\ 0 & 1 & -2 & 1 & 0 & 0 \\ 0 & 0 & 1 & -2 & 1 & 0 \\ 0 & 0 & 0 & 1 & -2 & 1 \\ & & & \cdots & & \end{pmatrix} \ddots$$

$$dx_n = \left(\sum_m a_{nm} x_m + \sum_m b_{nm} u_m \right) dt + \sum_m c_{nm} dw_m, \quad n \in \mathbb{Z}_N$$

$$dx = (Ax + Bu)\, dt + C dw$$

where $A, B, C \colon \mathbb{R}^N \to \mathbb{R}^N$ are linear operators, representable by finite matrices with elements a_{nm}, b_{nm}, c_{nm}, respectively. The state equation is an Ornstein–Uhlenbeck equation on the finite dimensional Hilbert space $\ell^2(\mathbb{Z}_N) = \mathbb{R}^N$.

Turing Instability

- A semi-arid system can be described in terms of spatiotemporal dynamics of three state variables: surface water, soil water, and plant biomass. Space is a circle and surface water is fixed by rainfall and uniformly distributed along the circle.
- Plant biomass is consumed in the process of producing cattle products. Cattle products are produced by a conventional production function with two inputs, plant biomass and grazing effort.

Semi-arid systems (Broke and Xepapadeas, 2010)

The model of the semi-arid ecosystem is

$$P_t(t, z) = G(W(t, z), P(t, z)) - b(P(t, z)) \tag{14}$$

$$- TH(t, z) + D_P P_{zz}(t, z) \tag{15}$$

$$W_t(t, z) = F(P(t, z), R) - V(W(t, z), P(t, z))$$

$$- r_W W(t, z) + D_W W_{zz}(t, z) \tag{16}$$

$$P(0, z), \ W(0, z) \text{ given}$$

$$P(t,0) = P(t,L) = \bar{P}(t),$$

$$W(t,0) = W(t,L) = \bar{W}(t) \ \forall t \tag{17}$$

where $P(t,z)$ is plant density (biomass), $W(t,z)$ is soil water at time $t \in [0,\infty)$ and site $z \in [0,L]$, R is fixed rainfall, $TH(t,z)$ is harvesting of the plant biomass through grazing, $G(W,P)$ is plant growth, increasing in soil water and plant density, $b(P)$ is plant senescence, $F(P,R)$ is water infiltration, $V(W,P)$ is water uptake by plants, r_W is the specific rate of water loss due to evaporation and percolation, and D_P and D_W are the diffusion coefficients for plant biomass (plant dispersal) and soil water.

A general reaction–diffusion system

$$\frac{\partial x_1(t,z)}{\partial t} = f_1(x_1(t,z), x_2(t,z), \quad \mathbf{u}(t,z)) + D_{x_1}\frac{\partial^2 x_1(t,z)}{\partial z^2}$$

$$\frac{\partial x_2(t,z)}{\partial t} = f_2(x_1(t,z), x_2(t,z), \quad \mathbf{u}(t,z)) + D_{x_2}\frac{\partial^2 x_2(t,z)}{\partial z^2}$$

$$\mathbf{x}(0,z) \text{ given}, \ \mathbf{x}(t,0) = \mathbf{x}(t,L) = \bar{\mathbf{x}}(t), \quad \forall t$$

Economic agents maximize utility or profits myopically in each z

$$u_j^0(t,z) = \arg\max_{u_j} U(\mathbf{x}(t,z), \mathbf{u}(t,z)), \quad j = 1,\ldots,m$$

$$u_j^0(z,t) = h_j^0(\mathbf{x}(t,z)), \quad j = 1,\ldots,m$$

Open access is defined as

$$\hat{\mathbf{u}}(t,z): \quad U(\mathbf{x}(t,z), \quad \hat{\mathbf{u}}(t,z)) = 0 \tag{18}$$

$$\hat{u}_j(t,z) = \hat{h}_j(\mathbf{x}(t,z)), \quad j = 1,\ldots,m \tag{19}$$

Reaction–diffusion system with optimizing agents is as follows:

$$\frac{\partial x_1(t,z)}{\partial t} = f_1(x_1(t,z), \quad x_2(t,z), \quad \mathbf{h}^0(\mathbf{x}(t,z)))$$

$$+ D_{x_1}\frac{\partial^2 x_1(t,z)}{\partial z^2}$$

$$\frac{\partial x_2 (t, z)}{\partial t} = f_2 \left(x_1 (t, z), \quad x_2 (t, z), \quad \mathbf{h}^0 \left(\mathbf{x} (t, z) \right) \right)$$

$$+ D_{x_2} \frac{\partial^2 x_2 (t, z)}{\partial z^2}$$

Local spatial stability

Define a spatially homogeneous or "flat steady state" for $D_{x_1} = D_{x_2} = 0$ as

$$\mathbf{x}^0 : f_1 \left(x_1^0, x_2^0, \mathbf{h}^0 \left(\mathbf{x}^0 \right) \right) = 0, \quad f_2 \left(x_1^0, x_2^0, \mathbf{h}^0 \left(\mathbf{x}^0 \right) \right) = 0$$

Let $\bar{x}(t) = \left(x_1(t) - x_1^0, x_2(t) - x_2^0 \right)' = (\bar{x}_1(t), \bar{x}_2(t))'$ denote deviations around $\mathbf{x}^0$ and define the linearization

$$\bar{x}_t(t) = J^P \bar{x}(t), \quad \bar{x}_t(t) = \begin{pmatrix} \dfrac{d\bar{x}_1(t)}{dt} \\ \dfrac{d\bar{x}_2(t)}{dt} \end{pmatrix}, \quad J^P = \begin{pmatrix} b_{11} & b_{12} \\ b_{21} & b_{22} \end{pmatrix} \quad (20)$$

Assume that $\operatorname{tr} J^P = b_{11} + b_{22} < 0$ and $\det J^P = b_{11}b_{22} - b_{12}b_{21} > 0$ which means that both eigenvalues of J^P have negative real parts. This implies that the FSS $\mathbf{x}^0$ is locally stable to spatially homogeneous perturbations.

Emergence of spatial patterns

Theorem: *Private optimizing behavior, as implied by choosing controls according to myopic optimization in the management of a reaction–diffusion system, generates spatial patterns around a flat steady state if*

$$\frac{b_{22} D_{x_1} + b_{11} D_{x_2}}{2 D_{x_1} D_{x_2}} > 0 \quad (21)$$

$$-\frac{(b_{22} D_{x_1} + b_{11} D_{x_2})^2}{4 D_{x_1} D_{x_2}} + \det J^P < 0 \quad (22)$$

Sketch of proof

Note that the elements of the Jacobian matrix, evaluated at $\mathbf{x}^0$, are defined as

$$b_{11} = \frac{\partial f_1}{\partial x_1} + \sum_{j=1}^{m} \frac{\partial f_1}{\partial u_j} \frac{\partial u_j}{\partial x_1}, \quad b_{12} = \frac{\partial f_1}{\partial x_2} + \sum_{j=1}^{m} \frac{\partial f_1}{\partial u_j} \frac{\partial u_j}{\partial x_2} \quad (23)$$

$$b_{21} = \frac{\partial f_2}{\partial x_1} + \sum_{j=1}^{m} \frac{\partial f_2}{\partial u_j} \frac{\partial u_j}{\partial x_1}, \quad b_{22} = \frac{\partial f_2}{\partial x_2} + \sum_{j=1}^{m} \frac{\partial f_2}{\partial u_j} \frac{\partial u_j}{\partial x_2} \quad (24)$$

Following Murray (2003), the linearization of the full reaction-diffusion system is

$$\bar{x}_t(t, z) = J^P \bar{x}(t, z) + D \bar{x}_{zz}(t, z), \quad \bar{x}_{zz}(t, z) = \begin{pmatrix} \dfrac{\partial^2 \bar{x}_1(t, z)}{\partial z^2} \\ \dfrac{\partial^2 \bar{x}_2(t, z)}{\partial z^2} \end{pmatrix}$$

$$D = \begin{pmatrix} D_{x_1} & 0 \\ 0 & D_{x_2} \end{pmatrix}$$

Spatial patterns emerge if the FSS is unstable to spatially *heterogeneous* perturbations which take the form of spatially varying solutions defined as

$$\bar{x}_i(t, z) = \sum_k c_{ik} e^{\sigma t} \cos(kz), \quad i = 1, 2, \quad k = \frac{2n\pi}{L}, \quad n = \pm 1, \pm 2, \dots,$$

$$(25)$$

where k is called the *wavenumber* and $1/k$, which is a measure of the wave-like pattern, is proportional to the wavelength $w : w = 2\pi/k = L/n$ at *mode n*. σ is the eigenvalue which determines temporal growth and c_{ik}, $i = 1, 2$ are constants determined by initial conditions and the eigenspace of σ.

Substituting (25) and noting that they satisfy circle boundary conditions at $z = 0$ and $z = L$, we obtain our result because the linearization becomes

$$\bar{x}_t(t, z) = J^L \bar{x}(t, z), \quad J^L = \begin{pmatrix} b_{11} - D_{x_1} k^2 & b_{12} \\ b_{21} & b_{22} - D_{x_2} k^2 \end{pmatrix} \quad (26)$$

Since $\operatorname{tr} J^L = b_{11} + b_{22} - D_{x_1}k^2 - D_{x_2}k^2 < 0$, the destabilization of the FSS under spatially heterogenous perturbations requires that

$$\det J^L = \phi\left(k^2\right) = D_{x_1}D_{x_2}k^4 - (b_{11}D_{x_2} + b_{22}D_{x_1})\,k^2 + \det J^P < 0 \tag{27}$$

where $\det J^P > 0$ by the stability assumption about the FSS.

Relationship (27) is a dispersion relationship. The instability condition will be satisfied if there exist wavenumbers k_1 and k_2 such that $\phi\left(k^2\right) < 0$ for $k^2 \in \left(k_1^2, k_2^2\right)$, which implies that matrix (26) has a positive eigenvalue $\sigma\left(k^2\right)$ for $k^2 \in \left(k_1^2, k_2^2\right)$ This in turn requires that (i) $k_{\min}^2$ which corresponds to the wavenumber which minimizes $\phi\left(k^2\right)$ be positive and, (ii) $\phi\left(k_{\min}^2\right) < 0$ or

$$\frac{b_{22}D_{x_1} + b_{11}D_{x_2}}{2D_{x_1}D_{x_2}} > 0$$

$$-\frac{(b_{22}D_{x_1} + b_{11}D_{x_2})^2}{4D_{x_1}D_{x_2}} + \det J^P < 0$$

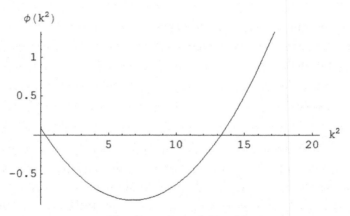

The dispersion relationship.

Long-run spatial patterns

- Linear instability is local.
- It is hypothesized that the nonlinear kinetics of the system bound the solution $\mathbf{x}\left(t, z\right)$, which eventually settles to a spatial pattern.

- A spatially heterogeneous steady state is obtained by

$$0 = f_i\left(\mathbf{x}\left(z\right), \quad \mathbf{h}^0\left(\mathbf{x}\left(z\right)\right)\right) + D_{x_i}\frac{\partial^2 x_i\left(z\right)}{\partial z^2}, \quad i = 1,2 \qquad (28)$$

- If persistence patterns emerge in this set-up, their creation is a result of the Turing mechanism.

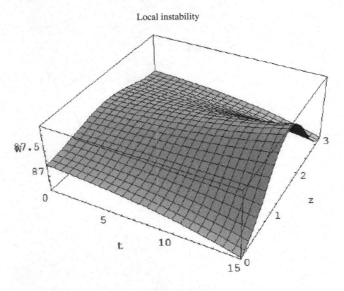

Local instability

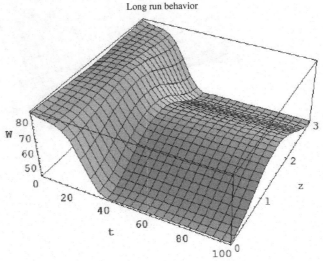

Long run behavior

Local instability

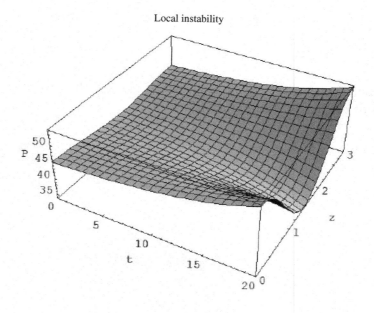

Long run behavior

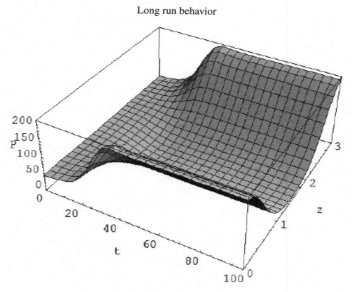

Optimal Instability

Differences from model in biology

- There is a large literature in mathematical biology (e.g., Murray, 2003) that study spatial agglomeration problems.
- To my knowledge, none of this literature deals with optimization problems as we do here. There are many differences between the "backward-looking" dynamics in mathematical biology problems and other natural science problems, and the "forward-looking" dynamics of economic problems.
- These suggest the possibility of a potential agglomeration at the social optimum or at a rational expectations equilibrium related to the incomplete internalization of the spatial externality by optimizing agents.

The planner's problem

$$\max_{\{\mathbf{u}(t,z)\}} \int_0^\infty \int_0^L e^{-\rho t} \left[U\left(\mathbf{x}\left(t,z\right), \quad \mathbf{u}\left(t,z\right)\right)\right] dz \, dt \qquad (29)$$

subject to

$$\frac{\partial x_1\left(t,z\right)}{\partial t} = f_1\left(x_1\left(t,z\right), \quad x_2\left(t,z\right), \quad \mathbf{u}\left(t,z\right)\right) + D_{x_1}\frac{\partial^2 x_1\left(t,z\right)}{\partial z^2}$$

$$\frac{\partial x_2\left(t,z\right)}{\partial t} = f_2\left(x_1\left(t,z\right), \quad x_2\left(t,z\right), \quad \mathbf{u}\left(t,z\right)\right) + D_{x_2}\frac{\partial^2 x_2\left(t,z\right)}{\partial z^2}$$

$$\mathbf{x}\left(0,z\right) \text{ given, } \mathbf{x}\left(t,0\right) = \mathbf{x}\left(t,L\right) = \bar{x}(t), \quad \forall t$$

Optimality conditions

$$u_j^*\left(t,z\right) = \arg\max_{u_j} \mathcal{H}\left(\mathbf{x}\left(t,z\right), \quad \mathbf{u}\left(t,z\right), \quad \mathbf{p}\left(t,z\right)\right) \text{ or} \qquad (30)$$

$$u_j^*\left(t,z\right) = g_j^*\left(\mathbf{x}\left(t,z\right), \quad \mathbf{p}\left(t,z\right)\right), \quad j = 1,\ldots,m$$

where $\mathcal{H}$ is the current value Hamiltonian function

$$\mathcal{H} = U\left(\mathbf{x}\left(t, z\right), \quad \mathbf{u}\left(t, z\right)\right)$$
$$+ \sum_{i=1,2} p_i\left(t, z\right)\left[f_i\left(\mathbf{x}\left(t, z\right), \mathbf{u}\left(t, z\right)\right) + D_{x_i}\frac{\partial^2 x_i}{\partial z^2}\right] \quad (31)$$

which is a generalization of the "flat" Hamiltonian function

$$H = U\left(\mathbf{x}, \mathbf{u}\right) + \sum_{i=1,2} p_i f_i\left(\mathbf{x}, \mathbf{u}\right) \quad (32)$$

The vector of the costate variables is
$\mathbf{p}\left(t, z\right) = \left(p_1\left(t, z\right), p_2\left(t, z\right)\right)$ and satisfies for $i = 1, 2$:

$$\frac{\partial p_i\left(t, z\right)}{\partial t} = \rho p_i - H_{x_i}\left(\mathbf{x}\left(t, z\right), \quad \mathbf{p}\left(t, z\right), \quad \mathbf{g}^*\left(\mathbf{x}, \mathbf{p}\right)\right) \quad (33)$$

$$- D_{x_i}\frac{\partial^2 p_i\left(t, z\right)}{\partial z^2} \quad (34)$$

where $\mathbf{g}^*\left(\mathbf{x}\left(t, z\right), \mathbf{p}\left(t, z\right)\right)$ is the vector of the optimal control functions defined by (30).[1]

Temporal and spatial transversality conditions are as follows:

$$\lim_{T \to \infty} e^{-\rho T}\int_0^L p_i\left(T, z\right) x_i\left(T, z\right) dz = 0, \quad i = 1, 2 \quad (35)$$

$$p_i\left(t, 0\right) = p_i\left(t, L\right), \quad i = 1, 2 \quad (36)$$

The reaction–diffusion system of $\left(x_1\left(t, z\right), x_2\left(t, z\right)\right)$, with $\mathbf{u}$ replaced by the optimal controls $\mathbf{g}^*\left(\mathbf{x}\left(t, z\right), \mathbf{p}\left(t, z\right)\right)$, and the system of

---

[1]To ease notation, we sometimes use subscripts to denote partial derivatives. Thus, $H_{\mathbf{v}}$ denotes a vector of partial derivatives, while $H_{\mathbf{vv}}$ denotes a matrix of second-order partial derivatives with respect to variables $\mathbf{v}$.

(33) constitute the Hamiltonian system of four partial differential equations:

$$\frac{\partial x_i\,(t,z)}{\partial t} = H_{p_i}\left(\mathbf{x}(t,z),\,\mathbf{p}(t,z),\,\mathbf{g}^*\left(\mathbf{x},\mathbf{p}\right)\right) + D_{x_i}\frac{\partial^2 x_i}{\partial z^2}$$

$$\frac{\partial p_i\,(t,z)}{\partial t} = \rho p_i - H_{x_i}(\mathbf{x}(t,z),\,\mathbf{p}(t,z),\,\mathbf{g}^*(\mathbf{x},\mathbf{p})) - D_{x_i}\frac{\partial^2 p_i}{\partial z^2}$$

$$i = 1, 2$$

Diffusion-induced instability

Theorem: *Assume that for problem (29) with $D_{x_1} = D_{x_2} = 0$, the FOSS $(x_1^*, x_2^*, p_1^*, p_2^*)$ has the local saddle point property with either two positive and two negative real roots, or with complex roots with two of them having negative real parts. Then there is a $(D_{x_1}, D_{x_2}) > 0$ and wave numbers $k \in (k_1, k_2) > 0$ such that if:*

(a)

$$\frac{\left[\sum_{i=1,2} D_{x_i}(2H_{x_i p_i} - \rho)\right]}{2\left(D_{x_1}^2 + D_{x_2}^2\right)} > 0 \tag{37}$$

$$\frac{\left[\sum_{i=1,2} D_{x_i}(2H_{x_i p_i} - \rho)\right]^2}{4\left(D_{x_1}^2 + D_{x_2}^2\right)} + K^0 > 0 \tag{38}$$

$$0 < \det J^S\left(k^2\right) \le (K/2)^2$$

then all the eigenvalues of the Jacobian matrix $J^S\left(k^2\right)$ are real and positive;

(b)

$$\det J^S\left(k^2\right) < 0 \tag{39}$$

then $J^S\left(k^2\right)$ has one negative real eigenvalue, while all the other eigenvalues have positive real parts;

(c)

$$K^2 - 4\det J^S\left(k^2\right) < 0 \tag{40}$$

$$\det J^S\left(k^2\right) < (K/2)^2 + \rho^2\left(K/2\right)$$

then all the eigenvalues of $J^S\left(k^2\right)$ are complex with positive real parts. In all the above cases, the optimal dynamics associated with the reaction–diffusion system are unstable in the neighborhood of the FOSS in the time-space domain and optimal diffusion-induced instability emerges.

Sketch of proof

Let $\bar{x}\left(t,z\right),\bar{p}\left(t,z\right)$ denote deviations from the FOSS, and define the linearization of the Hamiltonian system at the FOSS as

$$
\begin{pmatrix} \bar{x}_t\left(t,z\right) \\ \bar{p}_t\left(t,z\right) \end{pmatrix} = J^0 \begin{pmatrix} \bar{x}\left(t,z\right) \\ \bar{p}\left(t,z\right) \end{pmatrix} + D \begin{pmatrix} \bar{x}_{zz}\left(t,z\right) \\ \bar{p}_{zz}\left(t,z\right) \end{pmatrix} \tag{41}
$$

$$
J^0 = \begin{pmatrix} H_{\mathbf{px}} & H_{\mathbf{pp}} \\ -H_{\mathbf{xx}} & \rho I_2 - H_{\mathbf{xp}} \end{pmatrix}, \quad D = \begin{pmatrix} D_{\mathbf{x}}I_2 & \mathbf{0} \\ \mathbf{0} & -D_{\mathbf{x}}I_2 \end{pmatrix}
$$

$$
D_{\mathbf{x}} = \begin{pmatrix} D_{x_1} \\ D_{x_2} \end{pmatrix}
$$

where $H_{\mathbf{pp}}, H_{\mathbf{xx}}, H_{\mathbf{px}} = H_{\mathbf{xp}}$ are (2×2) matrices of second derivatives of the Hamiltonian with $\mathbf{u}^* = \mathbf{g}^*\left(\mathbf{x},\mathbf{p}\right)$, I_2 is the (2×2) identity matrix, $\mathbf{0}$ is a (2×2) zero matrix, and J^0 is the Jacobian of the flat Hamiltonian system $\left(D_{x_1} = D_{x_2} = 0\right)$.

Consider spatially heterogeneous perturbations of the FOSS of the form

$$
\bar{x}_i\left(t,z\right) = \sum_k c_{ik}^x e^{\sigma t}\cos\left(kz\right), \quad \bar{p}_i\left(t,z\right) = \sum_k c_{ik}^p e^{\sigma t}\cos\left(kz\right)
$$

$$
k = \frac{2n\pi}{L}, \quad n = \pm 1, \pm 2, \ldots,
$$

and define the following:

$$
K_i = \begin{vmatrix} H_{p_i x_i} - D_{x_i}k^2 & H_{p_i p_i} \\ -H_{x_i x_i} & \rho - H_{x_i p_i} + D_{x_i}k^2 \end{vmatrix}, \quad i = 1, 2
$$

$$K_3 = \begin{vmatrix} H_{p_1 x_2} & H_{p_1 p_2} \\ -H_{x_1 x_2} & -H_{x_1 p_2} \end{vmatrix} \tag{42}$$

$$K\left(k^2\right) = K_1 + K_2 + 2K_3 \tag{43}$$

Substituting the spatially heterogenous perturbations into the linearized Hamiltonian system, we obtain

$$\begin{pmatrix} \bar{x}_t\left(t, z\right) \\ \bar{p}_t\left(t, z\right) \end{pmatrix} = J^S \begin{pmatrix} \bar{x}\left(t, z\right) \\ \bar{p}\left(t, z\right) \end{pmatrix}$$

$$J^S = \begin{pmatrix} H_{\mathbf{px}} - D_{\mathbf{x}} k^2 I_2 & H_{\mathbf{pp}} \\ -H_{\mathbf{xx}} & \rho I_2 - H_{\mathbf{xp}} + D_{\mathbf{x}} k^2 I_2 \end{pmatrix}$$

Define the matrix

$$Z\left(\frac{\rho}{2}\right) = \begin{pmatrix} H_{\mathbf{px}} - D_{\mathbf{x}} k^2 I_2 - \frac{\rho}{2} I_2 & H_{\mathbf{pp}} \\ -H_{\mathbf{xx}} & -H_{\mathbf{xp}} + D_{\mathbf{x}} k^2 I_2 + \frac{\rho}{2} I_2 \end{pmatrix}$$

Following Kurz (1968, Theorem 2) we obtain that if σ_1, σ_2 are eigenvalues of J^S, then they satisfy $\sigma_{1,2} = \frac{\rho}{2} \pm \psi$, where ψ is a pair of eigenvalues for Z. The eigenvalues of matrix Z are determined by the solution of the characteristic equation

$$\psi^4 - M_3 \psi^3 + M_2 \psi^2 - M_1 \psi + \det Z = 0 \tag{44}$$

where $M_3 = \operatorname{tr}(Z) = 0$. By a rather tedious calculation, we can obtain $M_2 = \left(K - \frac{\rho^2}{2}\right)$, with K defined in (42), and with M_2 being the sum of six principal minors of Z of second order; $M_3 = 0$, with M_3 being the sum of four principal minors of Z of third order; and $\det Z = \left(\frac{\rho}{2}\right)^4 - \left(\frac{\rho}{2}\right)^2 K + \det J^S$.

Substituting in (44) and using the Kurz Theorem, we obtain the eigenvalues of J^S as

$$_1^3 \sigma_2^4 = \frac{\rho}{2} \pm \sqrt{\left(\frac{\rho}{2}\right)^2 - \frac{K}{2} \pm \sqrt{\left(\frac{K}{2}\right)^2 - \det J^S}} \tag{45}$$

which is an extension of Dockner's (1985) formula for the eigenvalues of the Hamiltonian system for optimal control problems with two state variables, for the case where the state variables diffuse in space.

- The FOSS will have the saddle point property (two positive and two negative eigenvalues) under spatially heterogenous perturbations if (i) $K < 0$ and (ii) $0 < \det J^S < \left(\frac{K}{2}\right)^2$.
- If $K > 0$ while (ii) is still satisfied, the two negative eigenvalues will become positive.

$$K\left(k^2\right) = -\left(D_{x_1}^2 + D_{x_2}^2\right) k^4 \tag{46}$$

$$+ \left[\sum_{i=1,2} D_{x_i}(2H_{x_i p_i} - \rho)\right] k^2 + K^0, \quad K^0 < 0 \tag{47}$$

where $K^0 < 0$ because of the saddle point assumption for the FOSS. For instability, we want $K\left(k^2\right) > 0$ for some wavenumber k, thus (46) is a dispersion relationship.

Let $\left(\sigma_3\left(k^2\right), \sigma_4\left(k^2\right)\right) > 0, k^2 \in \left(k_1^2, k_2^2\right)$ the eigenvalues that turn positive under spatial perturbation, then the patterned state and costate paths in the neighborhood of the FOSS can be approximated as

$$\begin{pmatrix} \bar{x}(t, z) \\ \bar{p}(t, z) \end{pmatrix}$$

$$\sim \sum_{n_1}^{n_2} \mathbf{c}_{3n} \exp\left[\sigma_3\left(k^2\right) t\right] \cos(kz)$$

$$+ \sum_{n_1}^{n_2} \mathbf{c}_{4n} \exp\left[\sigma_4\left(k^2\right) t\right] \cos(kz), \quad k = \frac{2n\pi}{L}, \quad n = 1, 2, \dots.$$

- Note that the two constants which correspond to eigenvalues σ_1, σ_2 with positive real parts should still be set equal to zero, so that the use of the temporal transversality condition at infinity will allow us to choose initial costates $\mathbf{p}$ for any initial state $\mathbf{x}$, which will set the system on the *spatially heterogeneous–spatiotemporally unstable* "optimal" manifold.

- The length L of space should be adequate to allow the existence of these unstable modes.

Identifying the spatial instability

- Fourier methods are used to reduce the original problem to a countable number of "ordinary" finite dimensional optimal control problems in which the dynamics are described by ordinary differential equations (Brock and Xepapadeas, 2008). These mode-n control problems correspond to each mode $k = 2n\pi/L$, $n = 0, 1, 2, \ldots$.
- Then the unstable nodes are identified through the dispersion relationship.
- Optimal pre-patterns occur along the *spatially heterogeneous–spatiotemporally unstable* "optimal" manifold.
- This steady state will satisfy the system of second-order differential equations in the space variable z, defined by

$$0 = H_{p_i}\left(\mathbf{x}\left(t, z\right), \quad \mathbf{p}\left(t, z\right), \quad \mathbf{g}^*\left(\mathbf{x}, \mathbf{p}\right)\right) + D_{x_i}\frac{\partial^2 x_i}{\partial z^2}$$

$$0 = \rho p_i - H_{x_i}\left(\mathbf{x}\left(t, z\right), \quad \mathbf{p}\left(t, z\right), \quad \mathbf{g}^*\left(\mathbf{x}, \mathbf{p}\right)\right) - D_{x_i}\frac{\partial^2 p_i}{\partial z^2}$$

- However, no convergence results.

Global Analysis

Objectives

- Use global analysis based on monotone operator theory, combined with local analysis based on spectral theory, to obtain insights regarding the endogenous emergence (or not) of optimal agglomerations at a rational expectations equilibrium and the social optimum of dynamic economic systems.

- The possibility of a potential agglomeration at a rational expectations equilibrium is related to the incomplete internalization of the spatial externality by optimizing agents.
- A "no agglomerations" theorem at the social optimum stems from the full internalization of the spatial externality by a social planner and the strict concavity of the production function.

A Ramsey-type growth model

- Production at time t and site z is given by the strictly concave production function $f : \mathbb{R} \times \mathbb{R} \to \mathbb{R}$ in terms of $f(x(t,z), X(t,z))$.

$$X(t,z) = \int_{\mathcal{O}} w(z,s)x(t,s)ds \qquad (48)$$

- $x(t,z)$ denotes the capital stock at point $z \in \mathcal{O}$ at time $t \in [0, +\infty)$.
- $w : \mathcal{O} \times \mathcal{O} \to \mathbb{R}$ is an integrable kernel function modeling the effect that position s has on position z. There is a mapping which takes an element $x(t, \cdot) \in \mathbb{H}$ and maps it to a new element $X(t, \cdot) \in \mathbb{H}$ such that (48) holds for every $z \in \mathcal{O}$.
- $\mathbb{H} = L^2(\mathcal{O})$, the space of square integrable functions on $\mathcal{O}$.

Budget constraints

$$c(t,z) + \frac{\partial x(t,z)}{\partial t} = f(x(t,z), \quad \check{X}(t,z)) - \eta x(t,z) - \frac{\alpha}{2}\left[\frac{\partial x(t,z)}{\partial t}\right]^2$$

$$\frac{\partial x(t,z)}{\partial t} = u(t,z)$$

$$0 = \mathcal{C}(z) := \int_0^\infty e^{-rt}\left[x_0 + f\left(x(t,z), \quad \check{X}(t,z)\right)\right. \qquad (49)$$

$$\left. - \lambda x(t,z) - c(t,z) - \frac{\alpha}{2}u^2(t,z)\right]dt$$

$$0 = \mathcal{C}^\diamond := \int_\mathcal{O} \int_0^\infty e^{-rt} \left[x_0 + f\left(x(t,z), \quad \check{X}(t,z)\right) \right] \tag{50}$$

$$- \lambda x(t,z) - c(t,z) - \frac{\alpha}{2} u^2(t,z)] dt\, dz$$

Rational expectations equilibrium (REE)

$$\max_c (J_{RE}(c))(z) := \int_0^\infty e^{-\rho t} U(c(t,z)) dt$$

$$0 = \mathcal{C}(z) := \int_0^\infty e^{-rt} \left[x_0 + f\left(x(t,z), \check{X}(t,z)\right) \right.$$

$$\left. - \lambda x(t,z) - c(t,z) - \frac{\alpha}{2} u^2(t,z)] dt \right.$$

$$\check{X}(t,z) = X^e \text{ exogenous}$$

Social optimum (SO)

$$J_{SO}(c) := \int_\mathcal{O} \psi(z)(J_s c)(z) dz$$

$$= \int_\mathcal{O} \int_0^\infty e^{-\rho t} \psi(z) U(c(t,z)) dt\, dz$$

$$0 = \mathcal{C}^\diamond := \int_\mathcal{O} \int_0^\infty e^{-rt} \left[x_0 + f\left(x(t,z), \check{X}(t,z)\right) \right.$$

$$\left. - \lambda x(t,z) - c(t,z) - \frac{\alpha}{2} u^2(t,z)] dt\, dz \right.$$

$$\check{X}(t,z) = X(t,z) = \int_\mathcal{O} w(z,s) x(t,s) ds$$

Main assumptions

- The influence kernel function $w \colon \mathcal{O} \times \mathcal{O} \to \mathbb{R}$ is continuous and symmetric, i.e., $w(z,s) = w(s,z) = w(z-s)$. Then the following integral operator is defined:

$$X(t,z) = (\mathsf{K}x)(t,z) := \int_\mathcal{O} w(z-s) x(t,s) ds \tag{51}$$

- The production function $f \colon \mathbb{R} \times \mathbb{R} \to \mathbb{R}$ is a strictly increasing, strictly concave function of the (real) variables (x, X).

- The second-order derivatives f_{xX}, f_{XX} are uniformly bounded below in $\mathcal{O}$,

$$-\mu := \inf_{(x,X)\in\mathbb{R}^2} f_{XX}, \quad \xi := \inf_{(x,X)\in\mathbb{R}^2} f_{xX}, \quad \mu, \xi \in \mathbb{R}_+$$

- The utility function $U\colon \mathbb{R}_+ \to \mathbb{R}$ is an increasing and strictly concave C^2 function in consumption c and satisfies the Inada conditions

$$\lim_{c\to 0} \partial_c U(c) = +\infty, \quad \lim_{c\to+\infty} \partial_c U(c) = 0$$

- The operator $\mathsf{K}\colon \mathbb{H} \to \mathbb{H}$ is strictly positive.
- It holds that $\mu/\xi < \mu_1$, where μ_1 is the largest (positive) eigenvalue of operator K.

Fisher separation: Optimal investment

$x(t,z) = x_0(z) + \int_0^t u(s,z)ds, \ u = k'$

Rational Expectations' Equilibrium:

$$\max_{x'} \int_0^\infty e^{-rt}\left(f(x(t,z),(\mathsf{K}x)(t,z)) - \lambda x(t,z) - \frac{\alpha}{2}(x'(t,z))^2 \right)dt \tag{52}$$

Social Optimum:

$$\max_{x'} \int_0^\infty \int_{\mathcal{O}} e^{-rt}\left[f(x(t,z),(\mathsf{K}x)(t,z)) \right.$$

$$\left. - \lambda x(t,z) - \frac{\alpha}{2}(x'(t,z))^2 \right]dz\,dt \tag{53}$$

Optimality conditions

Define the nonlinear operators $\mathsf{A}_\nu\colon \mathbb{H} \to \mathbb{H}$, $\nu = RE, SO$, by

$$\mathsf{A}_{RE}x := -\alpha^{-1}(f_x(x,\check{X}) - \lambda), \ \check{X} = \mathsf{K}x$$

$$\mathsf{A}_{SO}x := -\alpha^{-1}(f_x(x,\check{X}) + \mathsf{K}f_X(x,\check{X}) - \lambda), \ \check{X} = \mathsf{K}x$$

Theorem: *The first-order necessary condition for problems (52) and (53) is of the form*

$$x'' - rx' - A_\nu x = 0, \quad \nu = RE, SO \tag{54}$$

where A_ν *are the nonlinear operators above. The first-order necessary conditions have to be complemented with the transversality condition*

$$\lim_{t \to \infty} e^{-rt} x x' = \lim_{t \to \infty} \frac{1}{2} e^{-rt} (x^2)' = 0 \tag{55}$$

REE and SO

Definition: A solution $x : I \to \mathbb{H}$, if it exists, of the nonlinear integro-differential equation

$$x'' - rx' - A_\nu x = 0 \tag{56}$$

is called an *RE* equilibrium if $\nu = RE$ and an *SO* equilibrium if $\nu = SO$.

Sketch of proof

Consider

$$J = \int_0^\infty \int_{\mathcal{O}} e^{-rt} \Big[f(x(t,z), (Kx)(t,z)) \tag{57}$$

$$- \lambda x(t,z) - \frac{\alpha}{2} (x'(t,z))^2 \Big] \, dz \, dt \tag{58}$$

as a functional of $u = x'$ and $x = x_0 + \int_0^t u(s) ds$. The FONC will be of the form $(\nabla J, \phi) = 0$, where ∇ denotes the Gâteaux derivative and ϕ is a test function in $\mathbb{H}$.

The Gâteaux derivative: We fix any direction $v \in \mathbb{H}$, define $u_\epsilon = u + \epsilon v$, $V = \int_0^t v(s) ds$ and calculate

$$\frac{d}{d\epsilon} J(u_\epsilon)\Big|_{\epsilon=0} = \int_0^\infty \int_{\mathcal{O}} e^{-rt} \left[\partial_x f(x, Kx) + K^* \partial_X f(x, Kx) V \right.$$

$$\left. - \lambda V - \alpha u v \right] dz \, dt \tag{59}$$

Since $v = V'$, by integration by parts over t and using the transversality condition, the first-order condition becomes

$$\int_0^\infty \int_{\mathcal{O}} e^{-rt} \left[\partial_x f(x, \mathsf{K}x) + \mathsf{K}^* \partial_X f(x, \mathsf{K}x) \right.$$
$$\left. - \lambda + \alpha u' - r\alpha u \right] V \, dz \, dt = 0$$

This must be true for all v therefore for all V which implies that the first-order condition becomes

$$\partial_x f(x, \mathsf{K}x) + \mathsf{K}^* \partial_X f(x, \mathsf{K}x) - \lambda + \alpha u' - r\alpha u = 0$$

(a.e.) and keeping in mind that $u = x'$, we obtain

$$x'' - rx' - \mathsf{A}_{SO}x = 0 \tag{60}$$

- The operators $\mathsf{A}_\nu : \mathbb{H} \to \mathbb{H}$, $\nu = RE, SO$ are maximal monotone.[2]
- We now use Theorem 3.3 of Rouhani and Khatibzadeh (2009) to obtain convergence results. According to a special case of this theorem, a bounded solution of

$$x'' - rx' = \mathsf{A}_\nu x$$

for any initial condition, x_0, converges weakly as $t \to \infty$ to an element of $\mathsf{A}_\nu^{-1}(0)$, if A_ν is a maximally monotone.

Optimal agglomerations in the long run

The following theorem provides important information on the long-run dynamics.

Theorem (Convergence): (*a*) *The operator equations,* $\mathsf{A}_\nu x = 0$, $\nu = RE, SO$, *have unique solutions.* (*b*) *All bounded solutions of* $x'' - rx' - \mathsf{A}_\nu x = 0$ *have as weak limit the solution of* $\mathsf{A}_\nu x = 0$, $\nu = RE, SO$.

---

[2] A possibly nonlinear operator $\mathsf{A} : \mathbb{H} \to \mathbb{H}$ is called monotone if $(\mathsf{A}x - \mathsf{A}y, x - y) \geq 0$ for all $x, y \in \mathbb{H}$ and maximal monotone if its graph is not properly contained in the graph of any other monotone operator. Observe that monotonicity is related to positivity if the operator is linear.

Assumption P: The operator $\mathsf{K} : \mathbb{H} \to \mathbb{H}$ is strictly positive.[3]

It holds that $\mu/\xi < \mu_1$ where μ_1 is the largest (positive) eigenvalue of operator K.

$$-\mu := \inf_{(x,X)\in\mathbb{R}^2} f_{XX}, \quad \xi := \inf_{(x,X)\in\mathbb{R}^2} f_{xX}, \quad \mu, \xi \in \mathbb{R}_+$$

Implications of theorem

- The results of the theorem about convergence hold for *SO* without Assumption P. Assumption P is a sufficient condition for the theorem to hold in the *RE* case.
- Therefore, convergence to the *RE* steady state depends on the strength of diminishing returns with respect to spatial spillovers (f_{XX}), the strength of the complementarity between the capital stock and spatial spillovers in the production function (f_{xX}), and the structure of the spatial domain as reflected in the largest eigenvalue of K.
- Furthermore, relaxing the monotonicity assumption on operator K, there may exist multiple solutions for the *RE* steady-state equation for appropriate values of λ.
- For strictly concave production functions f, if the steady state equation $\mathsf{A}_{SO}x = 0$ admits a flat solution, then all bounded solutions of the time-dependent system will finally tend weakly to that flat solution as $t \to \infty$. Thus, agglomeration is not a socially optimal outcome in this case.
- The uniqueness of the solution of $\mathsf{A}_{SO}x = 0$ precludes the existence of any steady state other than the flat steady state as long as total spillover effects are the same across all sites of the spatial domain. Then the socially optimal spatial distribution of economic activity is the uniform distribution in space. This is always true in the case of periodic boundary conditions, when α is independent of z. This result is a generalization of classical turnpike theory to infinite dimensional spatial models.

---

[3]K is a positive operator if $(\mathsf{K}h, h) \geq 0$ for all $h \in \mathbb{H}$, and strictly positive if furthermore $(\mathsf{K}h, h) = 0$ implies $h = 0$.

- Convergence to the RE steady state is not guaranteed by the strict concavity of the production function, as in the SO case, but depends, according to part (a) of this theorem, on the relation between diminishing returns, complementarities, and the spatial geometry.
- If a unique globally stable RE steady state exists, it will be flat. Hence, for both the RE and SO, the unique steady state is the flat steady state.[4]
- If the conditions of this theorem leading to (a) are not satisfied, a more complex behavior is expected in the RE equilibrium. In this case, multiple RE steady states cannot be eliminated, and a potential agglomeration at the RE equilibrium takes the form of instability of the flat steady state.

Agglomeration emergence and local spillover-induced instability

- For a flat steady state $\bar{x}$, let

$$s_{11} := \alpha^{-1}\partial_{xx}^2 f(\bar{x}, \mathsf{K}\bar{x}), \quad s_{22} := \alpha^{-1}\partial_{XX}^2 f(\bar{x}, \mathsf{K}\bar{x})$$
$$s_{12} := \alpha^{-1}\partial_{xX}^2 f(\bar{x}, \mathsf{K}\bar{x}) > 0 \tag{61}$$

and define the linear bounded operators $\mathsf{L}_\nu \colon \mathbb{H} \to \mathbb{H}$ by

$$\mathsf{L}_{RE}\hat{x} := s_{11}\hat{x} + s_{12}\mathsf{K}\hat{x}$$
$$\mathsf{L}_{SO}\hat{x} := s_{11}\hat{x} + 2s_{12}\mathsf{K}\hat{x} + s_{22}\mathsf{K}^2\hat{x}$$

- These operators govern the behavior of spatiotemporal perturbations, $\hat{x}$, from the flat steady state $\bar{x}$: Inserting the ansatz $x = \bar{x} + \epsilon\hat{x}$ into the equilibrium condition

$$x'' - rx' - \mathsf{A}_\nu x = 0 \tag{62}$$

---

[4]The RE and SO steady states will in general be different from each other, which calls for spatially dependent economic policy if the SO steady state is to be attained.

and expanding in ϵ, we obtain the linearized equation for the evolution of the perturbation $\hat{x}(t, z)$ as follows:

$$\hat{x}'' - r\hat{x}' + \mathsf{L}_\nu \hat{x} = 0, \quad \nu = RE, \, SO \tag{63}$$

Let $\{\mu_j\}$ be the eigenvalues of operator K and $\{\phi_j\}$ the corresponding eigenfunctions. Then,

Proposition: *An arbitrary initial perturbation of the flat steady state of the form*

$$\hat{x}(0, z) = \sum_j a_j \phi_j(z), \quad \hat{x}'(0, z) = \sum_j b_j \phi_j(z)$$

evolves under the linearized system (63) to

$$\hat{x}_\nu(t, z) = \sum_j c_{\nu,j}(t) \phi_j(z)$$

where $\{c_{\nu,j}(t)\}$ *is the solution of the countably infinite system of ordinary differential equations*

$$c_{\nu,j}'' - r c_{\nu,j}' + \Lambda_{\nu,j} c_{\nu,j} = 0, \quad \nu = RE, SO, \; j \in \mathbb{N} \tag{64}$$

$$c_{\nu,j}(0) = a_j, \quad c_{\nu,j}'(0) = b_j$$

where

$$\Lambda_{RE,j} = s_{11} + s_{12}\mu_j$$

$$\Lambda_{SO,j} = s_{11} + 2s_{12}\mu_j + s_{22}\mu_j^2$$

Proposition:

(1) *If* $\Lambda_{\nu,j} < 0$, *then* $c_{\nu,j}(t) = \bar{A}_j e^{\sigma_1 t} + \bar{B}_j e^{\sigma_2 t}$ *where* $\sigma_1 < 0 < \frac{r}{2} < \sigma_2$ *(saddle path behaviour).*

(2) *If* $0 < \Lambda_{\nu,j} < \left(\frac{r}{2}\right)^2$, *then* $c_{\nu,j}(t) = \bar{A}_j e^{\sigma_1 t} + \bar{B}_j e^{\sigma_2 t}$ *where* $0 < \sigma_1 < \frac{r}{2} < \sigma_2$ *(unstable solutions).*

(3) *If* $\left(\frac{r}{2}\right)^2 < \Lambda_{\nu,j}$, *then* $c_j(t) = e^{\frac{r}{2}t} \left(\bar{A}_j \cos(\sigma t) + \bar{B}_j \sin(\sigma t)\right)$, $\sigma \in \mathbb{R}$

and $\bar{A}_j, \bar{B}_j$ *are constants related to the initial conditions.*

236 Advanced Mathematical Methods in Environmental and Resource Economics

- The perturbations from the flat steady state which contain modes ϕ_j such that $\Lambda_{\nu,j} < 0$ will die out and the system will converge to the flat steady state — no possible agglomeration is expected.
- The perturbations from the flat steady state which contain modes ϕ_j such that $\Lambda_{\nu,j} > 0$ will turn unstable and lead to possible potential agglomeration spatial patterns, either monotone in time or oscillatory in time.

Comparison with turing instability

This instability can be contrasted with the celebrated Turing instability mechanism (Turing, 1952), which leads to pattern formation in biological and chemical systems. The important differences here are that

(a) in our model, the instability is driven not by the action of the diffusion operator (which is a differential operator) but rather by a compact integral operator that models geographical spillovers, and

(b) contrary to the spirit of the Turing model, here, the instability is driven by optimizing behavior, so it is the outcome of forward-looking optimizing behavior by economic agents and not the result of reaction diffusion in chemical or biological agents. It is the optimizing nature of our model which dictates precisely the type of unstable modes which are "accepted" by the system, in the sense that they are compatible with the long-term behavior imposed on the system by the policy maker.

Periodic boundary conditions

Assume periodic boundary conditions, i.e., $\mathbb{H} = L_{\text{per}}(\mathcal{O})$, $\mathcal{O} = [-L, L]$. Then,

(a) The eigenfunctions of operator K are the Fourier modes $\phi_n(z) = \cos(n\pi z/L)$, $n \in \mathbb{N}$ with corresponding eigenvalues $W_n = \int_{-L}^{L} w(z)\,\phi_n(z)dz$.

(b) The action of operator K on a flat state returns a flat state, $\mathsf{K}\bar{x} = \bar{x} \int_{-L}^{L} w(z)dz$.

A Cobb–Douglas example

Cobb–Douglas and composite exponential kernels are as follows:

$$f(x, X) = C_0 x^a X^b, \quad a + b < 1$$

$$w(z) = \sum_{i=1}^{N} C_i \exp(-\gamma_i |z|), \quad \gamma_i \geq 0, \quad C_i \in \mathbb{R}$$

$$\bar{x}_{RE} = \left(\frac{\bar{\lambda}}{a}\right)^{\frac{1}{a+b-1}} W^{-\frac{b}{a+b-1}}$$

$$\bar{x}_{SO} = \left(\frac{\bar{\lambda}}{a+b}\right)^{\frac{1}{a+b-1}} W^{-\frac{b}{a+b-1}}$$

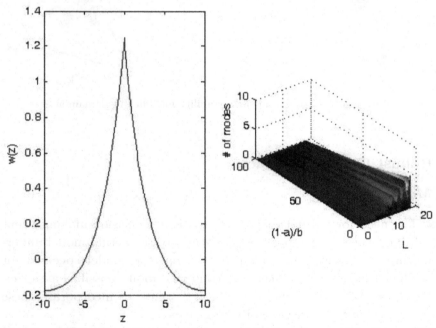

The shape of the composite kernel for $\gamma_1 = 0.3$, $C_1 = 2$, $\gamma_2 = 0.1$, $C_2 = -0.75$ (left panel). The number of unstable modes for this choice of kernel function, as a function of the parameter $\frac{1-a}{b}$ and L (right panel).

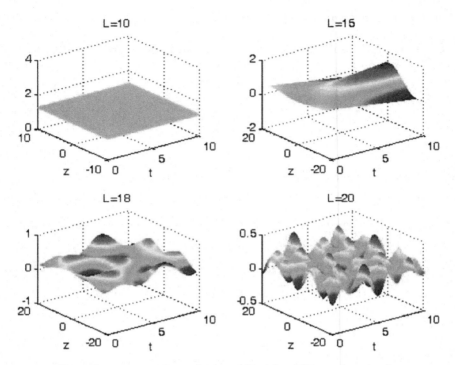

Emerging patterns from the instability for different domain sizes.

Robust Control in Space

Motivation

- The need for **robustness** emerges when a decision-making agent has concerns about possible deviations of the actual model underlying the decision-making process from the model specified, or when the decision maker has concerns about possible misspecifications of the reference model and wants to incorporate these concerns into the decision-making rules.
- A rule is robust if it continues to behave well even if the actual model deviates from a specified or a benchmark model.

Approaches to robust control

- Robust control problems have been traditionally analyzed in the context of

    o risk sensitive linear quadratic Gaussian (LEQG) models and
    o the H$^\infty$ models. The H$^\infty$ criterion implies decision-making for protection against the "worst case" and is related to a minimax approach.

- More recently, Hansen and Sargent interpreted concerns about model misspecification in economics as a situation where a decision maker or a regulator distrusts her model and wants good decisions over a cloud of models that surrounds the regulator's approximating or benchmark model, which are difficult to distinguish with finite data sets.
- There is a fictitious "adversarial agent" — Nature.
- Nature promotes robust decision rules by forcing the regulator, who seeks to maximize (minimize) an objective, to explore the fragility of decision rules to departures from the benchmark model.
- A robust decision rule means that lower bounds to the rule's performance are determined by Nature — the adversarial agent — which acts as a minimizing (maximizing) agent when constructing these lower bounds.
- Hansen and Sargent show that the robust control theory can be interpreted as a recursive version of max-min expected utility theory.
- Robust control methods have not been extended, as far as we know, to models that evolve both in time and space.

Robust Control and Spatial Models:

- Concerns about model misspecification refer now to the benchmark or reference model that describes the spatiotemporal dynamics of each specific site.
- If potential deviations from the specified model differ from site to site, then concerns for one site might affect the robust rules for other sites.

- Thus, robust rules should account not only for the spatial characteristics of the problem in a specific location, but also for the degree to which the regulator distrusts her model across locations.
- If concerns about the benchmark model in a given site differ from concerns in other sites, a spatially dependent robust rule should capture these differences.

Hot Spots:

- We formally identify spatial hot spots, which are sites, where
  - ◦ robust control breaks down.
  - ◦ robust control is very costly as a function of the degree of the regulator's concerns about model misspecification across all sites.
  - ◦ the need to apply robust control induces spatial agglomerations and break down spatial symmetry.
    - ■ This is, as far as we know, a new source for generating spatial patterns as compared to the classic Turing diffusion induced instability.
- Thus, hot spots are specific sites where uncertainties in these sites are such that when concerns about local misspecifications are incorporated into the decision rules for the entire spatial domain, the global rule **could break down**, **could be very costly** or **could induce spatial clustering**.

Spatial Interactions

The economy

- Our economy is located on a discrete lattice $\mathfrak{L}$. The "economy" is a collection of state variables $x = \{x_n\}$, $n \in \mathfrak{L}$.
- We consider an optimal linear regulator problem: optimization of a quadratic objective defined over the whole lattice by exerting on each lattice site a control $u_n \in \mathbb{R}$.

- The economy evolves according to an infinite dimensional stochastic differential equation

$$dx_n = \left(\sum_m a_{nm} x_m + \sum_m b_{nm} u_m \right) dt + \sum_m c_{nm} dw_m, \quad n \in \mathbb{Z}$$

where the last term describes the fluctuations of the state due to the stochasticity.

- In a compact form, this can be expressed as

$$dx = (\mathsf{A}x + \mathsf{B}u)\, dt + \mathsf{C} dw$$

where $\mathsf{A}, \mathsf{B}, \mathsf{C} : \ell^2 \to \ell^2$ are linear operators, related to the doubly infinite matrices with elements a_{nm}, b_{nm}, c_{nm}, respectively.

The economy

- The economy at point m has an effect on the state of the economy at point n. This effect is quantified through an influence "kernel" which assumes the form of a double sequence $\mathsf{A} = (a_{nm})$. The entry a_{nm} provides a measure of the influence of the state of the system at point m on the state of the system at point n.
  - If the economies do not interact at all, then $\mathsf{A} = a_{nm} = \delta_{n,m}$ where $\delta_{n,m}$ is the Kronecker delta.
  - If only next neighbor effects are possible, then a_{nm} is non-zero only if m is a neighbor of n.
- The controls at different point of the lattice u_m are assumed to have an effect on the state of the system at site n, through the term $\sum_m b_{nm} u_m$.
  - Fishing effort at a given site may affect fish biomass at other sites through biomass movements.
- The term $\sum_m c_{nm} dw_m$ tells us how the uncertainty at site m is affecting the uncertainty concerning the state of the system at site n.

Model uncertainty

- Assume now that there is some uncertainty concerning the "true" statistical distribution of the state of the system. This corresponds to a family of probability measures $\mathcal{Q}$ such that each $Q \in \mathcal{Q}$ corresponds to an alternative stochastic model (scenario) concerning the state of the system.
- By Girsanov's theorem, $\bar{w}_n(t) = w_n(t) - \int_0^t v_n(s)ds$ is a Q-Brownian motion for all $n \in \mathbb{N}$, where the drift term v_n may be considered as a measure of the model misspecification at lattice site n.
- The adoption of the family $\mathcal{Q}$ of alternative measures concerning the state of the system leads to a family of different equations for the state variable

$$dx_n = \left(\sum_m a_{nm}x_m + \sum_m b_{nm}u_m + \sum_m c_{nm}v_m \right)dt$$

$$+ \sum_m c_{nm}d\bar{w}_m, \quad n \in \mathbb{Z}$$

The control objective for the linear optimal regulator

$$\min_u \mathbb{E}_Q \left[\int_0^\infty e^{-rt} \sum_{n,m} (p_{nm}x_n(t)x_m(t) + q_{nm}u_n(t)u_m(t)) \, dt \right]$$

or in compact form

$$\min_u \mathbb{E}_Q \left[\int_0^\infty e^{-rt}(\langle \mathsf{P}x(t), x(t) \rangle + \langle \mathsf{Q}u(t), u(t) \rangle)dt \right]$$

where $\langle \cdot, \cdot \rangle$ is the inner product in the Hilbert space ℓ^2, and $\mathsf{P}, \mathsf{Q} : \ell^2 \to \ell^2$ are symmetric positive operators with infinite matrix representation $\mathsf{P} = \{p_{nm}\}$, $\mathsf{Q} = \{q_{nm}\}$.

If $p_{nm} = p\,\delta_{nm}$, $q_{nm} = q\,\delta_{nm}$, then

$$\min_u \mathbb{E}_Q \left[\int_0^\infty e^{-rt} \sum_n p(x_n(t))^2 + q(u_n(t))^2) dt \right]$$

First sum is the total deviation of the states of the system at each site from the desired state 0. Second sum is the total control cost to drive it to 0.

The Problem

Being uncertain about the true model, the decision maker will choose the strategy that will work in the worst case scenario

$$\min_u \max_v \mathbb{E}_Q \left[\int_0^\infty e^{-rt} \sum_n \sum_m (p_{nm} x_n(t) x_m(t) \right.$$

$$\left. + q_{nm} u_n(t) u_m(t) - \theta r_{nm} v_n(t) v_m(t)) dt \right]$$

or in compact form

$$\min_u \max_v \mathbb{E}_Q \left[\int_0^\infty e^{-rt} (\langle (\mathsf{P}x)(t), x(t) \rangle + \langle (\mathsf{Q}u)(t), u(t) \rangle \right.$$

$$\left. - \theta \langle (\mathsf{R}v)(t), v(t) \rangle) dt \right]$$

subject to the dynamic constraint. The third term corresponds to a quadratic loss function related to the "cost" of model misspecification.

Entropic constrained robust control

The optimization problem for the choice $R = I$ is related to a robust control problem with an entropic constraint of the form

$$\inf_u \sup_{Q \in \mathcal{Q}} \mathbb{E}_Q \left[\int_0^\infty e^{-rt} (\langle \mathsf{P}x(t), x(t) \rangle + \langle \mathsf{Q}u(t), u(t) \rangle) dt \right]$$

$$\times \text{ subject to } \ \mathcal{H}(P \mid Q) < H_0$$

and the dynamic constraint, where by $\mathcal{H}(P \mid Q)$ we denote the Kullback–Leibler entropy of the probability measures P and Q.

$$\mathcal{H}(Q \mid P) := \mathbb{E}_Q \left[\ln \left(\frac{dQ}{dP} \right) \right] = \frac{1}{2} \int_0^T \sum_n v_n^2(t) dt$$

We now consider the robust optimization problem

$$\sup_{Q \in \mathcal{Q}} J(x, u; v)$$

$$\text{subject to} \quad \mathcal{H}(Q \mid P) \leq H_0$$

and the dynamic constraint where

$$J(x, u; v) := \mathbb{E}_Q \left[\int_0^T e^{-rt} \left(\langle Px(t), x(t) \rangle + \langle Qu(t), u(t) \rangle \right) dt \right]$$

Using Lagrange multipliers for the equivalent minimization problem $\inf_{Q \in \mathcal{Q}} (-J(x, u; v))$, we see that a solution of the relative entropy constraint problem is equivalent to the solution of

$$\sup_{Q \in \mathcal{Q}} J(x, u; v) - \theta(\mathcal{H}(Q|P) - H_0)$$

Localized entropy constraint

The optimization problem is related to a robust control problem with an entropic constraint of the form

$$\inf_u \sup_{Q \in \mathcal{Q}} \mathbb{E}_Q \left[\int_0^\infty e^{-rt} (\langle Px(t), x(t) \rangle + \langle Qu(t), u(t) \rangle) dt \right]$$

$$\times \text{subject to} \quad \mathcal{H}(P_n \mid Q_n) < H_n, \quad n \in \mathbb{Z}$$

and the dynamic constraint, where by $\mathcal{H}(P_n \mid Q_n)$ is the Kullback–Leibler entropy of the marginal probability measures P_n and Q_n.

The localized relative entropy constraint problem is equivalent to the solution of

$$\sup_{Q \in \mathcal{Q}} J(x, u; v) - \sum_n \theta_n \left(\mathcal{H}(\bar{Q}_n \mid \bar{P}_n) - H_n \right)$$

- The introduction of the local entropic constraints means that the policy maker's concerns differ at various spatial points.
- The maximizing adversarial agent — Nature — chooses a $\{v_n(t)\}$ where $\theta_n \in (\underline{\theta}_n, +\infty]$, $\underline{\theta}_n > 0$, is a penalty parameter restraining the maximizing choice of Nature.
- θ_n is associated with the Lagrange multiplier of the entropy constraint, at each site. In the entropy constraint H_n is the maximum misspecification error that the decision maker is willing to consider given the existing information about the system at site n.

Hot spots and spatial connectivity

- The lower bound $\underline{\theta}_n$ is a so-called breakdown point beyond which it is fruitless to seek more robustness because the adversarial agent is sufficiently unconstrained so that she/he can push the criterion function to $+\infty$ despite the best response of the minimizing agent.
- Thus, when $\theta_n < \underline{\theta}_n$ for a specific site, robust control rules cannot be attained. In our terminology, this site will be **a hot spot** since misspecification concerns for this site will break down robust control for the whole spatial domain.
- On the other hand, when $\theta_m \to \infty$ or equivalently $H_m = 0$, there are no misspecification concerns for this site and the benchmark model can be used.
- The effects of spatial connectivity can be seen in this extreme example. The spatial relation of site m to site n breaks down regulation for both sites. If site m was spatially isolated from n, there would be no problem with regulation at m.

Translation Invariance

- Assume that $a_{nm} = a_{n-m}$, i.e., the effect that a site m has on site n depends only on the distance between n and m and not on the actual positions of the sites. Thus, the operators A, B and C are translation invariant.
- Denote the discrete Fourier transform by $\mathfrak{F}$. The Fourier transform has the property of turning a convolution operator into a

multiplication operator, i.e.,

$$\mathfrak{F}(\mathsf{A}u) = \mathfrak{F}(\mathsf{A})\mathfrak{F}(u)$$

- We will use the convention

$$\hat{u}_k := \mathfrak{F}(u)(k)$$

where now k takes values on the dual lattice, $k \in \mathfrak{L}$.
- Applying the Fourier transform $\mathfrak{F}$ and Plancherel theorem

$$d\hat{x}_k(t) = (\hat{a}_k\hat{x}_k(t) + \hat{b}_k\hat{u}_k(t) + \hat{c}_k\hat{v}_k(t))dt + \hat{c}_k\hat{w}_k(t)$$

$$\sum_n u_n^2 = \sum_k [\mathfrak{F}(u)(k)]^2 = \sum_k \hat{u}_k^2, \quad \mathsf{P} = pI \text{ and } \mathsf{Q} = qI$$

The decoupled problem

$$\min_{\hat{u}_k} \max_{\hat{v}_k} \mathbb{E}_Q\left[\int_0^\infty e^{-rt} p(\hat{x}_k(t))^2 + q(\hat{u}_k(t))^2 - \theta \sum_k (\hat{v}_k(t))^2)dt \right]$$

$\times\, k \in \mathfrak{L}$ subject to the state constraint.

Solution:

$$d\hat{x}_k^* = R_k\hat{x}_k^*dt + \hat{c}_k d\hat{w}_k$$

$$R_k := \hat{a}_k - \frac{\hat{b}_k^2 M_{2,k}}{2q} + \frac{\hat{c}_k^2\, M_{2,k}}{2\theta}$$

and $M_{2,k}$ is the solution of

$$\left(\frac{\hat{c}_k^2}{2\theta} - \frac{\hat{b}_k^2}{2q} \right) M_{2,k}^2 + (2\,\hat{a}_k - r)\, M_{2,k} + 2p = 0$$

The optimal controls are given by the feedback laws

$$\hat{u}_k^* = -\frac{\hat{b}_k M_{2,k}}{2q}\hat{x}_k^*, \quad \hat{v}_k^* = \frac{\hat{c}_k\, M_{2,k}}{2\theta}\hat{x}_k^*$$

Let $\mathcal{L}_k : C^2(\mathbb{R}) \to C(\mathbb{R})$ be the generator operator of the diffusion process $\{\hat{x}_k(t)\}$, $t \in \mathbb{R}_+$ defined by

$$(\mathcal{L}_k \Phi)(\hat{x}_k) = (\hat{a}_k \hat{x}_k + \hat{b}_k \hat{u}_k + \hat{c}_k \hat{v}_k)\frac{\partial \Phi}{\partial \hat{x}_k} + \frac{1}{2}\hat{c}_k^2 \frac{\partial^2 \Phi}{\partial \hat{x}_k^2}$$

The Hamilton–Jacobi–Bellman–Isaacs (HJBI) equation becomes

$$rV_k = \bar{H}\left(\hat{x}_k, \frac{\partial V_k}{\partial \hat{x}_k}, \frac{\partial^2 V_k}{\partial \hat{x}_k^2}\right)$$

$$\bar{H}\left(\hat{x}_k, \frac{\partial \Phi}{\partial \hat{x}_k}, \frac{\partial^2 \Phi}{\partial \hat{x}_k^2}\right) := \inf_{\hat{u}_k} \sup_{\hat{v}_k} \left(p\hat{x}_k^2 + q\hat{u}_k^2 - \theta\hat{v}_k^2 + \mathcal{L}_k\Phi\right)$$

The solution to the primal problem $(\min_{\hat{u}_k} \max_{\hat{v}_k})$ is the same as the solution to the dual $(\max_{\hat{v}_k} \min_{\hat{u}_k})$. **There is no duality gap**.

Hot Spots

We will call the qualitative changes in the behavior of the system **hot spots**.

Hot spots of type I

This is a breakdown of the solution procedure, i.e., a set of parameters where a solution to the above problem does not exist.

Proposition: *A hot spot of type I occurs for low enough values of θ. In particular, a mode k corresponds to a hot spot of type I if*

$$\theta < \theta_{cr} := \frac{p\hat{c}_k^2}{\left(\hat{a}_k - \frac{r}{2}\right)^2 + \frac{p}{q}\hat{b}_k^2}$$

In terms of regulatory objectives, this means that concerns about model misspecification make regulation impossible.

Hot spots of type II

This corresponds to the case where the solution exists but may lead to spatial pattern formation, i.e., to spatial instability similar to the Turing instability.

Proposition (Pattern formation for the primal problem):

There exists pattern formation behaviour for the primal problem if there exist modes k such that $R_k > 0$, i.e., if

$$\hat{a}_k - \frac{\hat{b}_k^2 M_{2,k}}{2q} + \frac{\hat{c}_k^2 M_{2,k}}{2\theta} > 0$$

θ may have a destabilizing effect on a mode, since it contributes a positive term to the expression for R_k. This effect is more pronounced the smaller θ is (but of course $\theta > \theta_{cr}$).

Optimal robustness-induced spatial instability:

- Assume that when $|\theta| \to \infty$, then $R_k < 0$ for all modes k. This means that the control problem is stable when there are no concerns about model misspecification.
- If there exists a $\hat{\theta}$, $\theta_{cr} < \left|\hat{\theta}\right| < \infty$ such that $R_k\left(\hat{\theta}\right) > 0$ for some mode k, then concerns about model misspecification induce the emergence of a type II hot spot.
- That is, the regulator's desire for robustness causes the emergence of spatial patterns.
- This result connects uncertainty aversion and the robust control with the emergence of spatial clustering and agglomerations.

We will call this result optimal robustness-induced spatial instability.

Hot spot of type III: The cost of robustness

This corresponds to the case where the cost of robustness becomes more than what it offers, i.e., where the relative cost of robustness may become very large.

$$\frac{1}{V} \frac{\partial V}{\partial \theta} = \frac{1}{M_{2,k}} \frac{\partial M_{2,k}}{\partial \theta}$$

Whenever $\frac{1}{M_{2,k}} \frac{\partial M_{2,k}}{\partial \theta} \to \infty$, then we say that the cost of robustness becomes more expensive than what it offers, and we will call that a hot spot of type III.

The General LQ Problem

- We relax the simplifying assumptions concerning the translation invariance property of the operators $\mathsf{A}, \mathsf{B}, \mathsf{C}$ as well as the assumption that $\mathsf{P} = pI$ and $\mathsf{Q} = qI$.
- We consider the solution of the general linear quadratic robust control problem under the state constraint, and comment on the possibility of hot spot formation working in real space directly rather than in Fourier transform space.

Solution in terms of operator Riccati equation

Theorem: *The general LQ robust control problem has a solution for which the optimal controls are of the feedback control form*

$$u = -\mathsf{Q}^{-1}\mathsf{B}^*\mathsf{H}^{\mathrm{sym}}x, \quad v = \frac{1}{\theta}\mathsf{R}^{-1}\mathsf{C}^*\mathsf{H}^{\mathrm{sym}}x$$

and the optimal state satisfies the Ornstein–Uhlenbeck equation

$$dx = \left(\mathsf{A} - \mathsf{B}\mathsf{Q}^{-1}\mathsf{B}^*\mathsf{H}^{\mathrm{sym}} + \frac{1}{\theta}\mathsf{C}\mathsf{R}^{-1}\mathsf{C}^*\mathsf{H}^{\mathrm{sym}}\right)x\,dt + \mathsf{C}dW$$

where $\mathsf{H}^{\mathrm{sym}}$ *is the solution of the operator Riccati equation*

$$\mathsf{H}^{\mathrm{sym}}\mathsf{A} + \mathsf{A}^*\mathsf{H}^{\mathrm{sym}} - \mathsf{H}^{\mathrm{sym}}\mathsf{E}^{\mathrm{sym}}\mathsf{H}^{\mathrm{sym}} - r\mathsf{H}^{\mathrm{sym}} + \mathsf{P} = 0$$

and $\mathsf{E}^{\mathrm{sym}} := \frac{1}{2}(\mathsf{E} + \mathsf{E}^*)$ *is the symmetric part of* $\mathsf{E} := \mathsf{B}\mathsf{Q}^{-1}\mathsf{B}^* - \frac{1}{\theta}\mathsf{C}\mathsf{R}^{-1}\mathsf{C}^*$.

- The operator Riccati equation is the generalization of the quadratic algebraic equation in the case where the operators A, B and C are not translation invariant, and thus amenable to analysis using the Fourier transform.
- When the state space is finite dimensional (i.e., in the case of finite lattices) the operator Riccati equation assumes the form of a matrix Riccati equation.

Hot spot formation in general linear quadratic systems

Proposition: *Let* $m = ||A||$ *be defined as* $m = \sup\langle Ax, x \rangle$ *and assume that* $m < r/2$. *Then, for small enough values of* $||E||$ *and* $||P||$ *the operator Riccati equation admits a unique bounded solution.*

- For the existence of a strong solution, we need $||E|| + ||P|| < d$. This condition breaks down for small enough values of θ, which in fact is the analogue of the **hot spot of Type I** that was obtained before.
- **Hot spots of Type II** will correspond to these eigenfunctions of the operator $\mathcal{R} := A - BQ^{-1}B^*H^{\text{sym}} + \frac{1}{\theta}CR^{-1}C^*H^{\text{sym}}$ that have positive eigenvalues.
- Assume for simplicity that C is diagonal and that the spatial domain is finite so that $\theta = (\theta_0, \ldots, \theta_{N-1})$ is the vector of local misspecification concerns.
- The low θ's will correspond to locations with the higher concerns.
- **Hot spot of Type I.** If one or more of these low θ's are such that the "smallness" condition on $||E||$ and $||P||$ is violated, then local concerns will cause global regulation to break down.
- **Hot spot of Type II.** If the low θ's are such that the operator $\mathcal{R}$ has positive eigenvalues, then local concerns may induce global spatial clustering.
- Even in the simple (2×2) case, it is not possible to obtain the solution of the Riccati equation in closed form, as we did in the special case where the operators are translation invariant.

Pattern formation through a "non-turing" mechanism

The mean field for the optimal state is

$$dx = \left[A - BQ^{-1}B^*H^{\text{sym}} + \frac{1}{\theta}CR^{-1}C^*H^{\text{sym}} \right] x = \mathcal{R}x$$

Assume that matrix A is invertible but matrix $\mathcal{R}$ which embodies optimization and misspecification concerns is not invertible. In this case, the steady state equation $0 = \mathcal{R}x$ will have more than one solution. This means that there will be vectors $x \neq \mathbf{0}$ that will satisfy

$0 = \mathcal{R}x$. These vectors will be ker $(\mathcal{R})$. If ker $(\mathcal{R})$ consists of vectors with spatially non-uniformity, then pattern formation emerges.

- This pattern formation mechanism is however a non-Turing mechanism.
- Distance-dependent utility. Models of travel behavior where the impact of distance on trip preferences underlies the choice of an individual to consume at locations which are away from his/her current location.
- The distance-dependent utility relates to the concept of spatial discounting.
- A representative consumer is located at $n = 0, 1, \ldots, N - 1$. Each location is characterized by a stock of natural capital $x_n(t)$, which generates environmental services that can be consumed only *in situ*.

Consumption at location n is the sum of consumption of all individuals or $u_n(t) = \sum_{m=0}^{N-1} u_{nm}(t)$, where $u_{nm}(t)$ is the consumption of services at location n of an individual located at location $m = 0, 1, \ldots, N - 1$.

$$dx_n(t) = \sum_{m=0}^{N-1} [\alpha_{nm} x_m(t) - \gamma_{nm} u_n(t)] \, dt + \sum_{m=0}^{N-1} c_{nm}(t) dw_m$$

Robust Control of *In-Situ* Consumption

Consumers

$$\max_{\{u_{nm}\}} \quad - \left[\sum_{m=0}^{n-1} \beta_{nm} (u_{nm}(t) - b_{nm}(t))^2 + I_n(t) \right.$$

$$\left. - \sum_{m=0}^{N-1} p_m(t) u_{nm}(t) \right] \text{ for all } n$$

$$\beta_{nm} \equiv \beta_{n-m} = \beta_{m-n} \equiv \beta_{mn}$$

Individual demand curves for consumption at each location are

$$2\beta_{nm}b_{nm}(t) - 2\beta_{nm}u_{nm}(t) = p_m(t)$$

The aggregate demand at location m and time t is

$$u_n(t) := \sum_{n=0}^{N-1} u_{nm}(t)$$

$$u_m(t) = \sum_{n=0}^{N-1} b_{nm}(t) - \left(\sum_{n=0}^{N-1} \frac{1}{2\beta_{nm}}\right) p_m(t) =: B_{0m}(t)$$
$$- B_{1m}(t)p_m(t)$$

The regulator

Site-dependent misspecification concerns:

$$\min_{u} \max_{v} \mathbb{E}_P \left[\int_0^\infty e^{-rt} \sum_{n=0}^{N-1} \left[\langle (BU)(t), U\rangle - \theta_n \langle (Rv), (v)\rangle\right] dt \right]$$

subject to $dx = (Ax + Zu + Cv)\, dt + Cdw$

Welfare: $\sum_{n=0}^{N-1} \sum_{m=0}^{N-1} \beta_{nm} (u_{nm}(t) - b_{nm}(t))^2$

Optimal supply of services for an individual located at m and consuming at n is

$$u_{nm}^*(t) = -\mathsf{B}^{-1}\mathsf{\Gamma}^*\mathsf{H}^{\mathsf{sym}}x_n(t)$$

Local equilibrium price at n will be

$$p_n^*(t) = B_{0n}(t) - \frac{1}{B_{1n}(t)} \left(\sum_{m=0}^{N-1} u_{nm}^*(t)\right)$$

Hot spot interpretation

- **Hot spot of type I:** Regulation breaks down for small θ. This means that because the regulator has very strong concerns about possible model misspecifications at specific site(s), the regulator cannot set up markets for consumption of *in situ* services.
- **Hot spot of type II:** The regulator, due to misspecification concerns, allows a non-homogeneous spatial pattern of the stocks to emerge. There exists a system of local prices that supports the pattern.
- **Hot spot of type III:** The cost of controlling the *in situ* consumption at each location becomes very high in terms of deviations from the desired bliss points due to misspecification concerns.

References

Brock, W. and Xepapadeas, A. 2010. Pattern formation, spatial externalities and regulation in coupled economic-ecological systems. *Journal of Environmental Economics and Management*, 59(2), pp. 149–164.

Brock, W.A., Xepapadeas, A. and Yannacopoulos, A.N. 2014. Optimal control in space and time and the management of environmental resources. *Annu. Rev. Resour. Econ.*, 6(1), pp. 33–68.

Brock, W. and Xepapadeas, A. 2008. Diffusion-induced instability and pattern formation in infinite horizon recursive optimal control. *Journal of Economic Dynamics and Control*, 32(9), pp. 2745–2787.

Brock, W.A., Xepapadeas, A. and Yannacopoulos, A.N. 2014. Robust control and hot spots in spatiotemporal economic systems. *Dynamic Games and Applications*, 4(3), pp. 257–289.

Turing, A.M. 1990. The chemical basis of morphogenesis. *Bulletin of Mathematical Biology*, 52(1), pp. 153–197.

Selected Bibliography

Arrow, K.J. and Kruz, M. 2013. *Public Investment, The Rate of Return, and Optimal Fiscal Policy*. Washington, DC: RFF Press.

Arutyunov, A.V. 2003. The Pontryagin maximum principle and sufficient optimality conditions for nonlinear problems. *Differential Equations*, *39*(12), pp. 1671–1679.

Athans, M. and Falb, P.L. 2013. *Optimal Control: An Introduction to the Theory and its Applications*. Chelmsford, MA: Courier Corporation.

Başar, T. and Olsder, G.J. 1998. *Dynamic Noncooperative Game Theory*. Society for Industrial and Applied Mathematics.

Bellman, R.E. and Dreyfus, S.E. 2015. Applied dynamic programming. In *Applied Dynamic Programming*. Princeton University Press.

Bertsekas, D. 2012. *Dynamic Programming and Optimal Control: Volume I* (Vol. 1). Belmont, MA: Athena Scientific.

Bertsekas, D.P. 2011. *Dynamic Programming and Optimal Control 3rd edition, Volume II*. Belmont, MA: Athena Scientific.

Bertsekas, D.P. 2014. *Constrained Optimization and Lagrange Multiplier Methods*. Cambridge, MA: Academic Press.

Brock, W.A. and Malliaris, A.G. 1989. *Differential Equations, Stability and Chaos in Dynamic Economics* (No. 90A16 BROd), North Holland.

Caputo, M.R. and Caputo, M.R. 2005. *Foundations of Dynamic Economic Analysis: Optimal Control Theory and Applications*. Cambridge, UK: Cambridge University Press.

Chang, F.R. 2004. *Stochastic Optimization in Continuous Time*. Cambridge, UK: Cambridge University Press.

Dockner, E.J., Jorgensen, S., Van Long, N. and Sorger, G. 2000. *Differential Games in Economics and Management Science*. Cambridge, UK: Cambridge University Press.

Hansen, L.P. and Sargent, T.J. 2011. Robustness. In *Robustness*. Princeton, NJ: Princeton University Press.

Hirsch, M.W., Smale, S. and Devaney, R.L. 2012. *Differential Equations, Dynamical Systems, and an Introduction to Chaos*. Cambridge, MA: Academic Press.

Intriligator, M.D. 2002. *Mathematical Optimization and Economic Theory*. Society for Industrial and Applied Mathematics.

Kamien, M.I. and Schwartz, N.L. 2012. *Dynamic Optimization: The Calculus of Variations and Optimal Control in Economics and Management*. Chelmsford, MA: Courier Corporation.

Malliaris, A.G. and Brock, W.A. 1982. *Stochastic Methods in Economics and Finance*. North Holland.

Murray, J.D. 2001. *Mathematical Biology II: Spatial Models and Biomedical Applications* (Vol. 3). New York: Springer.

Perko, L. 1990. *Differential Equations and Dynamical Systems*. New York: Springler-Verlag.

Samuelson, P.A. 1948. Foundations of Economic Analysis. *Science and Society*. Cambridge, MA: Harvard University Press.

Seierstad, A. and Sydsaeter, K. 1986. *Optimal Control Theory with Economic Applications*. Elsevier North-Holland, Inc.

Stokey, N.L., Lucas, R.E. and Prescott, E.C. 1989. *Recursive Methods in Economic Dynamics*. Cambridge, MA: Harvard University Press.

Takayama, A. and Akira, T. 1985. *Mathematical Economics*. Cambridge, UK: Cambridge University Press.

Takayama, A. 1993. *Analytical Methods in Economics*. Ann Arbor, MI: University of Michigan Press.

Verhulst, F. 2006. *Nonlinear Differential Equations and Dynamical Systems*. Berlin/Heidelberg, Germany: Springer Science & Business Media.

Index

Printed in the United States
by Baker & Taylor Publisher Services

Printed in the United States
by Baker & Taylor Publisher Services